Newman the Priest

A Father of Souls

Gerard Skinner

GRACEWING

First published in 2010

Gracewing
2 Southern Avenue
Leominster
Herefordshire HR6 0QF

ISBN 978 0 85244 736 9

Front cover: Photograph of Cardinal Newman taken in December 1861, reproduced by kind permission of the Fathers of the Birmingham Oratory

Typeset by Action Publishing Technology Ltd
Gloucester GL1 5SR

Contents

Part III

Appendices

Acknowledgements

I would like to thank the following for their kind assistance to me whilst writing this book: Fr Paul Chavasse, Fr Dermot Fenlon, Fr Alexander Master, Fr Nicholas Schofield, Br Francis McGrath, Sr Mary Dechant, FSO, Joan Bond, Gaynor Brown, Anthony Martin and Sue Regan. Special thanks to Sr Mary Joseph, OSB, for her editorial assistance and to Tom Longford of Gracewing Publishing for his kind support.

Introduction

They came on the day of his funeral as they had come for his lying in state: if he had spent much of his latter years hidden from public view, now they could come to be close to him. Up to twenty thousand people lined the route the cortege was to take from the Oratory at Edgbaston to his final resting place in the community cemetery at Rednal some eight miles away. Some would have read the works for which he is now so celebrated, but not many; others may have been attracted by the curiosity of witnessing the obsequies of a famous convert who became a Roman Cardinal, of these there must have been a few; but something of this man, now deceased, had obviously touched the hearts of many who lined those streets for a passing glimpse of his cortege – to explore what this was is the subject of this book.

Celebrated English priests, such as John Henry Newman or John Fisher, who have been outstanding theologians have at the same time been surrounded by a remarkably popular cult. And yet when one asks who Fisher or Newman were most would immediately recognize the men who were great theologians whilst struggling to see the men who were first and foremost great priests, priests moreover who can assist the Faithful of today to understand the priesthood by their insight and inspiration. In this regard Pope Benedict XVI, whilst himself still a Cardinal, noted,

> The characteristic of the great doctor of the Church, it seems to me, is that he teaches not only through his thought and speech, but

rather by his life, because within him thought and life are interpenetrated and defined. If this is so, then Newman belongs to the great teachers of the Church, because at the same time he touches our hearts and enlightens our thinking.[1]

My principal desire in bringing together many of Newman's writings on the priesthood is not to set out an academic treatise or attempt a systematic theological study of the subject but rather to present the words left to us by this eminent Victorian pastor, this hard-working priest.[2] Newman himself was not what we call today a 'systematic theologian', indeed he did not consider himself a theologian at all. Thus what he has left us is necessarily shaped by the various expediencies of the sermons, the letters or whichever literary form he was employing, usually determined by the needs of an inquiry or an occasion. The result, in terms of his written output, is unsurprisingly going to be uneven in that it may seem that he dwells too long on one aspect, too little on another or does not mention yet another.

In other places one may read in detail of such themes as Newman's Anglican ministry, his conversion or his Oratorian life, his theological and philosophical explorations or his educational vision: here these important facets are drawn upon only in as much as they illuminate Newman's years of service as a Catholic priest. In the first part of this book is recounted, in chronological order, the ministry of John Henry Newman, first as an Anglican and then as a Catholic. In the second section of the book various themes are presented. These themes present some of the aspects of Newman's priestly life be they what he did, thought, said or was strengthened by. These are a series of sketches of Newman, for the full lustrous portrait of him none is better than Ian Ker's magisterial *John Henry Newman – A Biography* (Oxford, 1988). Seven sermons of Cardinal Newman comprise the final section of this work.

---

[1]   Ratzinger, J., 'One of the "Great Teachers of the Church"', *L'Osservatore Romano* (English edition) 22, 1 June 2005, 9.

[2]   Having said that this is not an academic study of Newman's priesthood, it may seem strange for the reader to discover so many footnotes in the following pages. Copious footnotes have been employed throughout this work purely to facilitate the efforts of others to follow up the material that I have drawn from.

The subtitle of this book, *A Father of Souls*, is taken from the title of an appreciation of Cardinal Newman published soon after his death in 1890.[3] As a title it provides the key to understanding what essentially motivated John Henry Newman in all that he did, whilst also clearly declaring to priests today an epitaph to aspire to. It was crystal clear to him that 'the object of Christianity is to save souls'.[4] And this he did pre-eminently as a man of action, before being a man of letters.

Newman once wrote to his sister saying that, 'It has ever been a hobby of mine (unless it be a truism, and not a hobby) that a man's life lies in his letters ... Biographers varnish; they assign motives; they conjecture feeling; they interpret Lord Burleigh's nods; they palliate or defend. For myself, I sincerely wish to seem neither better nor worse than I am.'[5] In a similar vein he once had pondered,

On the other hand, when a Saint is himself the speaker, he interprets his own action; and that is what I find done in such fulness in the case of those early luminaries [the Fathers] of the Church to whom I am referring. I want to hear a Saint converse; I am not content to look at him as a statue; his words are the index of his hidden life, as far as that life can be known to man, for "out of the abundance of the heart the mouth speaketh." This is why I exult in the folios of the Fathers.[6]

Indeed, 'A Saint's writings are to me his real "Life"; and what *is called* his "Life" is not the outline of an individual, but either of the *auto-saint* or of a myth.'[7] In another place Newman wrote that 'Any Saint's life and works must be interesting and useful.'[8] I hope that there may be something in this book that is 'interesting and useful' and will encourage and

---

[3] Fr H. J. Coleridge, 'A Father of Souls', *The Month*, vol. 70, no. 316, October 1890, 153–64.
[4] *LD* xix. 422. To T. W. Allies, 22 November 1860.
[5] *LD* xx. 443. To Jemima Mozley, 18 May 1863; Cf. *LD* xxvi. 375. To H. A. Woodgate, 18 October 1873.
[6] *HS* ii. 220–1. Originally published in the 'Rambler' (May, 1859).
[7] Ibid. 227.
[8] *LD* xxxi. 103. To an Unknown Correspondent, 16 December 1885.

inspire so that every priest, religious or layperson reflecting on these lines might encounter Him who sends us and embody Him yet again to those to whom we are sent so that, perhaps, it may be said of us, as it was said of Newman, that

> Men thought he was the servant of the unseen and eternal powers, and when they came near him it was easier for them to believe in God and in God's nearness to mankind.[9]

Note: Throughout this book, editorial marks employed in the various editions of Newman's works have been retained; likewise Newman's own punctuation has been preserved. Newman's interlinear explanations are presented in angle brackets < >, after the word or phrase they explain.

---

[9] *Birmingham Daily Post*, 12 August 1890.

Abbreviations

References to Newman's writings are, unless otherwise noted, to the uniform edition of 1868–81 (36 vols.) which were published by Longmans, Green, and Co., London.

Apo.	*Apologia pro Vita Sua,* ed. Martin J. Svaglic (Oxford, 1967)
Ari.	*The Arians of the Fourth Century*
AW	*John Henry Newman: Autobiographical Writings,* ed. Henry Tristram (London & New York, 1956)
B.O.A.	Birmingham Oratory Archives
Campaign	*My Campaign in Ireland, Part I,* ed. W. Neville (privately printed 1896)
Card. C.	Such references are taken from Fr Zeno, O.F.M., *John Henry Newman – His Inner Life*, San Francisco, 1987. 'This [Card. C.] refers to the four cupboards in the Cardinal's study. Labelled A, B, C, and D, they respectively contain 54, 13, 7 and 18 pigeonholes, each filled with many items, most of them not published. The cupboards are indicated in the references by the letters A, B, C, D; then follows the number of the pigeonhole, and in the third place the number of the special item.'
CS	*Catholic Sermons of Cardinal Newman*, ed. at the Birmingham Oratory (London, 1957)
Clem.	*John Henry Newman. St. Clement's 1824.* Such references are taken from Fr Zeno, O.F.M., *John Henry Newman – His Inner Life*, San Francisco, 1987. "A record of the persons I attended in sickness, principally in St Clement's." (Not published; in Cardinal's cupboards A. 10. 3)

DA   *Discussions and Arguments on Various Subjects*
Dev.   *An Essay on the Development of Christian Doctrine*
Diff.* i, ii   *Certain Difficulties felt by Anglicans in Catholic Teaching,* 2 vols.
Ess.* i, ii   *Essays Critical & Historical,* 2 vols.
HS* i, ii, iii *Historical Sketches*, 3 vols.
Idea   *The Idea of a University*
Jfc.   *Lectures on the Doctrine of Justification*
LD   *The Letters and Diaries of John Henry Newman*, ed. Charles Stephen Dessain *et al.*, vols i-vi (Oxford, 1978–84), xi-xxii (London, 1961–72), xxiii–xxxii (Oxford, 1973–2008)
LG   *Loss and Gain: The Story of a Convert*
MD   *Meditations and Devotions of the late Cardinal Newman* (London, 1893)
Mix.   *Discourses addressed to Mixed Congregations*
NO   *Newman the Oratorian: His Unpublished Oratory Papers*, ed. Placid Murray, OSB (Dublin, 1969)
OS   *Sermons preached on Various Occasions*
Positio* i, ii *Positio super virtutibus – Report of the Relator of the Cause; Information on the Virtues of the Servant of God From the Acts of the Diocesan Investigation in the Archdiocese of Birmingham*, (Rome, 1989)
PS* i-viii   *Parochial and Plain Sermons,* 8 vols.
Prepos.   *Present Position of Catholics in England*
SD   *Sermons bearing on Subjects of the Day*
Sermons* i, ii *John Henry Newman: Sermons 1824–1843,* Oxford, 1992 & 1994
SN   *Sermon Notes of John Henry Cardinal Newman, 1849–1878,* ed. Fathers of the Birmingham Oratory (London, 1913)
VM* i, ii   *The Via Media,* 2 vols.
VV   *Verses on Various Occasions*
Ward* i, ii Wilfrid Ward, *The Life of John Henry Cardinal Newman*, 2 vols (London, 1927)

Chronology of the Life of John Henry Newman

as presented in the Positio super virtutibus

1801	21 February	John Henry Newman was born at Old Broad Street, London, England, the eldest of six children.
	9 April	Baptized in the church of St Benet Fink, London.
1808	1 May	Entered Dr Nicholas' school at Ealing.
1816	8 March	His father's bank failed.
	1 August – 21 December	Newman underwent his first Conversion.
	14 December	Entered Trinity College, Oxford, as a commoner.
1817	8 June	Came into residence at Trinity College.
	30 November	First communion in the Church of England.
1818	18 May	Elected a scholar of Trinity College.
1820	November	Examined for the Bachelor of Arts degree.
	5 December	He took his degree which was 'below the line', i.e. third.
1821	1 November	Newman's father declared bankrupt.
1822	11 January	Newman decides to take Orders in the Church of England.
	12 April	Elected a Fellow of Oriel College, Oxford.

1824	31 May	Completed article on 'Cicero' for *Encyclopaedia Metropolitana*.
	13 June	Ordained deacon in Christ Church cathedral, Oxford.
	23 June	Newman preached his first sermon at Over Worton, near Oxford.
	4 July	Began his pastoral ministry as curate in the parish of St Clement, Oxford.
	29 September	Newman's father died.
1825	26 March	Newman accepts position of Vice-Principal of Alban Hall, Oxford.
	29 May	Ordained priest in the Church of England at Christ Church cathedral.
	15 August	Began work for his article on 'Miracles' for the *Encyclopaedia Metropolitana*.
	9 September	Began work for his article on 'Apollonius of Tyana' for the *Encyclopaedia Metropolitana*.
1826	21 February	Resigns as curate of St Clement's and Vice-Principal of Alban Hall on his appointment as a tutor of Oriel College.
	2 July	Newman preached his first University Sermon.
1827	26 November	Collapsed while examining in the Schools.
1828	5 January	His youngest sister, Mary, dies suddenly.
	2 February	Newman appointed Vicar of St Mary's, the University Church.
	23 June	Began systematic reading of the Fathers of the Church, beginning with the Apostolical Fathers.
1829	February	Successfully supports the election of Sir Robert Inglis as member of Parliament for Oxford in opposition to R. Peel.
1830	15 June	Accepts Hawkins' gradual mode of removing him from the tutorship.
	25 March	Began Saints' day services in St Mary's church.
1831	June	Began work on the *Arians*.

1832	31 July	Finished work on the *Arians*.
	3 December	Set out on journey to the Mediterranean with R. H. Froude and his father.
1833	April–May	The Froudes having departed for England, Newman returns to Sicily alone and contracts a severe fever.
	16 June	On the ship from Palermo to Marseilles Newman wrote 'Lead Kindly Light'.
	9 July	Arrived back in England.
	14 July	Keble preached the Assize Sermon in St Mary's church on 'National Apostasy', which Newman considered the beginning of the Oxford Movement.
	9 September	Newman publishes the first of the *Tracts for the Times*.
	5 November	*The Arians of the Fourth Century* published.
1834	11 March	Volume One of the *Parochial Sermons* published.
	April–July	Newman takes prominent part in the debate on the admission of Dissenters to the University.
	30 June	Begins daily service at St Mary's.
	1 July	Declines to officiate at the marriage of Miss Jubber, a dissenter.
1835	27 March	Volume Two of the *Parochial Sermons* published.
1836	29 January	Volume Three of the *Parochial Sermons* published.
	10 February	Newman writes *Elucidations of Dr Hampden's theological statements* and opposes the appointment of Hampden as Regius Professor of Divinity at Oxford.
	May–July	Gives lectures on Romanism in the church of St Mary's.
	17 May	Newman's mother died.
	22 September	Dedication of the new church at Littlemore.

1837	11 March	Lectures on the *Prophetical Office of the Church* published.
	13 April	Began series of lectures in St Mary's on justification.
1838	20 January	Appointed editor of the *British Critic*, which he held until April 1841.
	24 February	First two volumes of Froude's *Remains* published.
	30 March	*Lectures on Justification* published.
	30 November	Volume Four of the *Parochial Sermons* published.
1839	July–September	First doubts about the position of the Anglican Church.
1840		Volume Five of the *Parochial Sermons* published.
1841	25 January	Completed work on *Tract 90*.
	February	Wrote 7 letters for the *Times* later published as the *Tamworth Reading Room* by Catholicus.
	27 February	*Tract 90* published.
	15 March	The hebdomadal Board of Oxford University censured Tract 90.
	July–September	Recurrence of doubts about the position of the Anglican Church.
1842	February	Volume Six of *Parochial Sermons* published.
	19 April	Newman goes to live a semi-monastic life at Littlemore. Part One of *Select Treatises of St. Athanasius in controversy with the Arians* published in the *Library of the Fathers*. Essay on the 'Miracles of early Ecclesiastical History' published as preface to the *Ecclesiastical History of M. L'Abbé Fleury*, of which Newman was editor.
1843	18 September	Newman resigned the benefice of St Mary's, Oxford.

	25 September	Preached in the church at Littlemore 'Parting of Friends', his last sermon as an Anglican.
		Published *Sermons, chiefly on the theory of religious belief, preached before the University of Oxford.*
		Published *Sermons bearing on Subjects of the Day.*
		Published Volume Five of *Plain Sermons* by contributors to the 'Tracts for the Times' (*PS* VII and VIII).
1844		Published Part Two of *Select Treatises of St. Athanasius in controversy with the Arians.*
1845	9 October	Newman received into the Catholic Church at Littlemore by Fr Dominic Barberi.
	1 November	Newman confirmed at Oscott.
1846	23 February	Left Littlemore for Old Oscott, renamed Maryvale.
	7 September	With Ambrose St John set off to Rome for studies at Propaganda.
1847	21 February	Pope approves Newman's decision to start an Oratory in England.
	30 May	Newman ordained priest.
	28 June	Newman and companions begin novitiate at Santa Croce under Fr Rossi.
	27 November	Receives Brief for the foundation of the Oratory.
	31 December	Arrives back at Maryvale.
1848		*Loss and Gain* published anonymously.
	1 February	The English Congregation of the Oratory set up at Maryvale.
	14 February	Newman admits Fr Faber and his Wilfridians at Cotton into the Oratory.
	31 October	Newman moves to St Wilfrid's, Cotton, having given up Maryvale.

1849 2 February Oratory opened at Alcester Street.

15 April Oratory divided into two: one remaining at Birmingham, the other going to London.

15 September Newman goes to Bilston to relieve parish priest during a cholera epidemic.

November *Discourses to Mixed Congregations* published.

1850 May–June Gives *Lectures on certain difficulties felt by Anglicans in submitting to the Catholic Church*.

22 August Newman receives honorary degree of Doctor of Divinity conferred by Pope Pius IX.

1851 30 June Begins *Lectures on the Present Position of Catholics in England* in response to the 'no popery' agitation.

28 July Newman denounces the apostate priest Achilli.

30 September Newman visits Ireland for the first time.

4 November Indicted for libel by Achilli.

12 November Newman appointed Rector of the proposed Catholic University of Ireland.

1852 16 February Oratory moves to new house in Edgbaston.

10 May–
7 June Newman delivers in Dublin first five of his *Discourses on the scope and nature of University education*.

21–24 June The Achilli trial in which jury decides Newman did not prove his charges.

13 July Newman preached 'The Second Spring' at the first synod of the new province of Westminster held at Oscott.

12 November Newman's lawyers request new trial in the Achilli case.

1853 31 January   Request for a new trial rejected.
                     Newman found guilty and fined £100.

      August   *Verses on Religious Subjects* published in
                     Dublin.

      17 October–   Newman gives Lectures *the History of*
      3 November   *the Turks* published in 1854.

      22 November Opening of the temporary church of the
                     Oratory.

1854 4 June   Newman installed as Rector of the
                     Catholic University in Dublin and begins
                     the *Catholic University Gazette*.

      3 November   Official opening of the Catholic
                     University.

1855 October–   Differences between Birmingham and
      November   London Oratory.

1856 12 January   Newman and St John arrive in Rome,
                     having visited Oratories en route.

      1 May   Newman's University Church opened in
                     Dublin.
                     Callista, a sketch of the third century
                     published.

1857 3 April   Newman announces to the Irish bishops
                     his intention of resigning the Rectorship
                     of the Catholic University.

      27 August   Receives request from Cardinal Wiseman
                     on behalf of the hierarchy to undertake
                     the supervision of a new translation of
                     the Scriptures into English.
                     Sermons preached on various occasions
                     published.

1858 12 November Newman formally resigns the Rectorship
                     of the Catholic University.

1859 21 March   Agrees to become editor of the *Rambler*
                     magazine.

      2 May   Oratory School opened in Edgbaston.

      22 May   Ullathorne asks Newman to give up
                     editorship of the *Rambler*.

	July	Newman publishes his article. 'On Consulting the Faithful in Matters of Doctrine', which is delated to Rome for heresy by Bishop Brown of Newport.
1863	30 December	Newman receives Macmillan's Magazine for January 1864 containing Kingsley's attack.
1864	12 February	Newman publishes correspondence with Kingsley arising out of the attack.
	20 March	Kingsley replies with pamphlet *What then does Dr. Newman mean?*
	21 April– 2 June	Newman publishes a history of his religious opinions in seven weekly parts entitled *Apologia pro vita sua*.
	24 October	Newman buys land in Oxford and prepares to build a church, having been offered the Catholic Mission there by Ullathorne.
	end December	Newman sells land in Oxford in view of Propaganda's opposition to Catholic youth going to Protestant universities.
1865	May–June	Newman's poem *The Dream of Gerontius* published in the *Month*.
1866	31 January	Publishes *A Letter to the Rev. E. B. Pusey, D.D. on his recent Eirenicon*.
	8 June	Accedes to Ullathorne's request that he take the Oxford Mission, erecting an Oratory there.
1867	6 April	Ullathorne informs Newman of confidential instruction from Propaganda that Newman not be allowed to take up residence at the proposed Oratory in Oxford.
	18 August	Newman gives up the Oxford mission and the proposed new Oratory.
1868	4 January	*Verses on Various Occasions* published.
	16 June	Newman and St John visit Littlemore for the first time since 1846.

1869		Newman declines the invitation of Bishop Dupanloup to attend the Vatican Council as his theologian.
1870	15 March	*An Essay in Aid of a Grammar of Assent* published.
	October	*Essays on Miracles* published.
1871	October	Newman begins to republish his Anglican works, starting with *Essays Critical and Historical*, 2 vols.
1873	29 April	Newman preaches at end of funeral Mass of Henry Wilberforce.
	5 May	Newman preaches in Farm Street Church at Hope Scott's funeral Mass, in the presence of Archbishop Manning.
1875	14 January	*A Letter to the Duke of Norfolk* published.
	24 May	Newman's closest friend and companion, Ambrose St John, dies.
1877	14 December	Newman invited to become the first Honorary Fellow of Trinity College, Oxford.
1878	26–28 February	Newman visits Oxford for the first time since 1846, staying at Trinity College.
1879	31 January	Newman receives news that the Cardinalate is to be offered to him.
	18 March	Newman receives official word from Cardinal Secretary of State, announcing he is to receive the Cardinalate.
	12 May	Newman delivers his 'Biglietto speech' in Rome.
	15 May	Newman receives the Cardinal's hat at a public consistory.
	1 July	Newman welcomed at the church of the Oratory on his arrival back in Birmingham.
1880	8–15 May	Newman guest of Duke of Norfolk in London where receptions and dinners are held in his honour. Preaches at London Oratory.

	22–23 May	Newman visits Trinity College, Oxford, and preaches morning and evening in St Aloysius's church, 23 May.
1881	25 June–6 July	Newman stays at London Oratory and preaches, 26 June.
1882	November	*Notes of Visit to the Russian Church* edited by Newman published.
1884	9 January	Newman visits Mark Pattison in Oxford.
	February	Newman's article 'On the Inspiration of Scripture' published in *Nineteenth Century*
1885	October	Newman's article 'On the development of religious error', published in the *Contemporary Review.*
1886	October	Newman has a fall and receives the anointing of the sick but recovers.
1889	c 14 November	Newman calls on George Cadbury about compulsory attendance of Catholic girl employees at daily prayer meeting.
	25 December	Newman says Mass for the last time.
1890	23 July	Newman gives out prizes in Oratory school and attends Latin play.
	10 August	Newman receives last Sacraments.
	11 August	Newman dies of pneumonia.
	19 August	Newman buried in Oratorian cemetery at Rednal near Birmingham.

Part I

1

Diaconal Ordination

*Thou must but hear the sound
Of the still voice divine.*[1]

Friday 11 January 1822 made up my mind to go into Orders.[2]

Like many a parent, the young John Henry Newman's father was none too keen to see his son enter the ordained ministry, rather hoping, in his son's case, that he would one day be called to the Bar:

After Church my Father began to speak to me as follows: – "I fear you are becoming etc ... Take care. It is very proper to quote Scripture, but you poured out texts in such quantities. Have a guard. You are encouraging a nervousness and morbid sensibility, and irritability, which may be very serious. I know what it is myself, perfectly well. I know it is a disease of mind. Religion, when carried too far, induces a softness of mind. You must *exert* yourself and do every thing you can. Depend upon it, no one's principles can be established at twenty. Your opinions in two or three years will certainly, *certainly* change. I have seen many instances of the same kind. Take care, I repeat. You are on dangerous ground. The temper you are encouraging may lead to something alarming. Weak minds are carried into superstition, and strong ones into infidelity. Do not commit yourself. Do nothing ultra. Many men say and do things, when young, which they would fain retract when older, but for shame they cannot. I know you write for the Christian Observer. My opinion of the Christian Observer is this, that it is a humbug. You must use exertions."[3]

[1] *VV* 25.
[2] *LD* i. 117.
[3] *AW* 179.

His father's precepts, delivered on Epiphany Sunday 1822, were to no avail. However a passage written by Newman in the third person, deleted in the autograph manuscript of his account records,

His father spoke from his general knowledge of the world; and, had he known his son's character thoroughly, he would have had a still greater right to anticipate a change in the religious views of the youth whom he so much loved and was so anxious about. For, as has been said above, the critical peculiarities of evangelical religion had never been congenial to him, though he fancied he held them. Its emotional and feverish devotion and its tumultuous experiences were foreign to his nature, which indeed was ever conspicuously faulty in the opposite direction, as being in a way incapable, as if physically, of enthusiasm, however legitimate and guarded.

One additional feature in Mr Newman's mind shall be noticed, which seemed to intimate from the first that the ethical character of Evangelical Religion could not lastingly be imprinted upon it. This was his great attraction to what may be called the literature of Religion, whether the writings of [the] Classics, or the works of the Fathers.[4]

And so, on the day before Newman was to return to Oxford for the Easter term,

Jany 11. Friday
My Father this morning said I ought to make up my mind what I was to be ... So I chose; and determined on the Church. Thank God, this is what I have prayed for.[5]

In fact Newman had privately decided during the previous year that this was the course that he was to take in life.[6] Indeed his mother had noticed a distinct crescendo in her son's devotion during the summer vacation of the previous year. Like her husband she was none too keen, accusing her son of 'verging upon enthusiasm' for the then unusual practice of going to Holy Communion once a fortnight. Not all of the young

[4] *AW* 82.
[5] *AW* 180.
[6] *AW* 49.

Newman's relatives were so reserved with regard to his vocation. Writing to his aunt after his priestly ordination he thanked her for her inspiration:

I in particular have cause to bless God for giving me such valuable and kind relatives. If I have been called of God to serve Him in His ministry, and if I am in any measure enabled by Him to fulfil my calling, it is to you two I must especially point as the instruments in His Providence in having from my youth turned my thoughts towards religion[7]

Having made up his mind to seek ordination, Newman was keen that it should happen as soon as possible, seeking advice as to the propriety of such a move whilst seeking to continue in academia.[8] He gave voice to his fervent desire in prayer:

Lord, Thou has blessed me with all goods, but make me Thine. Melt me down, mould me into the Divine Image. Let me be spent for Thee, Let me go through sickness, pain, poverty, affliction, reproach, persecution, any thing of worldly evil, if it is to promote Thy glory. O save me from a useless life, keep me from burying my talent in the earth.[9]

Newman prepared himself assiduously for ministerial service, attending to such faults and failings that he perceived he possessed and attempting to eradicate them. He accused himself of pride, tepidity in prayer, 'a great want of meekness and of gentleness', bad temper and being troubled by bad thoughts.[10] Throughout he led an ever deepening life of prayer and of charity whilst following the available theological lectures and seeking the guidance of the Scriptures as to the life of a minister of Christ, being 'much struck and humbled' by what he found.[11]

---

[7] *LD* i. 251. To Elizabeth Newman, 17 August 1825. The 'two' mentioned in this passage are Newman's aunt and his late grandmother. Cf. *AW* 205: Of his grandmother Newman records after her death in May 1825, 'Thou hast made her my earliest benefactor, and how she loved me!'

[8] *AW* 87, 192.

[9] *AW* 188.

[10] In order, *AW* 174, 165–6, 180, 188–9, 186.

[11] *AW* 177, 71, 192.

During these years Newman was seriously considering whether or not he was being called by God to be a missionary, a sentiment that ran deep as the first public speech that he ever made as an adult, given on 19 September 1825, had been to raise funds for the foreign missions.[12] However he did not think himself physically, mentally or spiritually equipped for the task yet he thought 'the Missionary office the highest privilege from God I can possess, though I speak blindly, it will not be wrong to pray to God to make me a Missionary – therefore in future I purpose to do so.'[13]

With an eye to possible missionary work, Newman began to learn tracts of the Bible off by heart at the same time as pursuing those most apposite to his ministerial calling and, as the day of his ordination approached, he found that the lines of Sacred Scripture had a 'tenfold force' over him.[14] 'I quite tremble,' Newman wrote on his twenty-third birthday, 'to think the age is now come, when, as far as years go, the ministry is open to me.'[15] Accepting the curacy of a nearby parish in May 1824, and having in these months prepared by fasting,[16] Newman was ordained as a deacon by Dr Legge, the Bishop of Oxford, on Trinity Sunday, 13 June of that year, at Christ Church Cathedral, Oxford, writing that day,

It is over. I am thine, O Lord; I seem quite dizzy, and cannot altogether believe and understand it. At first, after the hands were laid on me, my heart shuddered within me; the words "for ever" are so terrible. It was hardly a godly feeling which made me feel melancholy at the idea of giving up all for God. At times indeed my heart burnt within me, particularly during the singing of the Veni Creator. Yet, Lord, I ask not for comfort in comparison of

[12] Card. C., A.II.8. In *NO* 16, Placid Murray notes that in his later years as an Oratorian, Newman often spoke of an incident in St Philip's life when, after expressing a desire to become a foreign missionary, the saint was told by a Cistercian father that 'Rome was his India'. Murray notes the parallel in Newman's life with that of the Saint as being an example of how both were inspired to heroically work for the good of souls, both discerning that their missionary territory was in their respective native lands.

[13] *AW* 194.

[14] *AW* 199.

[15] *AW* 196.

[16] *AW* 198–9.

sanctification ... I feel as a man thrown suddenly into deep water.[17]

During the days immediately preceding his ordination, Newman vacillated between joy and anxiety writing on the Friday before the ceremony, 'As the time approaches for my ordination, thank God, I feel more and more happy.'[18] Yet the next day he notes, 'Now, on returning home, how hard my heart is, how dead my faith. I seem to have an unwillingness to take the vows, a dread of so irreparable a step.'[19] And on the day itself Newman later admitted, 'Alas, before the Ordination, from a most absurd feeling of shame, from pride, from other bad motives I wished it over.'[20] He was obviously overcome with awe at the path he was set upon, repeating the day after ordination those words that had so seared into him during the rite, 'For ever! words never to be recalled!'[21] In 1850 Newman remembered with honest emotion these days,

Can I forget, – I never can forget, – the day when in my youth I first bound myself to the ministry of God in that old church of St Frideswide [Christ Church Cathedral], the patroness of Oxford? nor how I wept most abundant, and most sweet tears, when I thought what I then had become; though I looked on ordination as no sacramental rite, nor even to baptism ascribed any supernatural virtue?[22]

Despite his appointment to a curacy, Newman was evidently still exploring the possibility of life as a missionary, calling at the Church Missionary House in London on Saturday 3 July, following up a letter that he had sent in March. In that letter he had outlined some of his physical attributes that he felt might disqualify him from missionary service such as the weakness of his voice, his shortness of sight and what he

---

[17] *AW* 200. Cf. *LD* xxxi. 64–5. To Anne Mozley, 15 May 1885.
[18] *AW* 200.
[19] Ibid.
[20] *AW* 201.
[21] *AW* 88.
[22] *Diff.* 81.

declared as his 'want of eloquence'. He discovered that none of these were considered impediments and, in fact, that 'the Stations most deficiently filled are such as, requiring scholastic attainments, do not require bodily vigour.'[23] The idea remained, fading gradually during his years as a curate although for many years after he remained an active member of the Church Missionary Society.

From the start, no matter how his ministry was to develop, Newman felt that 'he had left the secular line once for all, that he had entered upon a divine ministry, and for the first two years of his clerical life he connected his sacred office with nothing short of the prospect of missionary work in heathen countries as the destined fulfilment of it.'[24] Not for the foreign mission fields at this time, or later, Newman now pitched himself into parochial work perhaps fortified by a prayer he composed two days before his ordination:

Make me Thy instrument ... make use of me, when Thou wilt, and dash me to pieces when Thou wilt. Let me, living or dying, in fortune and misfortune, in joy and sadness, in health & Sickness, in honour and dishonour, be Thine.[25]

---

[23] *AW* 201.
[24] Ibid. On the day of his father's funeral in October 1824, Newman pondered, almost rhetorically, 'When I die, shall I be followed to the grave by my children? my Mother said the other day she hoped to live to see me married, but *I* think I shall either die within a College walls, or a Missionary in a foreign land – no matter where, so that I die in Christ.' *AW* 203.
[25] *AW* 200.

2

St Clement's and Priestly Ordination

I have the responsibility of souls on me to the day of my death.[1]

In May 1824 Newman, who had been recommended by Pusey, accepted the curacy of St Clement's, Oxford, a poor parish of two thousand inhabitants with a church that needed rebuilding. The parish was situated on the other side of Magdalen Bridge from the University. The Reverend John Gutch, Rector of the Parish and Registrar of the University, was in his eighties and in poor health. In becoming curate of St Clement's, Newman embraced a life of the kind of pastoral ministry that most clergymen would be familiar with. The sick were to be visited, the new born baptized, couples married, sermons prepared, meetings attended and building works to be arranged. Newman took his first service at St Clement's on 4 July, baptizing for the first time that same day and officiating at his first marriage the following Sunday.

By the Saturday of his first week at St Clement's, Newman was attempting to procure an up-to-date list of parishioners so that on the following Saturday, 17 July, his diary records 'began going through the parish, house by house, making a list of my parishioners.'[2] He kept note of the names and addresses of his flock in two pocket-books entitled, '*Speculum Gregis; or the Parochial Minister's Assistant,* by a Country Curate,

---

[1] *AW* 201.
[2] *LD* i. 179. Writing to R. F. Wilson on 3 July 1834, Newman recalled that 'When I was at St Clement's, I could visit sixteen people without inconvenience, taking half one day and half another, but then they were almost next door to each other.' *LD* iv. 289.

London 1823.'[3] From this little publication he learned that 'the readiest way of finding access to a man's heart, is to go into his house.'[4] Newman evidently agreed with this, remarking to his mother, 'I shall know my parishioners, and be known by them.'[5] By the middle of August he had visited all the houses of his parish and wrote with enthusiasm to his father, seeming to politely contradict an opinion expressed by him,

So far from this invasion of 'an Englishman's castle' being galling to the feelings of the poor, I am convinced by facts that it is very acceptable. In all places I have been received with civility, in most with cheerfulness and a kind of glad surprise, and in many with quite a cordiality and warmth of feeling.[6]

The visiting of the homes of the poor in Newman's parish seem to have met with real gratitude. He met with such comments as 'I was sure that one time or other we should have a proper minister' and 'the old man preached very good doctrine but he did not come to visit people at their houses as the new one did.'[7] And as for those parishioners of his who on principle would not attend Sunday services,

I have not tried to bring over any regular dissenter – indeed I have told them all, 'I shall make no difference between you and churchgoers – I count you all my flock, and shall be most happy to do you service out of Church, if I cannot within it.' A good dissenter is of course incomparably better than a bad Churchman – but a good Churchman I think better than a good dissenter.[8]

He often helped the poor of his parish by gifts of wine, loaves of bread, books or money if necessary, assisting one family to

---

[3]   *LD* i. 179, note 1. Inside the notebooks is written, 'given me by the Rev J. Gutch John Henry Newman July 1824 I can do all things through Christ which strengtheneth me –'; and 'Establish Thou the work of our hands upon us! yea, the work of our hands establish Thou it'. Occasionally Newman wrote comments in pencil next to some of the names.
[4]   Card. C., A. 12. 3.
[5]   *LD* i. 180. To Mrs Newman, 28 July 1824.
[6]   *LD* i. 184. To Mr Newman, 9 August 1824.
[7]   Ibid.
[8]   Ibid.

evade eviction.[9] Newman's enthusiasm for his work is palpable and he recorded in some detail the events of each day in his diary during these years:

Sunday 28 November [1824] – 1ˢᵗ in Advent   did duty morning and afternoon at St Clements   preached morning Mal iii, 1–3 (1) afternoon 1 Cor xv, 34   visited Mrs Flynn and Mrs Talboys, and went with Gutch to Harris who wished the sacrament administered to him – churched Mrs Marigold

Monday 29 November inquired after Mr Parsons, Mrs Flynn, Harris, and Mrs Pattenson   called on King and Gardner about probable increase of parish – [Appendix] Dec 1824   Mrs Pattenson – young married woman 22 in a decline – Happening to call by accident, I saw how ill she was and asked if I should visit her – she said no – called again and again – and fancied from her manner she did not like the thoughts of death. The last time was much pleased and prevailed on her to let me read constantly with her – but, being *much* engaged, was unable to go for ten days, when (the very morning I intended) she sent me *begging* to see her. She was *much* worse. I had no idea *how* ill she was. – I went: she had been much hurt at my absence – thought me ill etc. She seemed much comforted by my praying etc. Went next day – she still weaker – gave me her history – 'could not read – never went to school – a great trouble to her. Her father died when she was 5 – Her mother had to work hard to keep her family of five children – went out to service and then married' – (she was *always* sickly) 'had been very ill since marriage – given over after the first confinement – and God had brought her to Himself by sickness – had *always tried to do His will, as far as she knew it.* – she knew very little   Used to go to church when single, for it was a pleasure. Cared not whether God took her or not – He was all merciful and her soul was full of comfort.' – I read part of John iii, 14 and prayed – she *much* comforted, *particularly* with prayers. Her eyes looked at me with such a meaning, I felt a thrill I cannot describe – it was like the gate of heaven – I promised to call again in the evening – she was very thankful. – I did call in the evening – she had departed about an hour after I left her! – she seemed fainting the last few minutes I was there and I was obliged to get some one to bring water – etc – She told her friends she had had so pleasant a conversation with me – so glad she was alone with me – and looked

---

[9]   Clem., i.v. Edgington.

forward with such pleasure to my coming in the evening – The evening came and her joy was greater than she had anticipated. – This was written Sunday Dec 12 – the day after her death. – [10]

In fact Newman especially cherished the visits to his sick parishioners, as he confided in a letter to Pusey:

The most pleasant part of my duties is visiting the sick – I have seven or eight on my hands – and though there have been and are two or three most painful characters amongst them, yet on the other hand I have several most interesting cases. My visits quite hallow the day to me, as if every day were Sunday.[11]

The prayerbook that he took with him on these occasions, preserved at the Birmingham Oratory, shows signs of frequent use, particularly the section of prayers to be said before each visit. After attending to the sick person, Newman recorded his experiences in a large exercise book, also kept at the Oratory.[12]

From his very first years as a minister, Newman was frequently complimented on his preaching, although some thought him rather severe. As far as he was concerned, 'Those who make comfort the great subject of their preaching seem to mistake the end of their ministry. *Holiness* is the great end. There must be a struggle and a trial here. Comfort is a cordial, but no one drinks cordials from morning to night.'[13] Something of Newman's youthful zeal and Evangelical leanings comes across in a few lines he recorded of a conversation he had had with a fellow member of the Oriel Common Room, Edward Hawkins, after showing him a copy of his first sermon. Newman noted, 'The sermon divided the Christian world into two classes, the one all darkness, the other all light, whereas, said Mr Hawkins, it is impossible for us in fact to draw such a line of demarcation across any body of men ...'[14] In a different journal Newman made short notes of the same conversation with Hawkins:

[10] *LD* i. 199.
[11] *LD* i. 191. To E. B. Pusey, 17 September 1824.
[12] Zeno, *John Henry Newman – His Inner Life*, 39.
[13] *AW* 172.
[14] *AW* 77.

Had a conversation with Hawkins on real and nominal Christianity in fact on conversion. He admitted there was a line, but he put it much lower than I should. The majority, he said, of my congregation would not be touched by my preaching; for they would be conscious to themselves of not doing *enough*, not of doing *nothing*. May I get light, as I proceed.[15]

Importantly for the development of his thinking and the direction of his future ministry, Newman found that working in the parish, alongside the intellectual companionship of the Oriel Common Room, challenged and really did enlighten his theological opinions from leaning towards Evangelicalism to once again seeking to discover the writings of the ancient Fathers that he had first become aware of as a schoolboy on reading Milner's *Church History*.

The strains of beginning to preach regularly – and somewhat longer sermons than most are accustomed to today – quickly made its impact on the young curate: 'Two sermons a week are very exhausting. This is only the third week, and I am already running dry'.[16] The preaching was, he wrote, 'rather a drain upon my head'.[17] A further problem that Newman frequently encountered during his early days of preaching, and that he shared with his Rector, was simply not having a strong enough voice for his congregation to hear him. He overcame this deficiency and quickly the congregation increased from about fifty people to a greater number than the church could hold.

Not everything went well for the young curate – he had a quarrel with the choir, who walked out, for instance leaving the congregation to 'sing en masse'.[18] He found that he had 'little opportunity for devotion or private study of the Scriptures', sometimes he was 'reduced to neglect morning prayer, either from forgetfulness or excess of work'[19] and, most painfully, on 29 September 1824 his father died unexpectedly.

[15] *AW* 201.
[16] Ibid.
[17] *LD* i. 186. To Harriett Newman, 26 August 1824.
[18] *AW* 207.
[19] *AW* 204–6.

With just an examination for priest's orders on Wednesday 25 May 1825 and attending the bishop's charge the following Saturday, but without any other notable preparation, Newman returned to Christ Church Cathedral, Oxford, to be ordained priest by the Bishop of Oxford on 29 May, Trinity Sunday, 1825. Apart from the fact that he was ordained that day, his diary records a Sunday much like any other. In the morning he finished a sermon on I Cor xii, 4–6, then 'was ordained priest at Ch Ch [Christ Church] by Bishop of Oxford'.[20] After returning from the cathedral he conducted the afternoon service preaching the sermon he had completed that morning, he churched two ladies, conducted a baptism and then a burial, before settling down to dinner in his room – no guests are mentioned. Ordinations were, in those times, somewhat matter-of-fact occasions, excepting the ceremony itself, of course. Business-like or not, Newman paused to reflect on the great day:

I have this day been ordained priest. What a divine service is that of Ordination! The whole has a fragrance in it; and to think of it is soothing and delightful.

My feelings as to those ordained with me were somewhat different from those I had this time [last] year. I hope I was not exactly uncharitable then; still I certainly thought that there might be some among them who were coming to the Bishop out of their own heads, and without the Spirit of God. But when I looked round today, I could hope and trust that none were altogether destitute of divine influence, and, tho' there was difference of spirituality, yet all might be in some degree spiritual. Then, I thought there were many in the visible Church of Christ, who have never been visited by the Holy Ghost; now, I think there are none but probably, nay almost certainly, have been visited by Him.[21]

Newman had probably changed more than those whom he was looking upon and the change in his understanding of the real regenerative power of the Sacrament of Baptism, which is what he is referring to with regard to whether or not his fellow

[20] *LD* i. 234.
[21] *AW* 205–6.

ordinands had ever been 'visited by the Holy Ghost', came about precisely through his pastoral ministry as he noted the day after his ordination:

I may add to my above remarks on my change of sentiment as to Regeneration, that I have been principally or in great measure led to this change by the fact that in my parochial duties I found many, who in most important points were inconsistent, but whom yet I could not say were altogether without grace. Most indeed were in that condition as if they had some spiritual feelings, but weak and uncertain. [22]

Besides the pastoral work of the parish, Newman engaged himself with a project to rebuild St Clement's immediately upon his appointment to the parish. The old church was able to hold only 200 people and the decision for it to be rebuilt had been put off until the appointment of a curate who would be 'a kind of guarantee to the subscribers that every exertion will be made, when the Church is built, to recover the parish from meeting houses, and on the other hand alehouses, into which they [the parishioners] had been driven for want of convenient Sunday worship.' [23] This, unsurprisingly, took him 'an ocean of time', [24] yet it was a mark of his interest in his new parishioners that when he began his second visitation of the parish, this time to collect subscriptions for the new church, Newman found that there were very few houses of which he could not remember the owner's name. [25] He takes up the story in a Memoir:

Mr Newman held the curacy of St Clement's ... long enough to succeed in collecting the £5000 or £6000, which were necessary for the new Church. It was consecrated after he had relinquished his curacy, probably in the Long Vacation, when he was away from Oxford; but so

---

[22] *AW* 206.
[23] *AW* 198–9.
[24] *LD* i. 199. To Mrs Newman, 30 November 1824.
[25] *LD* i. 186. To Harriett Newman, 26 August 1824. This letter continues, 'If you love me, pray for me. I have found some religious persons in the parish, and it is a great consolation to me to believe that they remember me in their prayers.'

it happened by a singular accident that, neither while it was building, nor after it was built, was he ever inside it. He had no part in determining its architectural character, which was in the hands of a committee. The old Church, which stood at the fork of the two London roads as they join at Magdalen Bridge, was soon afterwards removed; and it thus was Mr Newman's lot to outlive the Church, St Bennet [sic] Fink, in which he was baptized, the School House & play grounds at Ealing, where he passed between eight and nine years of his boyhood, and the Church in which he first did duty.[26]

Once he had completed the task of raising funds for the new church Newman immediately set about launching an appeal for a Sunday school. In February the school opened and was soon housed in a specially built gallery for which Pusey provided a stove.

Thus during his ministry at St Clement's Newman was juggling with the spiritual and pastoral work of a parish and the practical care for its buildings whilst yet continuing to play an active role in the academic life of the University, being appointed Vice-Principal (meaning that he was Dean, Tutor and Bursar), of Alban Hall, a small institution, poorly thought of in the University, with about a dozen undergraduates in residence; Junior Treasurer of Oriel and writing an extensive article on Apollonius and miracles – 'parish, Hall, College, and Encyclopaedia go on together in perfect harmony', he wrote to his mother, after having visited his doctor.[27] However Newman's tenure as curate was not to last long as he had 'all along thought it was more' his 'duty to engage in College offices than in parochial duty'.[28]

Accepting the offer of being a tutor at Oriel he moved into the College on 21 March 1826 having resigned his curacy.[29]

[26] *AW* 72.
[27] *LD* i. 268. To Mrs Newman, 14 November 1825.
[28] *AW* 205.
[29] Writing to his mother later that year after he had taken up the tutorship, Newman commented, 'I have been and am very busy; but I can get through my business tolerably. It is *all of a* kind – not various, multiform, a convenience of which I have long been deprived.' *LD* i. 308. To Mrs Newman, 23 November 1826. To his sister Harriett he wrote in similar vein, 'I have felt much the delight of having but *one* business [[the College Tutorship]]. No one can tell the unpleasantness of having things

He had felt that the parish may have been suffering due to the demands made upon him by academia and was to have been assisted in his labours by Pusey, but Pusey was packed off to Germany for further theological studies. Newman's judgement on his personal parochial application was not shared by his parish clerk whose admiration for Newman's work was clear: 'Mr Hickman, the clerk of S. Clement's when Mr Newman was curate there ... says that Mr Newman's labours in that parish far exceeded any that could be named in other Oxford parishes at that date.'[30] In fact Newman was seriously overworking and his health had been suffering as a consequence.

In retrospect it seems that Newman recognized the intensity with which he threw himself into life at St Clement's as four years after having left the parish, whilst seeking leave of absence on doctor's orders from the Bishop of Oxford, Newman attributed his then weakness to overwork when he was a curate.[31] It was not until his arrival in Birmingham that he would experience once again the full sacerdotal round of parish life, and in Birmingham he met it on a scale hitherto unprecedented for him.

<matters> of different kinds to get through at once. We talk of its *distracting* the mind; and its effect upon me is indeed a *tearing* or *ripping open* of the coats of the brain and the vessels of the heart.' *LD* i. 309. To Harriett Newman, 25 November 1826.

[30] E. S. Ffoulkes, *A History of the Church of S. Mary the Virgin Oxford*, 457.

[31] *LD* iii. 141. To Richard Bagot, Bishop of Oxford, November [16 December] 1832.

3

Tutor at Oriel

*May it be! then well might I
In College cloister live and die.*[1]

From 1817 until his reception into the Catholic Church in 1845, Oxford was Newman's home, and its ancient university a singularly important factor in the shaping of his mind. Newman went up to Oxford as an undergraduate in June 1817, becoming a member of Trinity College. In 1822 he was elected a Fellow of Oriel College, becoming a tutor there in 1826 upon his resignation from St Clement's. In the Common Room at Oriel the young and impressionable Newman was intellectually formed in no small part through the everyday conversations with other Fellows.

From the moment of his appointment as a tutor of Oriel, Newman was clear as to the *raison d'être* of his being there:

When I was a Public Tutor of my college at Oxford, I maintained, even fiercely, that my employment was distinctly pastoral. I considered that, by the statutes of the University, a Tutor's profession was of a religious nature. I never would allow that, in teaching the classics, I was absolved from carrying on, by means of them, in the minds of my pupils, an ethical training; I considered a College Tutor to have the care of souls.[2]

Newman was committed, with creedal force, to the belief that the communication of knowledge was but only one part of his remit. His role was also fundamentally a pastoral one for

---

[1] *VV* 23.
[2] W. P. Neville (ed.), *Addresses to Cardinal Newman, with his replies, 1879–81*, 184.

as an ordained minister he had 'the care of souls.' Writing at
the time of his appointment he prayed,

And now, O Lord, I am entering with the new year into a fresh
course of duties (viz the Tutorship). May I engage in them in the
strength of Christ, remembering I am a minister of God, and have a
commission to preach the gospel, remembering the worth of souls,
and that I shall have to answer for the opportunities given me of
benefitting those who are under my care. May God be with me,
according to the prayer of my dear grandmother, "as He was with
Joseph", and may I see the fruit of my labour.[3]

What he found within the College was undoubtedly not new to
him, but he was resolved to do his best to reform the situation.
After four weeks in post Newman had judged that there was
much 'profligacy' in the place, particularly among the richer of
the undergraduates.

I think the Tutors see too little of the men, and that there is not
enough of direct religious instruction. It is my wish to consider
myself as the minister of Christ. May I most seriously reflect, that,
unless I find that opportunities occur of doing spiritual good to those
over whom I am placed, it will become a grave question, whether I
ought to continue in the Tuition.[4]

Beyond academic work, Newman sought to influence the
undergraduates by being their friend and trying to approach them
in terms 'almost of equality, putting off, as much as might be, the
martinet manner then in fashion with College Tutors.' He sought
out the society of his charges 'in outdoor exercises, on evenings,
and in Vacation.' Thus, Newman recalled,

when he became Vicar of St Mary's in 1828 the hold he had acquired
over them led to their following him on to sacred ground, and
receiving directly religious instruction from his sermons; but from
the first, independently of St Mary's he had set before himself in the
Tutorial work the aim of gaining souls to God.[5]

---

[3] *AW* 209.
[4] Ibid.
[5] *AW* 90.

This vision of the role of the Tutor was not without its critics, Newman standing accused of attempting to reduce the university to being simply a school of divinity. And yet Newman was seeking to resurrect a concept of the pastoral role of the Tutor that had, over the centuries, fallen into disuse. He pointed to the Laudian Statutes of the university (1636) for support for his ideal of the role of the college tutor.

James Anthony Froude, educated at Oriel from 1836, who became a noted historian, novelist and biographer, recorded in later life his reminiscences of Newman's conversations with undergraduates:

With us undergraduates Newman ... spoke ... about subjects of the day, of literature, of public persons and incidents, of everything which was generally interesting. He seemed always to be better informed on common topics of conversation than any one else who was present. He was never condescending with us, never didactic or authoritative; but what he said carried conviction along with it. When we were wrong he knew why we were wrong, and excused our mistakes to ourselves while he set us right. Perhaps his supreme merit as a talker was that he never tried to be witty or to say striking things. Ironical he could be, but not ill-natured. Not a malicious anecdote was ever heard from him. Prosy he could not be. He was lightness itself – the lightness of elastic strength – and he was interesting because he never talked for talking's sake, but because he had something to say.[6]

Of Newman's appearance at this time Froude recalled, 'His appearance was striking ... his face remarkably like that of Julius Caesar', and of Newman's character Froude saw

an original force of character which refused to be moulded by circumstances, which was to make its own way, and became a power in the world; a temper imperious and wilful, but along with it a most attaching gentleness, sweetness, singleness of heart and purpose. Both were formed by nature to command others .... *Credo in Newmannum* was a common phrase at Oxford, and is still

---

[6]   J. A. Froude, 'Oxford Counter Reformation, Letter III,' *Short Studies on Great Subjects*, vol. v. This letter was originally published as 'Letter III, John Henry Newman', in D. Macleod's *Good Words* (March 1881), 162–7.

unconsciously the faith of nine-tenths of the English converts to Rome.[7]

Other recollections of the time recognize this image of Newman. John Campbell Shairp, who became Professor of Poetry at Oxford and was a Scottish Presbyterian, noted that the influence that Newman had unconsciously invoked 'was unlike anything else in our time'. There was a 'mysterious veneration' that had gathered through the years around Newman's name 'till now it was almost as though some Ambrose or Augustine of elder ages had reappeared.' But even during Newman's Oxford years Shairp remembered that 'In Oriel Lane light hearted undergraduates would drop their voices and whisper, "There's Newman!" . . . Awe fell on them for a moment, almost as if some apparition had passed.' 'What were the qualities that inspired these feelings?' asked Shairp,

> There was of course learning and refinement, there was genius, not indeed of a philosopher, but of a subtle and original thinker, an unequalled edge of dialectic, and these all glorified by the imagination of a poet. Then there was the utter unworldliness . . . the tamelessness of soul, which was ready to essay the impossible.[8]

In the field of academia, Newman's work, along with that of like-minded colleagues, had a transformative effect on the results achieved by Oriel undergraduates. It is recorded that between 1821, when Newman began tutoring undergraduates privately, and 1831, fewer Gentlemen Commoners (students from backgrounds of either the landed gentry or the very rich) than before gained admittance to Oriel, more students actually graduated and the number of undergraduates sitting for honours increased. There was also an increase in the number of future clergy among his pupils.[9] Writing in February 1829 Newman

---

[7] Ibid. 196–7.

[8] John Campbell Shairp, *Studies in Poetry and Philosophy*, 3rd edition, 244–5.

[9] P. Lefebvre, 'The student population at Oriel and Newman's pupils (1821–1833)', Annexe 1.A, 'John Henry Newman tuteur: Tradition, rupture, développement (1826–1831)' (unpublished dissertation, Université de Paris III, 2004), 105–15. Quoted in *John Henry Newman In His Time*, edited by Philippe Lefebvre & Colin Mason.

was pleased and proud of the changes being worked at Oriel:
'We have gone through the year famously, packed off our
lumber, parted with spoilt goods, washed and darned when we
could, and imported several new articles of approved quality.
Indeed the College is so altered that you would hardly know it
again.'[10] Unprepared candidates had been rejected for admission
whilst vacancies had been offered to 'well recommended and
picked men', the 'Chapel Sermon at the Sacrament' had been
revived and a prize for Greek composition was instituted. A
'radical alteration' and 'The most important and far reaching
improvement', as seen by Newman, was that the students who
had been admitted to Oriel due to their academic potential and
were working conscientiously were to be placed in 'very small
lectures, and principally with their own Tutors' so that they
could converse about their subjects 'quite familiarly and
chattingly'. Furthermore, it was a development that 'a regular
lecture system *for the year* has been devised.'[11]

In all this progress Newman believed that he had the support
of the Provost of Oriel, Edward Hawkins, a man who had won
Newman's support over the candidacy of John Keble at the
time of Hawkins' election to the post, Newman famously
remarking that 'You know we are not electing an Angel, but a
Provost.'[12] Hawkins had been known as a strict disciplinarian
but to Newman's eyes he seemed to have been diminished by
his role. 'Hawkins' spirits are not what they used to be,' he
wrote, 'and persons who have known him long say he is aging.
I have sometimes been made quite sad at the sight of him.'[13]
This touching sympathy was soon to be tested as Newman
thought that Hawkins had 'always approved' his innovations,
even if the Provost didn't 'take the initiative' in them. During
examinations Hawkins had 'slain the bad men manfully', and it
was 'said in College by the Undergraduates that "now, alas,
the Provost is as bad as a Tutor"'.[14]

But all was not as it seemed and during 1829 differences

[10] *LD* ii. 117. To Samuel Rickards, 6 February 1829.
[11] Ibid. 117–18.
[12] *LD* xxx. 107. To E. B. Pusey, 29 June 1882.
[13] *LD* ii. 118. To Samuel Rickards, 6 February 1829.
[14] Ibid.

between Newman and Hawkins arose as to the organization of the college lecture system as well as matters ecclesiastical.[15] But it was the critical subject of admissions that brought their differences to a head. Newman, Hurrell Froude and Robert Wilberforce – the latter two being colleagues and close friends of Newman – decided to attempt to exercise greater control over Oriel's choice of undergraduate students. In this they were opposed by Hawkins and thus all three tutors resigned. The ruction that had occurred, however, was but the boiling over of the simmering disagreement between Newman and Hawkins as to the spiritual and pastoral influence of a tutor on his charges. In later life, Newman reflected that

Perhaps the Provost would have acted differently, had he been got to believe Mr Newman's blunt declaration, that there was not a chance of his remaining Tutor, if his scruples were not respected; but he was unable to comprehend the intensity of Mr Newman's feeling that, unless he could make his educational engagements a fulfilment of his ordination vow, he could have no part in them ... Mr Newman ... became simply indignant that, with the solemn consciousness which haunted him that he was a minister of Christ and a preacher of His gospel, the Provost should venture to press him on an occupation, which, while pressing it, he himself confessed was not properly clerical, and only to be tolerated for a time as an accident, and not the end and staple of a clergyman's life.[16]

Undoubtedly Newman had his failures as a tutor as any tutor must but accounts of these are extremely thin on the ground – the very occasional good story, perhaps, but nigh on worthless as an objective record of his tutorship. Two too frequently told vignettes of the Third Earl of Malmesbury reflect more of their author, it seems, than of Oriel's most famous tutor.[17]

---

[15] See K. C. Turpin, 'The Ascendency of Oriel', *The History of the University of Oxford*, vol. vi. *Nineteenth-century Oxford, Part I.* Edited by M. G. Brook and M. C. Curthoys (Oxford, 1997), 189.
[16] *AW* 103.
[17] Malmesbury, who had been Foreign Secretary and Lord Privy Seal, left an account in his *Memoirs of an Ex-Minister* that accused Newman of cowardice when, he alleged, students had forced Newman into a corner, jamming him there with a table and on another occasion being shouted down for mutilating, with his poor carving, a haunch of venison.

It would seem that Newman was never more 'a minister of Christ' for a large number of undergraduates than when he was indeed 'a preacher of His gospel'. In the words of one of Newman's university congregation,

If we ask by what means this power was gained at Oxford, the answer must certainly be that it was entirely by his sermons . . . . There was the style, always simple, refined, and unpretending, and without a touch of anything which could be called rhetoric, but always marked by a depth of feeling which evidently sprang from the heart and experience of the speaker . . . Then, as he entered into his subject more fully, the preacher seemed to enter into the very minds of his hearers, and, as it were, to reveal them to themselves, and to tell them their very inmost thoughts . . .

I question whether, as suited to a University audience, England has ever known a preacher of equal power.[18]

Richard William Church, who was to become Dean of St Paul's Cathedral in London and remained a lifelong friend of Newman, remarked that without Newman's sermons the Oxford Movement 'might never have gone on, certainly would never had been what it was', because 'While men were reading and talking about the Tracts, they were hearing the sermons; and in the sermons they heard the living meaning, and reason, and bearing of the Tracts, their ethical affinities, their moral standard.'[19]

William Lockhart, who after his conversion was to join Blessed Antonio Rosmini's newly-formed Institute of Charity, wrote later in life of 'the most wonderful effect' that Newman's sermons had on the undergraduates. 'It was to many of us as if God had spoken to us for the first time . . . I do not see how this could have been, unless he who spoke was himself a *seer*, who saw God, and the things of God, and spoke that which he had seen, in the keen, bright, intuition of faith'. The effect of the transmission of such divine illumination was

---

[18] Katherine Lake (ed.), *Memorials of William Charles Lake 1869–1894*, 40–1, 50.
[19] R. W. Church, *The Oxford Movement: Twelve Years 1833–1845*, 129–30.

profound: 'He had the wondrous, the supernatural power of raising the mind to God, and of rooting deeply in us a personal conviction of God, and a sense of His Presence.'[20]

The tutorship was, for Newman, indubitably an office that 'was of a Pastoral nature'[21] and without being permitted to express and practise accordingly the fullness of the office, Newman could not, as a matter of conscience, in consideration of his ordination vows, continue. This cutting away of the shoots of his academic branches, however, led to an abundance of growth, which could never have been foreseen. He was blessed with more time for study and the contemplation of the ancient Fathers, even with the care of St Mary the Virgin, where he continued as Vicar. Returning to England from travels through Italy and France on 8 July 1833, Newman arrived in Oxford the next day.

The following Sunday, July 14th, Mr. Keble preached the Assize Sermon in the University Pulpit. It was published under the title of 'National Apostasy'. I have ever considered and kept the day, as the start of the religious movement of 1833.[22]

A new phase in Newman's care of souls had commenced. One that began in the attempt to stir up the clergy to rediscover the treasures of Catholic life that had been lost to the Church of England but that continued, for Newman and through him for many others, in the fullness of Catholic Faith. Figuratively he never ceased to be a tutor for, as he himself noted,

Men live after their death – or, still more, they live not in their writings or their chronicled history, but in that ἄγραφος μνήμη exhibited in a school of pupils who trace their moral parentage to them. As moral truth is discovered, not by reasoning, but [by] habituation, so it is recommended not by books b[ut by] oral instruction.[23]

---

[20] W. Lockhart, *Cardinal Newman: Reminiscences of Fifty Years Since*, 24, 26–7.

[21] *LD* ii. 218. Memorandum. Letters to Henry Wilberforce, January 1876.

[22] *Apo.* 43.

[23] *LD* ii. 255. To S. Rickards, 20 July 1830 quoting Thucydides II, 43, the Greek meaning 'unwritten memory'.

4

Vicar of St Mary's

In 1828 I became Vicar of St Mary's. It was to me like the feeling of spring weather after winter; and, if I may so speak, I came out of my shell ...[1]

On Friday 14 March 1828, Newman was instituted by the Bishop of Oxford as Vicar of St Mary the Virgin, the University Church. His predecessor, Edward Hawkins, had just been elected, with Newman's support, Provost of Oriel. This had occasioned Hawkins' resignation from St Mary's two days earlier. The tradition of St Mary's was that the Rector should be a Fellow of Oriel College and thus Newman found himself well placed to be considered for the position, being inducted on Thursday 20 March. Newman brought to the prestigious parish some of the insights that he had gleaned at St Clement's, in the first instance visiting from house to house as had proved so successful in his first parish. The services at St Mary's consisted of two each Sunday (plus Christmas Day and Good Friday), one on the first day of Lent, every day during Holy Week and on various Saints' Days. These services were not Eucharistic – 'The Sacrament of the Lord's Supper' was 'administered 12 times in the year'.[2] He worked to bring together members of the different Colleges and founded a dinner club for the purpose, meeting once a fortnight.[3] His reputation was ever increasing and in July 1828 he was invited by the Bishop of London to take up one of the Whitehall Preacherships, an appointment that he regretted and only

---

[1] *Apo.* 27.
[2] *LD* iii. 11–12.
[3] *LD* ii. 68–9. To Jemima Newman, 10 May 1828.

accepted for 1828. It would bring Newman to London to preach at the palace chapel of Whitehall a number of times, including Christmas Day, which, he felt, greatly disrupted his ministry at the University Church and thus when invited at a later date to once again be a Whitehall Preacher, he declined.

From the time Newman left St Clement's his diary entries and letters contain much less detail of the parochial work in which he was engaged. Firstly this was due to his focus on attending to the needs of the University, and ultimately the Birmingham Oratory and all the different projects he was called upon to engage in. A simpler reason, however, why he wrote less about any parochial work that he was pursuing is that he had become accustomed to it – as he commented about the ancient Greek writers to his sister during a recuperative voyage to Greece, 'only I am astonished that they say so little about the scenery – of course they were used to it.'[4]

Newman had hoped that life as a Tutor at Oriel would have clarified the demands made on him and lessened their burdens but by May 1829 he was opining to his sister that

one of my growing infirmities is want of memory – the way things escape me is surprising – whether it is that the having College, Parish, and Bursarial duties distracts the attention or what else. I cannot tell – certain it is, I forget whom I spoke to even yesterday, what I said, and all about it[5]

Some six or so weeks earlier Newman had reflected, before his Sunday afternoon congregation, on his first year of ministry at St Mary's:

A year has now past since Christ (as I trust it was) called me to minister to you in this place – and, it is just a year this day, (as far as the calculation by weeks allows us to reckon) since I read the morning and evening prayers and the articles of the Church[6] as a pledge [of] what was to be the nature of my preaching and my teaching among you. –

---

[4] *LD* iii. 177. To Harriett Newman, 2 January 1833.
[5] *LD* ii. 141. To Jemima Newman, 7 May 1829.
[6] 'Sunday 23 March 1828 Lent 5 … read in (*i.e. read the 39 articles etc*) …', *LD* ii. 63.

How far I have faithfully fulfilled my promise to Christ and the Church, is to me a subject of vast importance – I pray God I may think much of it – But, My Brethren, *you* have not to think of it – for I have not to render my account to you but to the Lord – *I* am put over you by Christ to judge you in Christ's stead, to exhort, to convince, and teach you . . . yet it would be inconsiderate in me to have said what I have said concerning the awful situation and responsibility of the Christian Minister without adding that our high duties, trials, imperfections in God's sight are a call to you, not to talk critically of us, but *silently to* pray for us. And O that God would grant the clergy to feel their weakness as sinful men, and the people to sympathize with them and love them and pray for their increase in all good gifts of grace.[7]

Newman continues by 'lamenting the very imperfect intercourse' which he felt existed between a Parish Priest and his people. 'A Parish Priest it is obvious is intended to be living principle [*sic*] of religion among the people he is intrusted with.' And yet,

In short what is the intercourse between Minister and people reduced to, not here only but generally in towns? merely to addresses such as I am now making to you; – addresses, most useful in their way, but no fit substitute for familiar teaching, being too short in exposition to embrace the particularities of doctrine, and necessarily too general in exhortation to apply to the varieties of character and circumstances of those to whom they are spoken.[8]

An increasing concern for Newman was the pastoral care of the community at Littlemore, a hamlet near Oxford, and in the summer of 1829 he laid his plans before some of his friends to make it a separate parish once a chapel had been built there. In February of 1830 he wrote to Richard Bagot, the Bishop of Oxford, to formally request a Curate specifically for the care of Littlemore, a request denied.

[7]   *Sermons* i. 4–5. Sermon No. 191 – 'Sermon on the intercourse between Parish Priest and his charge – anniversary sermon of my entering into St Mary's', delivered at St Mary the Virgin, Oxford, Sunday afternoon 22 March 1829. The chosen text of the sermon was I Thess ii. 4: ' . . . As we were allowed of God to be put in trust with the gospel, even so we speak – not as pleasing men, but God which trieth our hearts.'
[8]   Ibid. 6.

Newman commenced 'Saints-day Services' at St Mary's in March 1830, thinking that these would be 'useful, both because it in some degree keeps up the memory of the Saints and so of old times' and 'because it gives me an opportunity of knowing the more religious part of my Congregation.'[9]

On Sunday 2 December 1832 Newman delivered the last university sermon he was to preach until, incredibly, 1839. This did not mean, however, that he was prevented from preaching to his parish, which he did with ever growing acclaim. As Ian Ker comments with regard to these sermons, 'there is no doubt that they constitute one of the great classics of Christian spirituality. It is certainly almost as hard to conceive of the Oxford Movement without the *Parochial and Plain Sermons* as without the *Tracts for the Times.*'[10] These mighty orations, delivered at 4 o'clock, tea time, are briefly explored elsewhere in this book.

Newman's care for his parish and enjoyment in parochial duties is once again seen in a letter to his mother written later in 1835. Having asked advice regarding the building of the new church at Littlemore that had been approved by the fellows of Oriel in April of that year, he turns to the subject of his fifteen candidates for Confirmation,

some very interesting ones. When I am employed in that sort of work, I always feel how I should like a parish with nothing but pastoral duties. One great advantage of a large parish is that *one can do nothing else.* Nothing is so hampering to the mind as *two* occupations; that is what I have found both at St. Clement's and when I was Tutor at Oriel. As it is, my parish is not large enough to employ me, so I necessarily make to myself two occupations – which, though necessary, is to me distracting. Some people can work better for a division of duties. Some persons cannot attend to one thing for more than two hours without a headache. I confess for myself I never do anything so well as when I have nothing else to do. I would joyfully give myself to reading or again to a parish. However, as to a large parish, there seem to me in the present state of things two special drawbacks: one, the amount of mere secular

[9] *LD* ii. 201–2. To Simeon Lloyd Pope, 5 April 1830.
[10] I. Ker, *John Henry Newman – A Biography*, 90.

business laid on a clergyman, attendance at vestries, etc.; the other, that really at the present day we are all so ignorant of our duties, that I should actually be afraid myself, without a great deal more learning, to undertake an extensive charge.[11]

The proposal for a chapel to be built at Littlemore met with great enthusiasm: 'Every one is full of hope and anxiety', wrote Harriett Newman, 'One man said, "If he could but live to be buried in Littlemore Churchyard, he should die happy."'[12] Newman set about raising the necessary capital with practiced panache, letting Henry Wilberforce know that, 'If you know any rich man furnished with ability, I have no objection to be indebted to him.'[13] It seemed as if a rich person were indeed required: Newman had hoped that the project would cost '£500 or £600',[14] but alas 'First the estimate, sent in by Fisher ... is £890!'[15] Yet by the time that Newman managed to conclude the same letter in which he had reported this devastating news – he was stopped by a bout of influenza – he was able to communicate that 'The estimate for the Church has suddenly sunk by £300!'[16]

Work began on the new chapel on 15 July 1835 and on Tuesday 21 July, 'in the presence of the whole village' its first stone was laid by Newman's mother with Newman himself delivering the address.[17] By 4 September Newman could report that 'The walls are rising of the Church – The arch of the door is finished, the windows are finishing and the roof is making – but the actual work put together is little.'[18]

On Thursday 22 September 1836, at half past eleven, the new church and churchyard at Littlemore was consecrated by the Bishop of Oxford, the land and part of the costs of building having been provided by Oriel College. The chapel was

[11] *LD* v. 111. To Mrs Newman, 31 July 1835.
[12] *LD* v. 61. From Harriett Newman, 23 April 1835.
[13] *LD* v. 64. To Henry Wilberforce, 3 May 1835.
[14] Ibid.
[15] *LD* v. 79. To Richard Hurrell Froude, 11 June 1835.
[16] Ibid. 80.
[17] *LD* v. 104–6. Newman's mother was not to live to see the church completed, dying on 17 May 1836.
[18] *LD* v. 135. To Jemima Newman, 4 September 1835.

dedicated to St Mary and St Nicholas as a monastery of that dedication had once been established at Littlemore. Whilst excavating the foundations, twenty-two skeletons were found laying east to west, it thus being supposed that a church had been formerly situated on the very same site. The Archdeacon read the Gospel and Newman preached, distributing buns to the children after the service. 'The day was fine, and, as you may suppose, the Chapel full ... The east end is quite beautiful,' wrote Newman. 'We had a profusion of bright flowers in bunches all about the Chapel The Bishop was much pleased.'[19] For the new church Newman had acquired 'a font large enough for immersion' intending 'to urge the people to suffer their children to be immersed – or at least in the summer'.[20] It was, in fact, the old font of St Mary's, 'once very beautiful with sculpture, which has been all hacked off by the Reformation or Rebellion mobs.'[21] Mercifully he saw 'no objection to the water having the chill taken off, and a large flannel might be ready to dry the infant,' and he reasoned that 'As children are *washed* all over, I cannot see why they might not be baptized by immersion.'[22]

I have Baptists at Littlemore and am quite sure they gain by our sprinkling – indeed it seems to me almost inexcusable. If it were only the danger incurred of not baptizing at all – for what with the infants cap and dress, it is a hard matter to scatter a few drops upon it at all. ... I think I never should *oblige* parents – but put it to them as a privilege[23]

The font was used on the very day of the consecration – the manner in which the two baptisms were administered, however, was not recorded.

Further developments back at St Mary's, inspired by his growing knowledge of the Fathers of the Church and their practices and a deeper appreciation of the sacraments, included

[19] *LD* v. 359–60. To John William Bowden, 23 September 1836.
[20] *LD* v. 342. To William Dodsworth, 23 August 1836.
[21] *LD* v. 366. To Elizabeth Newman, 10 October 1836.
[22] *LD* v. 342. To William Dodsworth, 23 August 1836.
[23] Ibid.

the institution in April 1838 of weekly Communion services each Sunday at 7 o'clock in the morning. He also gave an annual series of lectures, intended for his parishioners rather than for the university, in the Adam de Brome chapel at St Mary's.

Despite his obvious solicitude for his parish, by 1840 Newman was gravely concerned that he had not been attentive enough towards those in his care. Having temporarily exchanged St Mary's for Littlemore due to the resignation of his curate in March earlier that year, Newman had commented,

I am so drawn to this place ... that it will be an effort to go back to St Mary's. ... Every thing is so cold at St Mary's – I have felt it for years. I know no one. I have no sympathy. I have many critics and carpers – If it were not for those poor undergraduates ... and the Sunday Communions, I should be sorely tempted to pitch my tent here.[24]

Newman evidently enjoyed, albeit briefly, purely parochial work, writing to his Aunt Elizabeth saying: 'I came up here as a sort of penance during Lent; but though without friends or books, I have as yet had nothing but pleasure. So that it seems a shame to spend Lent so happily.'[25] Among other duties Newman had been spending some time reforming the school at Littlemore and leading singing practice with the aid of his violin. Writing to his friend and mentor, John Keble, he asked advice as to whether or not he should give up St Mary's, an idea that he had first aired to another friend the year before,

First, it is certain that I do not know my Oxford Parishioners; I am not conscious of influencing them; and certainly I have no insight into their spiritual state. I have no personal, no pastoral acquaintance with them. To very few have I any opportunity of saying a religious word. Whatever influence I exert on them is precisely that which I may be exerting on persons out of my parish. In my excuse I am accustomed to say to myself, that I am not adapted to get on with them, while others are. On the other hand, I am conscious that by

---

[24] *LD* vii. 261. To J. R. Bloxam, 15 March 1840.
[25] *LD* vii, 286. To Elizabeth Newman, 1 April 1840.

means of my position at St Mary's I do exert a considerable influence on the University, whether on Undergraduates or Graduates. It seems then, on the whole, that I am using St Mary's, to the neglect of its direct duties, for objects not belonging to it; I am converting a parochial charge into a sort of University office.

I think I may say truly that I have begun scarcely any plan but for the sake of my parish; but every one has turned, independently of me, into the direction of the University. I began Saints' Days services, daily services, and Lectures in Adam de Brome's Chapel for my parishioners; but they have not come to them. In consequence I dropped the last mentioned, having, while it lasted, been naturally led to direct it to the instruction of those who did come, instead of those who did not.[26]

Other reasons for which Newman considered himself unsuitable to continue at St Mary's included knowing the dislike of the university authorities of his preaching and that Newman could not any longer disguise from himself that his preaching was 'not calculated to defend that system of religion which has been received for 300 years, and of which the Heads of Houses are the legitimate maintainers in this place.'[27] A further reason was Newman's fear that his preaching was disposing his listeners towards Rome.

Keble thought it ill-advised for Newman to resign, offering as reasons that the scandal that such a resignation would cause was as likely as anything else to suggest to people the idea that all that was left to them now was to look to Rome. They would also assume that he had recanted the beliefs that he had espoused through the Tracts. By staying at St Mary's, Keble thought that Newman would be a stabilizing influence for all. Newman was, for the time, reassured, writing to another friend that 'there are so many reasons making it a duty to remain, so as soon as one comes to the conclusion that it is not a duty to go.'[28]

The turmoil and the increasing backlash caused by Newman's publication of Tract 90, his interpretation of the

---

[26] *LD* vii. 416–17. To John Keble, 26 October 1840.
[27] Ibid.
[28] *LD* vii. 450. To Frederic Rogers, 25 November 1840.

Thirty-nine articles, were ultimately to bring about the end of his days at St Mary's. As he tried to ascertain the exact measure of the opposition to him from his bishop and the Heads of Houses he resolved that he could not stay at St Mary's if they were against him – 'I cannot be a demagogue, or a quasi schismatiser',[29] he wrote to Keble. By January of 1842 he had to admit that

My present purpose is from sheer despondency lest I should be doing harm, to give over, at least for the present, preaching at St Mary's. Nothing I can say, though I preach Sermons 17 years old, but is made to have a meaning – much more when I write fresh ones. And I think it may be of use in itself, in the present excited state of Oxford and the country. My going to be at Littlemore, which has long been in contemplation and progress, will be an excuse, to save appearances.[30]

The temptation to depart St Mary's was further enhanced by the fact that Newman had 'bought nine or ten acres of ground at Littlemore, the field between the Chapel and Barne's – and, so be it, in due time shall erect a Monastic House upon it – but I do not wish this mentioned. This may lead *ultimately* to my resigning my fellowship – but these are visions as yet.'[31] He was indeed to resign his fellowship – six days before his conversion.

On 6 February Newman wrote to his sister, Jemima, informing her of his moving to Littlemore. 'It makes me very downcast,' he wrote,

it is such a nuisance taking *steps* – but for years three lines of Horace have been in my ears ...

>   Lusisti satis, edisti satis, atque bibisti
>   Tempus abire tibi est – ne potum largius æquo
>   Rideat et pulset lasciva decentiùs ætas[32]

[29] *LD* viii. 120. To John Keble, 25 March 1841.
[30] *LD* viii. 441. To R. I. Wilberforce, 26 January 1842.
[31] *LD* vii. 334. To Mrs John Mozley, 28 May 1840.
[32] *LD* viii. 456. To Mrs John Mozley, 6 February 1842, quoting Horace, *Epistles*, II, 2, 214–16. ''Tis Time for thee to quit the wanton Stage,/ Lest Youth, more decent in their Follies, scoff/ The nauseous Scene, and hiss thee reeling off.'

He secured the services of David Lewis to be his resident curate at St Mary's. By the end of March 1842 plans were seemingly coming together as Newman noted to Maria Giberne: 'P.S. . . . Do you know we are trying to set up a half College half monastery at Littlemore, which does very well as far as it has gone, i.e. without inmates yet. Men enough are *willing* – but parents, friends etc. are in the way.'[33]

It was not only to Miss Giberne that Newman had intimated that there was to be a monastic element to his new place of residence at Littlemore. Even without the turmoil that had accompanied the publication of Tract 90 the mention of the word 'monastery' or anything similar was utterly incendiary in the Oxford of the early 1840s for monasteries were unequivocally understood as Romish institutions. In response to his Bishop's polite inquiry as to the exact nature of his proposed intentions Newman replied,

I purpose to live there [Littlemore] myself a good deal, as I have a resident Curate in Oxford. . . . In doing this, I believe I am consulting for the good of my Parish, as my population at Littlemore is at least equal to that of St Mary's in Oxford, and the *whole* of Littlemore is double of it. It has been very much neglected; and in providing a parsonage house for Littlemore, as this will be, and will be called, I conceive I am doing a very great benefit to my people. At the same time it has appeared to me that a partial or temporary retirement from St Mary's Church might be expedient under the prevailing excitement.[34]

Newman continued by outlining changes that he hoped to make to improve the parish school and simply told the Bishop that he was as yet unsure how the other rooms at Littlemore might be used in the future.

Once again, in the mid-March 1843, Newman wrote to Keble proposing that he should resign from St Mary's. He felt that the almost 'unanimous condemnation' by the bishops of *Tract 90* meant that he could not continue to hold the position 'with any sense of propriety'. Positive reasons also suggested

---

[33] *LD* viii. 497. To Miss M. R. Giberne, 30 March 1842.
[34] *LD* viii. 506. To Richard Bagot, Bishop of Oxford, 14 April 1842.

that he should now resign: he was increasingly occupied 'directing ... the consciences of persons' and thought that he would be enabled to do a great deal more pastoral work at Littlemore if he were freed of his responsibilities to the University Church.[35] In this he was hoping that it might be possible to retain a position at Littlemore.

Keble now was not against Newman's plan to resign as long as his ministry at Littlemore was not also lost in the process. But on the same day that Newman heard from Keble, the most likely successor to the benefice of St Mary's, C. P. Eden, made it clear that Newman would no longer be allowed to take weekday prayers at Littlemore should he actually resign as Vicar. With his ever gathering conviction that the Roman Catholic Church was 'the Church of the Apostles, and that what grace is among us ... is extraordinary, and from the overflowings of His Dispensation'[36] Newman understandably fretted that his opinions would be discovered to the certain distress of everyone concerned. Furthermore he held that 'Such opinions' were not 'compatible with holding situations of trust in the Church'. His 'present position' was 'a cruelty', he thought, to many in the Church of England. How was it 'compatible with my holding St Mary's, being what I am'?[37]

By the end of July Newman had decided: he would resign from St Mary's. The unexpected news of the conversion of William Lockhart that summer brought forward the day of the resignation. Lockhart lived in the small community that Newman had founded at Littlemore and had promised Newman that he would remain an Anglican for at least three years after joining. Yet whilst on holiday, without any indication to Newman whatsoever, Lockhart converted to Catholicism. Lockhart had not only been sheltered by Newman's community at Littlemore but he had also been teaching in the school and Newman knew that he would be implicated in what would be considered the scandal of Lockhart's conversion. Thus on 7 September he sent his letter of resignation to the Bishop of

---

[35] *LD* ix. 279–81. To John Keble, 14 March, 1843.
[36] *LD* ix. 328. To John Keble, 4 May 1843.
[37] *LD* ix. 349–50. To John Keble, 18 May 1843.

Oxford, Richard Bagot, signing his resignation from St Mary's, after a sleepless night, before a notary on 18 September. He delivered his last Anglican sermon, 'The Parting of Friends', on 25 September, the anniversary of the consecration of the church at Littlemore taking as the text for his sermon the same verse of the Psalms which he had employed for the first sermon that he had ever given: 'Man goeth forth to his work and to his labour until the evening.'

5

Collegio di Propaganda
and Ordination

My Lord, I offer Thee myself in turn
as a sacrifice of thanksgiving.[1]

Newman was received into the Catholic Church at Littlemore
by (Blessed) Fr Dominic Barberi on 9 October 1845. He was
not to leave Littlemore until the afternoon of 22 February
1846, going to live at Old Oscott (now called Maryvale). One
aspect in particular made this time a not completely congenial
existence: 'How dreary,' he thought, was 'my first year at
Maryvale ... when I was the gaze of so many eyes at Oscott,
as if some wild incomprehensible beast, caught by the hunter,
and a spectacle for Dr. Wiseman to exhibit to strangers, as
himself being the hunter who captured it!' Newman also
encountered a 'strangeness of ways, habits, religious
observances, to which, however, I was urged on to conform
without any delicacy towards my feelings'.[2]

By April it had been decided that Newman was to go to
Collegio di Propaganda, the Roman college for students from
missionary countries. He himself had hoped for this as he
wanted 'a regular education'[3] thinking that at Propaganda he
would 'be under the discipline of all but a school boy'.[4]
Despite his understanding that Rome was the best place for him
to prepare for Catholic priesthood, Newman also knew that it

---

[1] *MD* 406.
[2] *AW* 255.
[3] LD xi. 152. To James Hope, 18 April 1846.
[4] *LD* xi. 151. To Mrs J. W. Bowden, 18 April 1846.

was going to be 'a very great trial' at his 'time of life' considering his 'stationary habits'.[5]

On 7 September he and Ambrose St. John departed from Brighton for France on the first leg of their journey to the Eternal City. They reached Milan on 20 September and after a stay of some five weeks, Newman and St John continued their journey to Rome. Writing to Henry Wilberforce from his new residence at Collegio di Propaganda, Newman was able to say, 'I was happy at Oriel, happier at Littlemore, as happy or happier still at Maryvale – and happiest here.'[6] At some length, but with evident enjoyment, Newman related to Henry Wilberforce a day in his life in Rome:

Community Mass was at $^1/_2$ past 6 when we first came here and now is at 7. After this we go down to a sort of small kitchen or pantry, where coffee and milk, or on fast days coffee and chocolate is served to all comers, very much in the Littlemore way, upon a dirty dresser by candlelight – they allow us burnt bread too, as much as we want – and the Rector insisted we should, à l'Anglaise, have butter – but we have gradually dispensed with that. Then we are to ourselves for an hour and a half, during which St John goes up for a while to Father Repetti, one of the two Confessors to teach him a little English, or a Swede comes to him to be taught Catholicism. Meanwhile I am, as now, writing a letter, or collating Pallavicino and Sarpi with the text of the Council[7] ... Two lectures follow of an hour each, first on morals, second on dogmatics (at which N. goes to sleep and nods)[8] – and then we are within half an hour of dinner, which is now at 12, and used to be at 11½. The quarter of an hour before is spent by the whole community in chapel ending with the Angelus, the bell ringing briskly the while for dinner. We are in the organ Tribune, and, while the youths file off below in Cameratas into Hall, we manage to join in at the end, and get into our places between the Professors and the Scholars just as (the Breviary) grace is said. Then the reading begins, a passage from Scripture, followed at once by some missionary correspondence or ecclesiastical history, – and ending with the Martyrology. Meanwhile in comes first a large plate of broth or soup, either macaroni, or plain

5 *LD* xi. 238. To Lord Adare, 31 August 1846.
6 *LD* xi. 294. To Henry Wilberforce, 13 December 1846.
7 Of Trent, interpreted in a different manner by the authors mentioned.
8 Note added by Ambrose St. John.

bread, or barley, or Indian corn, or pease, or cabbage, bouilli follows
. . . then roast veal or a made dish – on holidays another dish, pudding
or the like follows – and two apples or chestnuts conclude the banquet.
Wine ad libitum. All go to chapel to visit the B.S. [Blessed Sacrament]
immediately after dinner, and then the cameratas file off to the
recreation rooms reciting the Psalm Miserere. . . . After dinner we go
to a small miserable school room for recreation. . . . On great days we
have coffee, cakes, and a liqueur. Then we generally walk out, if the
weather permits – go to the Churches, or make a call, or go to a Shop,
returning by three to go to Lecture in dogmatics. You see we have
hardly had an hour for reading as yet, all through the day, except
perhaps after breakfast – This is a serious evil, though not as great as it
seems – because there are a great many vacation days, every Thursday,
e.g. and a number of Saints' days and (then not Thursday –) the
Apostles, St Stanislaus and St Francis Xavier, and of course the
Conception B.M.V. Also when snow falls, when there is a Cardinal's
Capella in Chapel; and when we skip, which we do frequently,
particularly on Saturdays, when there is nothing but examination in the
week's lectures. But on ordinary days I hardly get to work till 4 pm.
and I have hardly been at work an hour (if so much, for perhaps Talbot,
or Ryder, or some Monsignor, or some French Vicar Apostolic, or
Father Costa comes in) when a knock comes at the door, and in walks
Cesar Mola, a young Lombard Priest, who is going to Ceylon in
January, and whom I am meanwhile teaching English. He stops from
one to two hours, and I get a good deal of Italian talk in the time. . . .
After tea, I go to read again – and get stupid from cold – not sleepy as
much as torpid. Then if I have courage, I rouse, and go upstairs to
Father Repetti . . . [who] lets me talk about my matters . . . By this time
it is within a 1/4 of an hour of supper time. The Rosary is said in chapel,
and we go to supper, (at 8 or now 8 1/2) which consists of soup or broth,
a dish of meat, and apples or chestnuts, with wine. Then we go to
Chapel. Then the youths file off, as before, with the Miserere to
recreation. I go to my rooms and prepare for bed.[9]

The timetable and the studies were not the only novelties that
Newman came upon – Roman dress was equally worth
commenting upon. He thought his cassock etc.

---

[9] *LD* xi. 298–302. To Henry Wilberforce, 18 December 1846. Life for
Newman at Collegio di Propaganda must have been a pleasant surprise
considering the briefing that he had been given by one Dr Fergusson
about it. See *LD* xi. 200–1. To Ambrose St. John, 8 July 1846.

... very warm, but for outdoors most incommodious. In our rooms we wear a Roman Cassock of cloth with a biretta – over this, a thick coarse great-coat, very warm, of which the Propaganda has made us a present. But out of doors we are miserable – two dresses are possible. The most convenient, because the less trouble, is to keep our cassock on and to put over it the mantella – which is a thin stuff cloke, reaching, as the cassock, down to the heels. I have described the streets of Rome in a letter to Bowles – now it is bad enough to have to hold up *one* garment in the midst of such mire, but to manage two is almost impossible. If however one wishes to be saved from the dirt, then one is at liberty to wear a coat, a sort of dress clerical coat, it is, with a piece of silk < a fareolina > something like an undergraduate's back, hanging down behind – so far well – but shorts, and buckles; I assure you it is hard work to keep one's stockings up without wrinkles. If it rains or is cold, we wear our fareola, a very very full large handsome cloke, reaching down to the feet, – also the gift of Propaganda, – with a velvet collar, and frogs at the neck. Above all, a stupendous triangular hat – so contrived as to be susceptible of every puff of wind, but cocked so high in front as to afford the face no protection against the sun.[10]

Beyond the timetable and the dress Newman could not but be impressed with the catholicity of the community into which he and St John had been received. 'There are 32 languages spoken here,' he noted, and at Mass, 'It is most affecting to see the youths embrace each other in chapel at the Pax; it recalls Pentecost, especially as one knows that the chance is that some of them may be martyrs.'[11] Although he thought that 'The lecturers are men quite up with their subject,'[12] on the whole Newman was unimpressed by their theological and philosophical quality remarking that 'There is a deep suspicion of *change*, with a perfect incapacity to create any thing *positive* for the wants of the times.'[13] Newman was not hoping for unconstrained imaginings from Rome's theologians but rather creative thinking that naturally developed the concepts of faith

[10] *LD* xi. 301. To Henry Wilberforce, 18 December 1846.
[11] *LD* xi. 283. To Mrs John Mozley, 25 November 1846.
[12] *LD* xii. 48. To Richard Stanton, 21 February 1847.
[13] *LD* xii. 104. To Mrs John Mozley, 25 July 1847.

and was able to transmit them in a manner relevant to the times. Many years later when writing of the seminary system he thought that,

I cannot help thinking that the education of men for any profession, legal, medical, as well as clerical, must in a certain sense be narrow, if it is to be effective for the purposes of that profession, and that absolute freedom of word and deed in religious matters, is as inconsistent with the duties of a parish priest as a like liberty in military matters with the duties of a soldier, or in parliamentary action with those of a member of the Cabinet.[14]

Propaganda's programme of studies was a world apart from that which Newman had undergone and, to a certain degree, he realized that part of his difficulty with the proffered academic programme was that it was tailored for men many years younger and much less qualified than him. Newman had himself overseen the formation of young men for orders and in a letter to one John Marriott, written over fifteen years previously, had outlined the line of studies in some detail:

In your reading for orders, I should recommend your making the Bible itself your chief subject of study – and of its diversified contents, the Gospels. I am persuaded we do not sufficiently study our Savior's character and mode of teaching. Surely he is our pattern as *pastors* as well as *private* Christians. It must be our duty to imitate the *chief* shepherd. And, again, the persons he addresses were so numerous and various, and the scenes He went through – and moreover the circumstances in which He was placed bore so great a resemblance to ours at the present day, that (putting aside all thoughts of His dignity) His example must be preferable to St Paul's who *wrote* not *conversed* (i.e. *we* have only his *writings*), and addressed (for the most part) *confirmed* Christians not the confused mass (except indeed in his epistles to the Corinthians) and discordant elements of a Christian (so-called) country – the Scribes, Herodians, and Essenes with whom our Savior was engaged. – I should advise your *mastering* the four gospels – and (as far as you find interesting) harmonizing them – and neglecting the division of chapters, dividing

[14] *LD* xxviii. 5. To Matthew Arnold, 3 January 1876.

the narration into the scenes which it is made up of – observing the *order* of our Savior's teaching – His various answers to various persons – and seeing what instruction may be gained from it.[15]

As he surveyed the curriculum of Propaganda, Newman surely related his new experience with that which he had become accustomed to and perhaps noted, as has ever been the wont of English seminarians in Rome, that a key difference between the two systems was that in Oxford there was an emphasis on a Scriptural curriculum studied in depth whilst in Rome there was a greater field of studies, in part imposed through attempting to relate the various philosophical and the theological disciplines developed over two thousand years and impart them in seven years to the students. Newman was also realistic about what he had left behind. In 1838, on receipt of an anthology of texts drawn from the Anglican Divines on Tradition,[16] he wrote appreciatively to the editor saying,

It is not to be expected that the multitude even of Clergymen, when they get into active employment, will set to upon the works of our Divines, and the only thing that can be done by way of making an impression upon their opinions is to collect testimonies from them. One must hope that theological acquirements will be more an object provided for in the next generation, but I speak of the Church as it is.[17]

No small part of Newman's Roman sojourn was to settle upon the nature of his vocation. Wiseman had first suggested the idea of Newman joining the Oratory and so Newman procured a copy of the Rule of St Philip but St Philip was no stranger to him: 'I have long felt special reverence and admiration for the character of St Ph. [Philip] Neri, as far as I knew it, and was struck by your saying that his Church at Rome was in Vallicella – [18] I wish we could all become good

---

[15] *LD* xxxii. 3–4. To John Marriott, 15 August 1830.

[16] John Fuller Russell, ed., *The Judgement of the Anglican Church (posterior to the Reformation) on the Sufficiency of Holy Scripture, and the Authority of the Holy Catholic Church in matters of Faith.*

[17] *LD* vi. 182. To John Fuller Russell, 3 January 1838.

[18] This church is known as Santa Maria in Vallicella, the Italian for St Mary's in the Little Valley or, indeed, Mary Vale.

Oratorians, but that, I suppose, is impossible.'[19] He had visited the Roman Oratory on the day after Christmas with St John and was attracted by what he perceived as being a similarity of life with Oxford colleges with regard to the sets of rooms and the magnificent library that that Oratory possessed. Newman did not feel called to take a vow of poverty but was certain that he was being called to actively continue academic and pastoral work. He was seeking, it seems, a good measure of continuity with his life up until his conversion – even the life of the Oratory's founder, the greatly loved sixteenth-century Roman priest, St Philip Neri, reminded Newman of Keble due to what Newman reckoned as the saint's mixture of 'extreme hatred of humbug, playfulness, nay oddity, tender love for others, and severity, which are the lineaments of Keble'.[20] And so, after having considered the Dominicans, the Jesuits and life as a secular priest, Newman settled on the idea of the Oratory as being his calling and began to make plans for the establishment of the new foundation.

At the same time as his Oratorian vocation was being ultimately worked out, Newman was unsure as to exactly when he was to be ordained but was content enough to write in December 1846 that 'We [Newman and St John] cannot help thinking it gain that there is no talk yet of our ordination ... considering there is so much to read and think about, we are glad to remain as we are.'[21] He was of the same opinion one month later. His words, writing to a friend, reminiscent of his bearing at the time of his reception of Anglican orders:

As to ordination, among their other privileges here, they can confer the different degrees of orders without interval – so that probably we should be ordained sub-deacon, deacon, priest, in the course of 10 days, and just before our return. I am glad of my liberty, for the responsibilities of orders grow greater and greater upon me, as I approach them – and this without seeing any great ground in reason to think differently of my Anglican orders than before.[22]

---

[19] *LD* xi. 105. To F. W. Faber, 1 February 1846.
[20] *LD* xii. 25. To Mrs John Mozley, 26 January 1847.
[21] *LD* xi. 292–3. To W. G. Penny, 13 December 1846.
[22] *LD* xii. 15. To Mrs J. W. Bowden, 13 January 1847. The extract is from a P.S. dated 14 January.

On becoming a Catholic Newman was still unclear as to the validity of his Anglican ordination. This troubled him greatly for the repetition of such a sacrament, if sacrament it was (like in the case of baptism), would have been sacrilegious. Newman's mind was temporarily put at rest by Dr Griffiths who advised him, as Newman had been advised at Oscott, that 'the English Orders are no more than doubtful.' Bishop Griffiths informed him that when Anglican clergymen received ordination the bishop ordained them conditionally, something that would have happened to a cradle Catholic if there was any doubt as to the manner in which the original rite had been carried out.[23]

From April 8–17, 1847, Newman made his pre-ordination retreat at St Eusebio, his notes of which are still extant, notes which, according to the great twentieth-century member of the French Oratory, Louis Bouyer, throw an almost unbearably pitiless light on the workings of [Newman's] inmost conscience:

The piercing ray which Newman directs upon himself is his accuser, and an accuser such as no devil's advocate could have rivalled. But, then, the same piercing ray is the only physician with power to heal the wounds it inflicts. How easily here such a spiritual experience as this overtakes and outstrips the results of modern psychology. In that calm and unwavering insistence on the truth by which Newman is actuated, and which he directs upon himself, lies his solace and his peace. It is its own cure. Suffering no hidden evil to lurk in the recesses of his being, he lances it calmly and with terrifying resolution, and cures it as a miracle, or rather proclaims it triumphantly downtrodden. He who has the will and the courage to bring such a light to bear upon his conscience puts all his weakness to rout. Only to the Saints is it granted thus to bring the detecting ray to bear on all their soul's distress, all their sins and failings; but the very fact that they behold them so clearly is a sign that they have already got the better of them.[24]

---

[23] *LD* xi. 41. To Henry Wilberforce, 23 November 1845.

[24] Louis Bouyer, *Newman – His Life and Spirituality*, 271. Bouyer, who in the original French edition of the cited book published Newman's retreat notes for the first time, proceeds from page 272 to analyze the document paragraph by paragraph.

The notes, written by Newman in Latin, begin with the lines, 'I have in my mind a wound or cancer, the presence of which prevents me from being a good Oratorian. It cannot be described in a few words, for it is many-sided.' Several paragraphs on he reflects,

> Although I have the fixed habit of referring all things to the will of God, and desire to do His will, and although in practice I really observe this principle in greater matters, yet I do not in practice seek His will in lesser things. And even in those greater matters, although I have often prayed earnestly to do His will, yet my actions have proceeded rather from a kind of conscientiousness which forbade me to act otherwise, from a sense of correctness, from perceiving what became me, and doing which I should be consistent, than from faith and charity.[25]

Given the nature of the multifaceted tasks that the Bishops were to present to Newman during the years of his priestly ministry it is all the clearer that he did indeed refer all things to God as it is so evident that he would never have chosen such missions by himself in the light of the confession made during his retreat that

> In almost everything I like my own way of acting; I do not want to change the place or business in which I find myself, to undertake the affairs of others, to walk, to go on a journey, to visit others, since I prefer to remain at home. I am querulous, timid, lazy, suspicious; I crawl along the ground; feeble, downcast and despondent.[26]

The retreat was a further conversion experience for Newman, it seems, a throwing down of himself before providence in much the same way as he had, less than two years earlier, laid bare his life kneeling at the feet of Blessed Dominic Barberi. His retreat notes, his 'calm and unwavering insistence on the truth' provides an exemplary pattern of such a critical aspect of a priestly retreat.[27]

---

[25]   *AW* 245–8. The original Latin text of the complete notes is given in *AW* 239–42.

[26]   *AW* 246.

[27]   The complete text of Newman's retreat notes, translated into English, form Appendix 2 of this book.

Before travelling to Rome, Newman, St John and some others had, on Saturday 6 June 1846, received tonsure and minor orders. After having been examined for orders on 22 May, Newman and St John received subdiaconate in Cardinal Fransoni's private chapel on Wednesday 26 May (St Philip's Day) 1847, they were both ordained deacons at the Basilica of St John Lateran on Saturday 29 May by the Cardinal Vicar of Rome and ordained to the priesthood the following day, Trinity Sunday, by Cardinal Fransoni in the Chapel of the Three Kings at Propaganda. Apart from noting that on the day of his diaconal ordination he left the College at 6 a.m., returning at 12 noon (Lateran ceremonies of this type were incredibly long due to both the number of candidates and the fact that both minor and major orders were conferred upon the various men, hence many rites being joined together), Newman had little else to say in either diary or in his letters – beyond noting that he hoped to celebrate his first Mass on Corpus Christi and that indulgences were attached to his first three Masses.

Newman's first Mass was indeed celebrated on the solemnity of Corpus Christi in the small Jesuit's chapel at Propaganda, William Clifford (who was to become Bishop of Clifton) serving. That evening there was a festal meal for both Newman and St John. The next day, Friday 4 June, Newman said the Community Mass in the College Chapel, receiving the customary kissing of the newly ordained priest's hands afterwards. The following day he said Mass at St Thomas's altar at the English College, later going on to be present with St John 'at the admission of a novice into his [St Vincent Pallotti's] religious brotherhood . . .'[28]

A month after his ordination, Newman left Propaganda having enjoyed some 'happy months' there.[29] He was joined in Rome by other members of the Maryvale community in order to embark on the Oratorian novitiate – 'room-sweeping, slop-emptying, dinner-serving, bed making, shoe blacking' – 'How dreary,' he found it all.[30]

---

[28] *LD* xii. 84–6.
[29] *AW* 256.
[30] *LD* xii. 97. To T. F. Knox, 17 July 1847. *AW* 256.

6

Birmingham

Paradise was not made for sluggards.[1]

On New Year's Day 1848, Newman celebrated Mass at Maryvale for the first time, having arrived back there the previous day. He had completed his novitiate with his companions at Santa Croce in Rome under the tutelage of Fr Rossi and, on 27 November 1847, had received the Brief for the foundation of the Oratory. Thus on 1 February 1848, the Eve of the Feast of the Purification, the English Congregation of the Oratory was set up at Maryvale. The community consisted of five fathers, one novice and three lay brothers. Two weeks later Newman received Fr Frederick Faber and his community into the English Congregation of the Oratory. Faber's community remained settled at St Wilfrid's, Cotton, where Newman gathered all the English Oratorians, temporarily, at the end of October of that year. In the month before the transfer, Newman was able to procure a property in Alcester Street, Birmingham, of which he began to oversee the renovation, and the setting up of a chapel there. Although a provisional posting until they finally moved to Birmingham, the Oratorians threw themselves into action.

On Christmas Eve the Fathers imposed an unrelenting schedule on themselves: 'We have had masses going on literally *through* the night, 36 in all – as if in emulation of the Angels who sang through the night 1800 years ago "Glory to God, peace on earth." Some of us have not been to bed at all.'[2]

---

[1] A saying of St Philip Neri quoted by Newman: *LD* xxix. 357. To Lord Coleridge, 3 April 1881.

[2] *LD* xii. 382. To Henry Wilberforce, 9 [25] December 1848.

The Midnight Mass concluded at 3 a.m., the sacristan, Fr Ambrose, finally getting some rest at about 5.30 a.m. having attached a note to his door saying, 'Please don't call me, and don't knock'.

If this were in the centre of a town, I declare I think it would convert a good half of it by its very look. We have had a number of most splendid functions – but we shall soon (many of us) leave it for Birmingham – for a gloomy gin distillery of which we have taken a lease, fitting up a large room for a Chapel. ... Lately several of our Fathers held a mission in this neighbourhood. They heard between 700 and 800 confessions, and received 22 persons into the Church. Never surely were the words more strikingly exemplified, 'The Harvest is great, the labourers are few' than in England. We could convert England, humanly speaking, at least the lower classes, had we priests enough.[3]

On Friday 26 January 1849, Newman recorded in his diary, 'set off for Birmingham (Alcester Street) for good'.[4] He had been to Birmingham for the first time back in January of 1834 when he recorded in his diary, 'breakfasted at Birmingham', adding at a later date the note, 'the first time I saw Birmingham.'[5] By February 1847 he had to reflect on the nature of the place where he was to set up the Oratory:

the City of Birmingham, a most thickly populated place, remarkable for its recent flock of converts, but full of every sort of heresy, with its youth skilled in their trades but holding a false religion or none at all. This City was for many years the centre of those organizations which were actively hostile to the laws of nature and society; and also of those Associations, the Mechanics' Institutes, devoted to the perverse cultivation of literature (good in itself) and of an unhealthy science, which that English lawyer, Lord Brougham, for these twenty years has spread all over England, in order to teach the people Science, and make them unlearn their religion.[6]

---

[3] Ibid.
[4] *LD* xiii. 16.
[5] *LD* iv. 176.
[6] *NO* 153–4. A translation from the original Latin letter printed in *LD* xii. 36–40. To Cardinal Fransoni, 14 February 1847.

Ten years later, Newman's thought on his adopted city had developed, even if he still held that 'nearly everyone is a nothingarian, an infidel, a sceptic, or an inquirer ...' Yet, 'Here Catholic efforts are not only good in themselves, and do good, but cannot possibly do any even incidental harm – here, whatever is done is so much gain.'[7]

Some years earlier, as an Anglican, Newman had noted that, 'It is scarcely too much to say, that our great cities require even a missionary establishment.'

If the vice, the ignorance, the wretchedness there existing are to be anyhow met, it is not by the labours of a few parochial Clergymen, however exemplary and self-denying, occupied (as they are) with the services of their churches, the management of their vestries, the visitation of their sick, the administration of alms, and their domestic duties and cares, but by one of disengaged mind, intent upon the signs and the exigencies of the times, and vested with authority to promote co-operation among his fellow-labourers, and to conduct the Christian warfare on a consistent plan.[8]

This seems quite a good description of how Newman hoped the Birmingham Oratory, with his oversight, might develop and be leaven for all the good that the Diocesan clergy were achieving. The critical difference between the Newman who spoke as an Anglican about 'the great cities' and the Catholic priest who actually began to live in one was that such a plan, as there undoubtedly was, was subservient to the needs of real people whom Newman met, albeit in great numbers. As a successor of Newman as Superior of the Birmingham Oratory, Fr Paul Chavasse, memorably put it, Newman sought to save souls 'not by number but by name',[9] reflecting the motto that he took when created a Cardinal – St Francis de Sales' line, '*cor ad cor loquitor*' ('heart speaks to heart').

---

[7] *LD* xix. 352. To Canon Estcourt, 2 June 1860.
[8] *VM* ii. 68–9.
[9] Fr Paul Chavasse, Homily to Commemorate John Henry Newman's Ministry at Alcester Street 1849–1852, given at St Anne's, Digbeth, Wednesday 22 April 2009.

The community's new abode had been in its recent history a gin distillery and a marine store. Having, in one day, got his room 'perfectly in order', Newman felt that he was ready to work with 'greater zeal and spirit for the good of others.'[10] Just over a week later, on Friday 2 February, the chapel was opened, St John celebrating the Mass and Newman preaching.[11] 'We began with forgetting to light the Altar Candles, and ended by having to hunt for a corporal for the Tabernacle.'[12] The chapel was crammed full, though the collection was poor, £1.13. But Newman lived in hope, 'We have another collection this evening. We expect a row this evening, and are sending for two policemen – The boys (Wesleyans, I suppose) are frontis perfricatisissimi'.[13] There was no trouble and the service was attended by five to six hundred people.

The area that Newman and the Oratory had come to had the highest density of population in Birmingham and was, according to the Victoria County History of Warwickshire, 'an area of piecemeal development on small sites, in courts and narrow streets, while the proximity of the Warwick and Birmingham Canal encouraged the building of workshops and warehouses.'[14] A closer impression of the area is gained from Newman's comment to Ambrose Lisle Phillips of 'me and mine in Birmingham amid our labyrinth of lanes and beneath our firmament of smoke.'[15] Deritend, where Alcester Street was, was an impoverished area with a high percentage of recently arrived Irish immigrants.

Religious instruction began on 6 February, Newman, on that day, placing himself in the confessional there for the first time. Immediately it was clear to Newman that demand for instruction outstripped the number of catechists available and that this new

---

[10] *LD* xiii. 16–17. To R. A. Coffin, 28 January 1848.
[11] This sermon was published in *Mix.* as 'The salvation of the hearer the motive of the preacher.'
[12] *LD* xiii. 24. To F. W. Faber, Purification 1849.
[13] *LD* xiii. 24. To F. W. Faber, 4 February 1849.
[14] W. B. Stephens, ed., *The Victoria County History of the County of Warwick*, vol. vii, 13.
[15] *LD* xiii. 445. To Ambrose Lisle Phillips, 17 March 1850.

form of pastoral work for him and the community was going to be unwieldy. The children over seven years old in this area would have worked until 8 p.m., hence 'Our work seems to be this, a *rush* of all sorts from 7 to 9 P.M. and comparatively nothing else, unless in the way of the mission.'[16]

Newman describes the first months to a friend:

up to our coming here, we had time but nothing to say; since, we have much to say but no time. I trust we are making progress. We have a decent chapel, it was a gin distillery – it holds 600 persons when crammed – which it commonly is on Sundays – Last night people came an hour before the time, and a number had to go away. We have lectures on Monday and Thursday, well attended – confessions morning and evening and at all hours, daily. An evening school of 100 children, we might have 200, had we hands. We hope to begin a day school soon. We have not yet begun the Oratory[17] – We have made a number of converts, and have many under instruction. The house itself is bad, but it has seven bedrooms, and three sitting rooms beside the kitchen. The Chapel which is detached is 80 feet long, the ceiling low (15 feet) – we have hung curtains at the end and made it decent for the altar.[18]

In the midst of all this new work, Faber was persistently proposing setting up another community in London, and so on 15 April the community divided into two: one remaining in Birmingham, the other going to London. At the opening of this new mission, Newman preached of the task set before the London Fathers 'In this huge city, amid a population of human beings, so vast that each is solitary, so various that each is independent, which, like the ocean, yields before and closes over every attempt made to influence and impress it'.[19]

By October of the Oratory's first year at Alcester Street, Newman was writing, 'We are over laden with work here, and have every prospect, unless St Philip tires of us, of doing a good deal in the course of a few years.'[20] The church, not

---

[16] *LD* xiii. 44. To F. W. Faber, 13 February 1849.
[17] i.e. the Oratorian evening devotions.
[18] *LD* xiii. 101. To Miss M. R. Giberne, 3 April 1849.
[19] *Mix.* 238.
[20] *LD* xiii. 269. To Mrs J. W. Bowden, 8 October 1849.

being large, could not contain those who wished to enter for services: 'the congregation forcibly pushes back the Church doors,' wrote Newman, 'the porch is crowded, and we give Benediction right into the street, people kneeling on the opposite pavement.'[21] And yet, due to the poverty of the Alcester Street congregation, the Oratory Fathers were funding the Oratory from their own personal resources, with the result in Newman's case that 'I have not been able to buy shoes or stockings for the year past, and am ashamed to think how little I have given in charity.'[22]

During the summer of 1850 plans were drawn up for what was to become Newman's home for the rest of his life and the permanent site of the Birmingham Oratory – they were to settle in Edgbaston. This was an area of Birmingham where many professional and wealthy citizens lived, the population doubling within the first twenty years of the Oratory's existence there. Newman had some sense of the kind of church he hoped would be built at the new site in Edgbaston. He wanted something in the 'Roman style' with 'a smack of moorish and gothic – ... the beauty of Greece with something of the wildness of other styles – yet without the extravagance of the moor and the gloom of the Goth.'[23] In order to raise funds, Newman wrote a circular letter to anyone he felt reasonably confident might contribute to help fund the project:

Every order and congregation in the Church has its own work, and ours specially lies among the population of great towns and still more directly with the educated or half-educated or professedly educated portion of it. Here in Birmingham our object will be to influence the tone of thought and opinion prevalent in the various circles of society, high or low; to recommend Catholicism, to expose Protestantism, and especially to take care of young men.[24]

Despite the perhaps fanciful ideas that Newman harboured with regard to the hoped for Oratory Church, his own life was

---

[21] Ibid.
[22] *LD* xiii. 352. To Richard Stanton, 30 December 1849.
[23] *LD* xiv. 290. To Richard Stanton, 23 May 1851.
[24] *LD* xxxii. 43.

clearly rooted in the reality of the life of the Oratory.
According to Fr Paul Chavasse,

Newman's workload was now so intense that he often succumbed to
heavy colds, which showed his whole system was overtaxed. The
timetables for these Alcester Street days have survived and they reveal
Newman taking his turn week after week and month after month with
preaching and instructing and confessing. Indeed, at Christmas 1850 he
doubled and then tripled his hours in the often bug-ridden confessionals
in order to give the other Fathers a respite.[25]

In Edward Bellasis's recollections, published under the title
Coram Cardinali, the author records of Newman that,

One night he instructed, baptized, and prepared a member of the
flock for the death that came a few hours later. He stayed in many
days, expecting a Greek lady from abroad, thus missing much
outdoor exercise. The visitor came, was received into the Church,
returned to her distant home. "What would have been my feelings,"
he said, "had I listened to your expostulations about remaining
indoors?" thus missing her. On her death three months later, her
husband returned his letters. He bade him keep them: they had helped
her, and might aid him.[26]

By the time that the house adjoining what was to be the
temporary church was built – only after Newman's death was
the present church built – 1,700,000 bricks had been used. On
16 February 1852 the Oratorian Fathers moved in – 'we are to
fight the workmen out by our presence,' Newman ruefully
determined, adding, 'You recollect we were obliged to fight
out drunken Jim Blesy and the painters at Littlemore – so too
we fought them out at St Wilfrid's,'[27] the whole community,

[25] P. Lefebvre & C. Mason (eds), *John Henry Newman in his Time*, 90.
According to a Memorandum written by Newman himself, he ceased
going to the Confessional in the Oratory during the mid 1850s, principally
due to the pressure of work that he was under both at home and abroad.
The existence of the Memorandum demonstrates his concern over whether
or not his motivation for doing this was good or not. See *NO* 378–9
quoting BOA Oratory Letters, Jan-June 1857.
[26] E. Bellasis, *Coram Cardinali*, 64.
[27] *LD* xv. 37. To J. D. Dalgairns, 15 February 1852.

therefore, not being able to finally congregate together once again until two months later.

In the meantime Newman had defended himself and his community against the most bizarre rumours as to what the purpose of the new house was to be, in particular its cellars. He had sprung to the defence of the Church, attempting to allay the deep suspicions that were ignited by the restoration of the Hierarchy, in a series of Lectures in Birmingham that were subsequently published as the *Present Position of Catholics in England.* Newman was caught in a whirlwind of activity, saying to one correspondent that he would have written sooner 'were I not in such suffocation of business, from the lectures I am delivering.'[28]

In the summer of 1852, the Bishop of Birmingham, William Bernard Ullathorne, requested the Oratory Fathers to provide pastoral care for the Catholics ensconced at the New Workhouse which was situated a mile and a half from the Oratory at Edgbaston. By 1858 it was recorded that at any one time there might be around 150 Catholics, not including the children, living there but as the population of the Workhouse was ever changing it was thought that as many as 600 Catholics lived there in the space of a year, most desiring to make a general confession, the pastoral care being increased by the fact that a large proportion of the inmates were sick or elderly.[29]

Six years later, responding to a request that he write 'upon some subject of the day',[30] Newman, who had evidently taken responsibility for the sacristy, replied,

Thank you for the beautiful lace which you have worked for me. It is not the way to make me give up the Sacristy, thus to bribe me to stay there. But I would gladly give it up, but, when you talk as you do about it, *you do not realize our great want of hands.* We have the home mission which includes Harborne. We have Smethwick with schools on it, two miles off. We have the work house with 600 general confessions a year in it, and with old men and women, young careless women, and a lot of children. We have poor schools at the

[28] *LD* xiv. 329. To William Froude, 11 August 1851.
[29] *LD* xviii. 268–70. Circular Letter. 24 February 1858.
[30] *LD* xxi. 54. From Mrs T. W. Allies, 21 January 1864.

Oratory. We have the duties of the Church and the confessional, with a host of penitents who live out of our parishes and must be visited in sickness. We have the gentlemen Boy's School with 60 to 80 boys and its masters, dames and servants; we have our own community duties including Fr Minister's, Sacristan's, Prefect of Music's, Novice Master's and the Ruling Deputatio – none of these duties sham, – and together with me we have but seven Fathers. The consequence is that we are all over worked. The day before yesterday two Fathers had to go to bed, and a third had to go to a doctor.[31]

The 'gentlemen Boy's School' to which Newman refers had been opened at Edgbaston in May 1859 and was an establishment that Newman continued to show a lively interest in until the time of his death. The genesis of the idea of the school had come about due to the needs of converts from the Oxford Movement. They neither wished their children to become, in effect, minor seminarians nor to be influenced by what they considered the 'un-English' customs at other Catholic boarding schools. The school flourished, having become a boarding school with a roll call of seventy boys by the mid 1860s. This was the first Catholic public school and the first explicitly lay Catholic boarding school in England. Newman was adamant that the school's role was one of supporting the parents in their duty and care. To further this aim he introduced the then relatively novel system of sending the parents written reports twice a year. He would write the reports, respond to parents' enquiries and meet them whenever they were coming to Birmingham to either collect or drop off their sons at the end or beginning of term time.

For the school, Edward Bellasis records that Newman read 'all the New Testament outside the Epistles and the Apocalypse' to the pupils 'every Sunday, year after year,' and that Newman gave 'the weekly addresses, not remembered in detail, in St Philip's Chapel, Sunday after Sunday, during the simultaneous sermon going on in the church, his own remarks closing on a signal that the inaudible ones elsewhere were over.'[32]

---

[31] *LD* xxi. 54–5. To Mrs T. W. Allies, 20 February 1864.
[32] E. Bellasis, *Coram Cardinali*, 79.

Another aspect of Newman's involvement in education was with regard to the laity at large. At various times and places, as both Anglican and Catholic, he demonstrated the truth of his remark that 'from first to last, education, in this large sense of the word, has been my line.'[33] Newman's hopes for an educated laity are clearly expressed in his *Lectures on the Present Position of Catholics in England*:

I want a laity, not arrogant, not rash in speech, not disputatious, but men who know their religion, who enter into it, who know just where they stand, who know what they hold, and what they do not, who know their creed so well, that they can give an account of it, who know so much of history that they can defend it. I want an intelligent, well-instructed laity; I am not denying you are such already: but I mean to be severe, and, as some would say, exorbitant in my demands. I wish you to enlarge your knowledge, to cultivate your reason, to get an insight into the relation of truth to truth, to learn to view things as they are, to understand how faith and reason stand to each other, what are the bases and principles of Catholicism, and where lie the main inconsistencies and absurdities of the Protestant theory. I have no apprehension you will be the worse Catholics for familiarity with these subjects, provided you cherish a vivid sense of God above, and keep in mind you have souls to be judged and saved. . . .[34]

Humility was a requirement for the laity, as for any cleric, before Divine Revelation and its transmission by the Church:

No one desires more earnestly than the writer of these lines, that free discussion should be allowed us on all matters which the Church has not ruled. No one laments more than I do that bigotry and jealousy which would enthrone the decisions of individuals, or of parties, or of schools, as if divine truths, unassailable and irreversible.[35]

---

[33] *AW* 259.

[34] *Prepos.* 390.

[35] *LD* xix. 554–5. Letter to the editor of the *Rambler*, 14 August 1860. As Avery Cardinal Dulles, SJ, commented in 2002, 'In the past thirty years a great deal has been written about the problem of dissent, which occurs when the faithful do not receive, or even reject, the official teaching [of the Church]. Neither Newman nor Vatican II confronts that problem directly. So far as I am aware, Newman never dissented from any official teaching of the Church, nor did he encourage others to do so.' A. Dulles, *Newman*, 159.

Increasingly with age, Newman sought to influence and educate men and women by virtue of his writings rather than series of speeches. But the Oratory itself was a vehicle in Birmingham to educate those who came to its classes.

With such a pressure of work pressing on so few at the Oratory it is even more a wonder that Newman could begin to imagine, let alone spring into action, with regard to the slander of Charles Kingsley that resulted in Newman's publication of the history of his religious opinion in seven parts, issued weekly from 21 April until 2 June, the *Apologia pro vita sua*.[36] In the aftermath of the publication of Newman's Apologia, Bishop Ullathorne wrote,

We have now been personally acquainted, and much more than acquainted, for nineteen years, during more than sixteen of which we have stood in special relation of duty towards each other. This has been one of the singular blessings which God has given me amongst the cares of the Episcopal office. What my feelings of respect, of confidence, and of affection have been towards you, you know well, nor should I think of expressing them in words. But there is one thing that has struck me in this day of explanations, which you could not, and would not, be disposed to do, and which no one could do so properly or so authentically as I could, and which it seems to me is not altogether uncalled for, if every kind of erroneous impression that some persons have entertained with no better evidence than conjecture is to be removed.

It is difficult to comprehend how, in the face of facts, the notion should ever have arisen that during your Catholic life, you have been more occupied with your own thoughts than with the service of religion and the work of the Church. If we take no other work into consideration beyond the written productions which your Catholic pen has given to the world, they are enough for the life's labour of another. There are the Lectures on Anglican Difficulties, the Lectures on Catholicism in England, the great work on the Scope and End of University Education, that on the Office and Work of Universities, the Lectures and Essays on University Subjects, and the two Volumes of Sermons; not to speak of your contributions to the Atlantis, which you founded, and to other periodicals; then there are

---

[36] Cf. *LD* xxi. 62. To John Hardman, 27 February 1864.

those beautiful offerings to Catholic literature, the Lectures on the Turks, Loss and Gain, and Callista, and though last, not least, the Apologia, which is destined to put many idle rumours to rest, and many unprofitable surmises; and yet all these productions represent but a portion of your labour, and that in the second half of your period of public life.

These works have been written in the midst of labour and cares of another kind, and of which the world knows very little. I will specify four of these undertakings, each of a distinct character, and any one of which would have made a reputation for untiring energy in the practical order.[37]

Ullathorne continues by citing as the first two of Newman's undertakings the foundation of the Congregation of the Oratory and his involvement in the establishing of the University of Ireland (the fourth being the foundation of the Oratory School). He then turns to Newman's parochial work:

The original plan of an oratory did not contemplate any parochial work, but you could not contemplate so many souls in want of pastors without being prompt and ready at the beck of authority to strain all your efforts in coming to their help. And this brings me to the third and the most continuous of those labours to which I have alluded. The mission in Alcester Street, its church and schools, were the first work of the Birmingham Oratory. After several years of close and hard work, and a considerable call upon the private resources of the Fathers who had established this congregation, it was delivered over to other hands, and the Fathers removed to the district of Edgbaston, where up to that time nothing Catholic had appeared. Then arose under your direction the large convent of the Oratory, the church expanded by degrees into its present capaciousness, a numerous congregation has gathered and grown in it; poor schools and other pious institutions have grown up in connexion with it, and, moreover, equally at your expense and that of your brethren, and, as I have reason to know, at much inconvenience, the Oratory has relieved the other clergy of Birmingham all this while by constantly doing the duty in the poor-house and gaol of Birmingham.

More recently still, the mission and the poor school at Smethwick owe their existence to the Oratory. And all this while the founder and

---

[37] *Apo.* 316–17.

father of these religious works has added to his other solicitudes the toil of frequent preaching, of attendance in the confessional, and other parochial duties.

I have read on this day of its publication the seventh part of the Apologia, and the touching allusion in it to the devotedness of the Catholic clergy to the poor in seasons of pestilence reminds me that when the cholera raged so dreadfully at Bilston, and the two priests of the town were no longer equal to the number of cases to which they were hurried day and night, I asked you to lend me two fathers to supply the place of other priests whom I wished to send as a further aid. But you and Father St. John preferred to take the place of danger which I had destined for others, and remained at Bilston till the worst was over.

To spare, my dear Dr. Newman, any further pressure on those feelings with which I have already taken so large a liberty, I will only add one word more for my own satisfaction. During our long intercourse there is only one subject on which, after the first experience, I have measured my words with some caution, and that has been where questions bearing on ecclesiastical duty have arisen. I found some little caution necessary, because you were always so prompt and ready to go even beyond the slightest intimation of my wish or desires.[38]

Even in the midst of the most terrible loss of his later life, the death of Fr Ambrose St. John, Newman put first the needs of his parish. Fr Neville, a fellow Oratorian, recalled that Newman 'came back from Fr Ambrose's grave the day of the funeral to go to Fr Ambrose's Confessional though he would have like[d] so very much indeed to have stayed over Sunday there and Monday too and to have seen everything made tidy – but no – he is going to work.'[39]

Whilst much of Newman's parochial life is unremarkable when set beside the equally heroic efforts of so many of the English clergy at that time, one episode has caught the imagination and admiration of those who heard of it. As mentioned in Bishop Ullathorne's letter quoted above, in September 1849, whilst suffering from a heavy cold and a loss of hearing, Newman together with Fr Ambrose St. John and Br

[38] *Apo.* 317–18.
[39] *LD* xxvii. 304, note 2 July 1875.

Aloysius Boland left their house at Alcester Street to lend support to the priest at nearby Bilston who was, with great difficulty and personal courage, ministering to his parishioners in the midst of an outbreak of cholera in his town. As incredible as it may seem to many today, such outbreaks could cost the lives of many people in one town and also the lives of those brave enough to minister to them such as Bishop William Riddell, Vicar Apostolic of the Northern District, who had died just under two years previously from an infection he was exposed to during a similar epidemic in Newcastle. However, by the time Newman and his companions had arrived in Bilston the danger of the disease was abating and he found that there was little work for them to do.[40] Not only is Newman's courage marked by this account but the alarm of the newly-formed congregation at Alcester Street for the safety of Newman and his companions whilst away on their mission more than suggests that the Oratory Fathers had quickly won the hearts and minds of those to whom they ministered.

Another account, from late in his life, once again shows the kindness of Newman's heart. In November 1889, less than a year before his death, the elderly and frail Cardinal Newman drove through the snow-laden lanes to intercede on behalf of the female employees of the local Cadbury chocolate factory who were holding out against having to attend daily Bible classes as organized by the Quaker Cadbury brothers. Newman restored peace to the situation and a room was set aside to enable the women to partake in Catholic prayers. It was noted at the time that the Cadbury brothers were 'charmed by the loving Christian spirit with which [Newman] entered into the question.'[41]

This intervention on behalf of the good ladies of Cadbury's was an uncharacteristically yet necessarily public action. Beyond all doubt it betokened a hidden life of charity and

---

[40] Cf *LD* xiii. 258–60. Newman had had indirect experience of the dangers of cholera previously during an outbreak at Oxford in 1832, although no deaths were reported in his parish: see *LD* iii. 75–6. Memorandum About the Cholera, 14 October 1874.

[41] *LD* xxxi. 278, note.

almsgiving that has persistently been related yet is hard to unearth in detail. Fr Neville related,

Indeed, our Cardinal's thought about the poor was, how much he could give them discreetly; and in some cases, whether they were known to him personally or not, after learning well how things stood with them, he would give five pounds, even ten pounds, to one person at a time, chuckling at the thought of the pleased surprise they would feel on realising what they were holding. ... No matter to whom the Cardinal's gifts were made, it was always as though he felt it a privilege to make them. ...[42]

A similar sense of the caring pastor is conveyed in a letter from Rev. Robert Hodge, O.C.R., to the editor of the *Tablet* regarding the persevering tradition in Birmingham of Newman's love for the poor:

Not many years ago one of my brethren, Fr Ailred McPike, now deceased, told me with emphasis of the esteem in which Newman was held by the ordinary people of Birmingham, among whom he was proud to be numbered. ... If memory serves, what I believe he said was that the ordinary people of Birmingham adored him; and in those days the ordinary people of Birmingham were invariably poor. ... According to Fr. Alban's family tradition, the ordinary people of Birmingham doted on Newman. And why? Because, so he told me, quietly and behind the scenes he would help the unemployed, and especially women, to get work, and would sometimes ask persons in high positions to provide employment.[43]

There are other similar accounts of Newman's charity, even one of a Birmingham doctor's surgery, bombed during the Second World War, which proudly displayed the doctor's bills for the poor that Newman had paid.[44] His devotion to the poor remained consistent from when he first set out to serve the Lord. A letter records a response to his brother, Frank's, criticism of the comfort with which Newman had, at that time, placed his mother and sister when they came to live near

---

[42] *Positio* i. 395 – Extract from Fr Neville's recollections held in B.O.A.
[43] *Positio* i. 396, quoting The *Tablet* (24 July 1971), 723.
[44] *Positio* ii. 111, cf. 141 & 143.

Littlemore. In responding to the criticism he lifts the veil from his kindness: 'then where would be the kitchen for Littlemore, with broth and messes? where the rice and tapioca from a housekeeper's closet? in a word, they enable me to spend a large sum upon the poor which I could not spend satisfactorily myself.'[45]

Few were as aware of Newman's commitment to the souls under his care in Birmingham than Bishop Ullathorne. These two eminent Victorian pastors and friends held each other in affection and admiration for by far the greater time of their acquaintance. Three years before his death in 1889, Ullathorne dedicated to Newman a book, the title of which seems so apposite for the dedicatee, the book being called *Christian Patience*. Of Newman, Ullathorne wrote, 'Deeply sensible of the incalculable services which you have rendered to the Church at large by your writings, and to this Diocese of your residence in particular by the high and complete character of your virtues, by your zeal for souls, and by your influence of your presence in the midst of us'.[46] Having seen something of a priest at work amongst his flock, it is to Newman's virtues and his 'zeal for souls', expressed principally in his preaching and administration of the sacraments, that we now turn.

---

[45] *LD* iv. 330.
[46] *LD* xxxi. 160, note 1. Bishop Ullathorne, *Christian Patience*.

Part II

7

Prayer

Every thing that one does honestly, sincerely,
with prayer, with advice, must turn to good.[1]

The most important and consistent thread that binds together
Newman's ministry, first as an Anglican and then as a
Catholic priest, is his life of prayer, especially with regard
to prayers of intercession. Three small notebooks of his,
bearing the thumb marks of constant use, bear eloquent
testimony to this fact.

One of these books contains the prayers that Newman wrote
out to be said before and after Mass. These are drawn from
those recommended to priests to say along with Newman's
own addition of the *Dies Irae*. There is a prayer dated from the
day of his first communion as an Anglican yet copied out again
many years later as a Catholic:

Lord I praise Thee for calling me to the light of Thy Gospel – for my
birth in a country where Thy true religion is found, and for Thy
goodness in enlightening my soul with the knowledge of Thy truth,
that, whereas I was proud, selfrighteous, impure, abominable, Thou
wast pleased to turn me from such a state of darkness and irreligion,
by a mercy which is too wonderful for me, and make me fall down
humbled and abased before Thy footstool. O let me so run the race
that is set before me that I may lay hold of everlasting life, and
especially let me make Thee, O Holy Jesus, my pattern in my
pilgrimage here, that Thou mayest be the portion of my soul to all
eternity.[2]

[1] *LD* ix. 490. To Mrs John Mozley, 31 August 1843.
[2] B.O.A., C.5.12 (copied from A.10.4). Cited in *NO* 60.

As well as containing prayers, the notebooks record Newman's intercessions. They too had originally been set down many years before his conversion, indeed during the months following his ordination as an Anglican deacon in 1824, yet these petitions were also rewritten about 1875, with some amendments, into his Mass intention notebook. For each day of the week (here Tuesday's intercessions come from the original set that Newman inscribed whilst at St Clement's) Newman set out the intentions in the same pattern: Pray for ... Pray against ... Intercede for ...

Tuesday – ... Intercede for flock at St Clements – churchmen – dissenters – romanists – those without religion – pious, worldly – rector, churchwardens and other offices – sick, old, young, women labouring with child – rich and poor – schools – that the church may be rebuilt and well – for unity – for the extension of godliness.

Wednesday – Pray for *Purity*, sobriety – chastity – temperance – self denial – simplicity – sincerity – truth – openness – candour – Pray against excess, – uncleaness – worldlymindedness – lying – insincerity. ...

Friday – Pray for *Zeal* – Pray for In church – singleness of heart – I Cor. x, 31[3] 2 Cor. iii. 5[4] Gal. vi. 14.[5] Phil iv. 13[6] a view to God's glory – simple dependence on the grace of Christ – regarding myself as an *instrument*. For liveliness and fervency of prayer – for a deep sense of the awful nature of my sacred office – regarding myself as the voice of the people to God, and of God to the people, for the spirit of devotion, affection towards my people – love, faith, fear, confidence towards God ... for strength of body, nerves, voice, breath &c – earnestness of manner, distinctness of delivery.[7]

---

[3] 'Therefore, whether you eat or drink, or whatsoever else you do, do all to the glory of God.'
[4] 'Not that we are sufficient to think any thing of ourselves, as of ourselves: but our sufficiency is from God.'
[5] 'But God forbid that I should glory, save in the cross of our Lord Jesus Christ; by whom the world is crucified to me, and I to the world.'
[6] 'I can do all things in him who strengtheneth me.'
[7] B.O.A., C.5.12. Quoted in *NO* 16, 28 & 61–2. In setting out this pattern of intercessory prayer Newman seems to have been influenced by the devotions of Bishop Andrews that he freshly translated to become Tract 88 in 1840 entitled 'The Greek Devotions of Bishop Andrews, translated and arranged'.

As Dom Placid Murray notes in his book *Newman the Oratorian*, Friday's prayer for fervour is magnified by Newman in lines from his *Meditations and Devotions* 'where the recurring phrase "in asking for fervour" hammers home his prayer until the final demand':[8]

Lord, in asking for fervour, I am asking for Thyself, for nothing short of Thee, O my God, who hast given Thyself wholly to us. Enter my heart substantially and personally, and fill it with fervour by filling it with Thee. Thou alone canst fill the soul of man, and Thou hast promised to do so. Thou art the living Flame, and ever burnest with love of man: enter into me and set me on fire after Thy pattern and likeness.[9]

In the second notebook lists of names of those to be prayed for are recorded under short headings:

> Auld lang Syne
> Protestants (1864)
> Dear to me; kind to me; Cold to me; No how to me
> Godchildren
> Cousins
> St Mary's and Littlemore
> Faithful Women
> Old and Catholic
> Old and Protestant (*cancelled*)
> With claim on me
> Loyal to me
> Catholics 1; Catholics 2; Catholics 3
> Benefactors to Congr.
> Irish friends
> About Oratory
> Ecclesiastical
> Converts
> The Dead[10]

---

[8] *NO* 62.
[9] *MD* 431.
[10] *NO* 62.

The dates on which the names were recorded range from 1850 to 1864 and up to 1882. Existing similar lists by Newman date from 1839 and it is clear that upon his travelling to Rome to pursue his Catholic ecclesiastical education he was continuing to pray for many of his Anglican friends and acquaintances as he ever had done before.

Two sermons in particular explore Newman's deepest thoughts on the role and the necessity for intercessory prayer. Both are to be found published in *Parochial and Plain Sermons* – "The Christian Ministry" and "Intercession". In the former sermon Newman writes that

the office of intercession, which though not a peculiarity, is ever characteristic of the Priestly Order, is spoken of in Scripture as a sort of prerogative of the Gospel Ministry. For instance, Isaiah, speaking of Christian times, says, "I have set watchmen upon thy walls, O Jerusalem, which shall never hold their peace day nor night. Ye that make mention of the Lord, keep not silence; and give Him no rest, till He establish, and till He make Jerusalem a praise in the earth." [Isa. lxii. 6, 7.] In the Acts of the Apostles, we find Christ's ministers engaged in this sacred service, according to the prophecy. "There were in the Church that was at Antioch certain prophets and teachers, as Barnabas, and Simeon called Niger, and Lucius of Cyrene, and Manaen, foster brother to Herod the Tetrarch, and Saul. As they *ministered* to the Lord, and fasted," [Acts xiii. 1, 2.] the Holy Ghost separated two of them for His work. This "ministering" to the Lord with fasting was surely some solemn intercessory service. And this agrees with a passage in St. James's Epistle, which seems to invest the Elders of the Church with this same privilege of the priesthood. "Is any sick among you? Let him call for the Elders of the Church, *and let them pray over him* (not pray *with* him merely), anointing him with oil in the name of the Lord; and *the prayer of faith* (not the oil merely) shall save the sick, and the Lord shall raise him up." In like manner St. Paul speaks of Epaphras as "our dear fellow-servant, who is *for* you," that is, for the Colossians to whom he is writing, "a faithful minister of Christ." Presently he explains what was the service which Epaphras did for them: "always *labouring fervently for you in prayer*, that ye may stand perfect and complete in all the will of God." [James v. 14, 15. Col. i. 7; iv. 12.][11]

[11] *PS* ii. 312–14.

Newman's sermon on intercession speaks in unequivocal
terms of this type of prayer that is 'characteristic of Christian
worship, the privilege of the heavenly adoption, the perfect
and spiritual mind'.[12] Having traced the Scriptural inspiration
of intercessory prayer Newman reflects,

Such is the lesson taught us by the words and deeds of the Apostles
and their brethren. Nor could it be otherwise, if Christianity be a
social religion, as it is pre-eminently. If Christians are to live
together, they will pray together; and united prayer is necessarily of
an intercessory character, as being offered for each other and for the
whole, and for self as one of the whole. In proportion, then, as unity
is an especial Gospel-duty, so does Gospel-prayer partake of a social
character; and Intercession becomes a token of the existence of a
Church Catholic.[13]

Newman concludes,

Surely He did not die for any common end, but in order to exalt man,
who was of the dust of the field, into "heavenly places." He did not
die to leave him as he was, sinful, ignorant, and miserable. He did
not die to see His purchased possession, as feeble in good works, as
corrupt, as poor-spirited, and as desponding, as before He came.
Rather, He died to renew him after His own image, to make him a
being He might delight and rejoice in, to make him "partaker of the
divine nature," to fill him within and without with a flood of grace
and glory; to pour out upon him gift upon gift, and virtue upon
virtue, and power upon power, each acting upon each, and working
together one and all, till he becomes an Angel upon earth, instead of
a rebel and an outcast. He died to bestow upon him that privilege
which implies or involves all others, and brings him into nearest
resemblance to Himself, the privilege of Intercession. This, I say, is
the Christian's especial prerogative; and if he does not exercise it,
certainly he has not risen to the conception of his real place among
created beings. ... Beloved, clad in the garments of righteousness,
anointed with oil, and with a crown upon his head, in royal and
priestly garb, as an heir of eternity, full of grace and good works, as
walking in all the commandments of the Lord blameless, such an

---

[12] *PS* iii. 350–1.
[13] *PS* iii. 352–3.

one, I repeat it, is plainly in his fitting place when he intercedes. He is made after the pattern and in the fulness of Christ – he is what Christ is. Christ intercedes above, and he intercedes below.[14]

And while the gift of intercessory prayer is granted to all Christians, the priest, 'the spokesman of the saints far and near, gathering together their holy and concordant suffrages, and presenting them by virtue of his priesthood,'[15] has a most critical role in interceding on behalf of his people:

This, then, is what I felt and feel: – it is commonly said, when weekday prayers are spoken of, "You will not get a congregation, or you will get but a few;" but they whom Christ has brought near to Himself to be the Stewards of His Mysteries depend on no man; rather, after His pattern, they are to draw men after them. He prayed alone on the mountain; He prays alone (for who shall join with Him?) in his Father's presence. He is the one effectual Intercessor for sinners at the right hand of God. And what He is really, such are we in figure; what He is meritoriously, such are we instrumentally. Such are we by His grace; allowed to occupy His place visibly, however unworthily, in His absence, till He come; allowed to depend on Him, and not on our people; allowed to draw our commission from Him, not from them; allowed to be centres, about which the Church may grow, and about which it really exists, be it great or little.[16]

Before taking on any major endeavour, and attempting to do so before any minor activity, Newman would refer to God in prayer, seeking guidance. His intercessions as a Catholic included the Holy Souls, remembering departed friends whom he recorded in an Obituary Book that 'dear Mrs Pusey' had made for him in her last illness.[17] As a Cardinal, Newman collected together many small photographs of Catholic friends (and one of his mother) that had died and hung them on one side of his altar, including them in the intention of his daily Mass.[18] He seems to have remembered many people during his

---

[14] *PS* iii. 361–3.
[15] *PS* iii. 313.
[16] *PS* iii. 314.
[17] *LD* xxx. 153. To Mrs Edward Hawkins, 21 November 1882.
[18] *LD* xxix. 294. To Isy Froude, Baroness Anatole von Hügel, 4 August 1880.

Masses. Into old age Newman wrote to friends and acquaintances, as he had done from the time of his ordination, promising to offer Mass for their intentions, the death of the mother of one friend reminding him 'that the time must soon come, when I must need from others what I give to her.'[19]

As a Catholic cleric Newman was obliged to recite the Divine Office, the Breviary as it is also known, discovering this compendium of prayers as an Anglican and treasuring it, writing that 'if asked what *I* should wish Services formed upon, I should unhesitatingly say the model of the Breviary'.[20]

At a comparatively early date I drew up the Tract on the Roman Breviary ... It was an apparent accident which introduced me to the knowledge of that most wonderful and most attractive monument of the devotion of saints. On Hurrell Froude's death, in 1836, I was asked to select one of his books as a keepsake. I selected Butler's *Analogy*: finding that it had already been chosen, I looked with some perplexity along the shelves as they stood before me, when an intimate friend at my elbow said, 'Take that.' It was the Breviary which Hurrell had had with him at Barbados. Accordingly I took it, studied it, wrote my Tract from it, and have it on my table in constant use till this day.[21]

The breviary in question, a set of four volumes, is preserved at the Birmingham Oratory along with some other breviaries that Newman acquired as a Catholic. From the time that he received Froude's Breviary, Newman began to use the offices as part of his daily prayer.[22] At first he omitted those parts that invoked the Blessed Virgin Mary and the saints but, at the suggestion of Frederick Oakeley and soon after the publication of the ground breaking Tract 90, he began to use the Breviary in full. He recited the psalms, readings and prayers slowly, telling his friend Henry Wilberforce that it would take him between three and four hours a day to pray the offices.

---

[19] *LD* xxx. 309. To Mrs John Kenyon, 13 February 1884.
[20] *LD* vi. 48. To Henry Wilberforce, 25 March 1837.
[21] *Apo.* 75–76. The Tract referred to is Tract 75.
[22] *LD* vi. 10.

I like them uncommonly. They are very unexciting, grave and simple. They are for the whole year, varying day by day more or less. This again I like much; it keeps up attention and rouses the imagination towards the course of the Christian year, without exciting it ... Latin devotions are majestic and austere ... they are better fitted for praise and earnest expostulation. The great advantage of a dead language is that it keeps one sober.[23]

Other aspects of the Breviary were equally admired by Newman:

The Psalms should be the basis of all devotion – the more one knows of them, the more surprising they are – of course, being inspired. .... Another peculiarity of the Breviary is that the bulk and stress of the Service is in the morning – viz when our time is more our own and our mind most fresh. To leave the body of our prayers for night, is like putting off religion to a deathbed. ... Further the Breviary Services simplify as the day proceeds – Compline is all but invariable through the year – here is something beautiful in this – Another characteristic of the Breviary Services is the shortness of the prayers they contain.[24]

His delight in discovering such a cornucopia of prayers and meditations led Newman to write a Tract (Number 75) on the subject of the Breviary and, with two friends, to commence an attempt to publish a translation of it, a massive undertaking that was eventually abandoned. The Tract, which was surprisingly popular and in Newman's estimation 'the most promising event that has happened since the Tracts began',[25] set out to present to the Church of England the 'excellence and beauty' of the Breviary, despite the practice of imploring the intercession of the Blessed Virgin Mary and the saints – an area that Newman was yet to discover as praiseworthy. Newman opened his remarks on the Breviary with four lines of verse:

[23] *LD* vi. 47. To Henry Wilberforce, 25 March 1837.
[24] Ibid.
[25] *LD* vi. 18. To J. F. Christie, 29 January 1837.

Teach her to know and love her hour of prayer,
  And evermore,
  As faith grows rare,
Unlock her heart, and offer all its store,
In holier love and humbler vows,
As suits a lost returning spouse.[26]

Newman then writes,

There is so much of excellence and beauty in the services of the
Breviary, that were it skilfully set before the Protestant by Roman
controversialists as the book of devotions received in their
communion, it would undoubtedly raise a prejudice in their favour,
if he were ignorant of the circumstances of the case, and but
ordinarily candid and unprejudiced.[27]

Chief among his purposes in publishing the Tract, he declares,
is to avoid the 'Roman Church' having the benefit of the
Divine Office and thus letting it attract the faithful by means of
its beauty, particularly with regard to the 'excellence and
profitableness of those inspired compositions', the psalms.

In a word, it will be attempted to wrest a weapon out of our
adversaries' hands; who have in this, as in many other instances,
appropriated to themselves a treasure which was ours as much as
theirs; and then, on our attempting to recover it, accuse us of
borrowing what we have but lost through inadvertence. The
publication then of the selections, which it is proposed presently to
give from these Services, is, as it were, an act of re-appropriation.
Were, however, the Breviary ever so much the property of the
Romanists, by retaining it in its ancient Latin form, they have
defrauded the Church of that benefit which, in the vernacular tongue,
it might have afforded to the people at large.[28]

The publication of Tract 75 was not the only attempt by
Newman and his friends to bring the principles of the Breviary

---

[26] Tract No. 75, *On the Roman Breviary as Embodying the Substance of the
Devotional Services of the Church Catholic*, 1.
[27] Ibid.
[28] Ibid.

to a wider congregation, as they were preparing for the republication of Bishop John Cosin's *A Collection of Private devotions: in the practice of the Ancient Church, called the Hours of Prayer* first published in 1627.[29] The preface written for the 1838 edition described the aim of the work as

to recover or retain, at least in private devotion, a portion of that undoubtedly Catholic and Apostolic system which forms so beautiful a feature in the Breviaries; a portion which had survived the Reformation, forming a conspicuous part of the Primers of Henry VIII. and Edward VI., and which was preserved in that of Elizabeth of 1560, on which this book is professedly founded.

Responding to criticism of his publication of Tract 75, Newman complained to his Bishop that 'as far as its object is concerned, it is not very unlike the publication of Bishop Cosin's Hours of Prayer', a book promoted with the authority of the Church of England.[30] However he did concede to Pusey that the translation of the Breviary that they had been working on 'will tend to prepare minds for the Church of Rome'. 'I do not think our system will bear it. It is like sewing a new piece of cloth on an old garment.'[31]

Having resigned the living of the University Church, and having retired to Littlemore to lead a life of quasi-monastic prayer and study, Newman was at pains to assure the Bishop of Oxford that he was not setting up a monastery but rather a 'parsonage house' where he and others planned to live quietly for a while. Whilst he worked upon *Essay on Development* he was nourished by the community recitation of the Breviary, although the Antiphons to the Blessed Virgin Mary and certain other prayers were omitted and the Latin was declaimed according to English pronunciation. From the day of his reception into full communion with the Catholic Church, the Marian Antiphons were recited and the prayers once omitted reinstated. Even the pronunciation of the Latin was now Italianized.

---

[29] Eleventh edition published in London, 1838.
[30] *LD* viii. 133. To Richard Bagot, Bishop of Oxford, 29 March 1841.
[31] *LD* x. 40. To Edward Bouverie Pusey, 2 December 1843.

Being firmly established as a basic element of his daily life, Newman had little cause to write further about the Breviary that he recited day after day for the rest of his long life until no longer able. This privation, when it occurred, was softened by his substituting the Rosary for the Breviary at the suggestion of Bishop Ullathorne.[32]

Newman's prayer life was sustained by other forms of prayer too, the written evidence for his contemplative and meditative prayer are his magnificent sermons and ultimately the testimony of his life.

The Christian lives in the past and in the future, and in the unseen; in a word, he lives in no small measure in the unknown. And it is one of his duties, and a part of his work, to make the unknown known; to create within him an image of what is absent, and to realise by faith what he does not see. For this purpose he is granted certain outlines and rudiments of the truth and from thence he learns to draw it out into its full proportions and its substantial form, – to expand and complete it; whether it be the absolute and perfect truth, or truth under a human dress, or truth in such a shape as is most profitable for him. And the process, by which the word which has been given him, 'returns not void,' but brings forth and buds and is accomplished and prospers, is Meditation.[33]

He wrote meditations himself, a large number being post-humously published together by Fr Neville in *Meditations and Devotions*. However Newman was in no doubt that

[The Bible] is the best book of meditations which can be, because it is divine. This is why we see such multitudes in France and Italy giving up religion altogether. They have not impressed upon their hearts the life of our Lord and Saviour as given us in the Evangelists. They believe merely with the intellect, not with the heart. Argument may overset a mere assent of the reason, but not a faith founded in a personal love for the Object of Faith.[34]

---

[32] *Ward* ii. 533. Eventually even the Rosary had to be abandoned too, due to a lack of sensitivity in the Cardinal's fingers preventing him from its use.

[33] *LD* x. 801. From *Lives of the English Saints*, i. A Legend of St Gundleus, Hermit in Wales, about A. D. 500.

[34] *LD* xxvi. 87. To Mrs J. W. Bowden, 12 May 1872.

Devotion to the Sacred Heart of Jesus was, according to Fr Neville, 'a very special devotion to him [Newman], and it is remembered that he spoke of it in years long gone by as affecting him far more powerfully than other devotions which he named, though to those also he was known to be drawn.'[35] Once the Oratory had settled at Edgbaston, Newman built the Chapel of the Sacred Heart with his own money.

In all, prayer was the heart of all the good that was of John Henry Newman. He taught that it simply was '(if it may be said reverently) *conversing* with God'[36] and that 'it is plain to common sense that the man who has not accustomed himself to the language of Heaven will be no *fit* inhabitant of it when, in the Last Day, it is perceptibly revealed.'[37] It is the duty and the glory of the followers of Christ to

live in Heaven in their thoughts, motives, aims, desires, likings, prayers, praises, intercessions, even while they are in the flesh; to look like other men, to be busy like other men, to be passed over in the crowd of men, or even to be scorned or oppressed, as other men may be, but the while to have a secret channel of communication with the Most High, a gift the world knows not of; to have their life *hid* with Christ in God.[38]

Such an intelligent man as Newman humbly recognized that it was in prayer that his strength, such as he felt it was, lay, and he advises against putting our trust in any lesser means: 'Quarry the granite rock with razors, or moor the vessel with a thread of silk; then you may hope with such keen and delicate instruments as human knowledge and human reason to contend against those giants, the passion and the pride of man'.[39] Prayer in all its forms is one of the greatest of God's gifts to us and brings about our interior transformation, as it did in the priestly heart and soul of John Henry Newman:

35 *Ward* ii 364.
36 *PS* iv. 227.
37 *PS* iv. 229.
38 *PS* vi. 214.
39 *Idea* 121.

So a habit of prayer, the practice of turning to God and the unseen world, in every season, in every place, in every emergency (let alone its supernatural effect of prevailing with God), – prayer, I say, has what may be called a *natural* effect, in spiritualizing and elevating the soul. A man is no longer what he was before; gradually, imperceptibly to himself, he has imbibed a new set of ideas, and become imbued with fresh principles. He is as one coming from kings' courts, with a grace, a delicacy, a dignity, a propriety, a justness of thought and taste, a clearness and firmness of principle, all his own. Such is the power of God's secret grace acting through those ordinances which He has enjoined us . . . As speech is the organ of human society, and the means of human civilization, so is prayer the instrument of divine fellowship and divine training.[40]

[40] *PS* iv. 230–1.

8

Consecrated to Christ

Simply to His grace and wholly
Life and light and strength belong,
And I love, supremely, solely,
Him the Holy, Him the Strong.[1]

From a young age it seemed clear to Newman that he was called by God to lead a single life. This self-understanding first came during the autumn of 1816 and seems to have been inspired, in part, by his belief that his 'calling in life would require such a sacrifice as celibacy involved; as, for instance, missionary work among the heathen, to which I had a great drawing for some years. It also strengthened my feeling of separation from the visible world'.[2]

This sense of separation being intrinsic to the aspiration to live celibately was given a less idealized hue by a more mature Newman during his time as a Fellow of Oriel College, Oxford, when he related in a letter that he felt 'more strongly than ever the necessity of there being men in the Church, like the R Catholic friars, free from all obstacles to their devoting themselves to its defence.'[3]

The illumination of 1816, Newman later recorded, had 'held its ground almost continuously ever since, – with the break of a month now and a month then, up to 1829, and, after that date, without any break at all.'[4] Indeed after February 1829 Newman had 'the continuous will and resolution, with divine aid, to live and die single. I determined to be 'a pilgrim pale

---

[1] *VV* 327.
[2] *Apo.* 20
[3] *LD* ii. 133. To Jemima Newman, 17 March 1829.
[4] *Apo.* 20.

in Paul's stern girdle bound'.[5] 'For years,' he wrote, 'I have
made up my *mind* to remain in single blessedness – but
whether my *heart* be equally made up, time alone can tell.'[6]
All these thoughts were written whilst Newman was an
Anglican and while holding for himself that he was called to
the celibate life, the 'severing vow'.[7] Yet he wrote in 1832,
'You mistake me, if you think I consider clergymen, as such,
should not marry, I only think there should be among the
clergy enough unmarried, to give a character of strength to the
whole – and that therefore, every one should ask himself
whether he is called to the celibate.'[8]

Later that year he remarked to a friend that 'country parsons
ought, as a general rule, to be married.' Celibacy was 'a high
state of life, to which the multitude of men cannot aspire – I do
not say, that they who adopt it are necessarily better than
others, though the noblest ηθος is situated in that state.'[9]

In 1840 Newman still held to this principle, asking, 'As to
celibacy, does not the notion that it is not a holier state than
matrimony tend to Pelagianism? Does not the conclusion that it
is, follow from the words of the Article 'concupiscence has the
nature of sin'? and what is the meaning of 'In sin hath my
mother conceived me'?[10]

Writing to Faber later that same year Newman concurs with
an opinion expressed in a letter sent to Faber:

I subscribe to its principles heartily in the abstract, especially to his
principal view, of celibacy as a penance for past sin. I consider it also
as a more holy state [than marriage]; but could not urge this strongly
on another, this view being so much a matter of feeling. But
regarding it as penance, I could urge it strongly, did I know on whom

---

[5] B.O.A., C. 5. 12. quoted in *NO*.
[6] *LD* iii. 66–67.
[7] *VV* 66.
[8] *LD* iii. 23. To Henry Wilberforce, 26 February 1832. Cf. *LD* iii. 40. To
Robert Isaac Wilberforce, 5 April 1832. For more information as to the
influence of earlier writers on the concept of celibacy in the Church of
England see the article 'The Anglican Origins of Newman's Celibacy' by
B. W. Young, *Church History* (Chicago) 64 (1996) 15–27.
[9] *LD* iii. 70. To George Ryder, 22 July 1832.
[10] *LD* vii. 331. To Henry Moore, 21 May 1840.

to urge it. . . . One thing is quite plain, that we are not to judge one another, but to give each other credit for determining agreeably to God's will in his own case.[11]

In the years after ordination as a Catholic priest Newman, like the majority of his co-religionists at that time, was clear as to 'the superiority of celibacy to marriage.'[12] This understanding of Newman was undoubtedly rooted in his desire to imitate Christ: 'Christ was born of a Virgin; He remained a virgin; His beloved disciple was a virgin . . . and He said that there were those who for the kingdom of heaven's sake would be even as He.'[13]

As a Roman Catholic, Newman observed the motives for celibacy amongst some of the clergy and clearly found them wanting: 'To make a single life its own end, to adopt it simply and solely for its own sake, I do not know whether such a state of life is more melancholy or more unamiable, melancholy from its unrequited desolateness and unamiable from the pride and self-esteem on which it is based.'[14]

Whilst acknowledging that being free from the responsi-bilities of marriage and family life was in part meant to free the cleric to pursue the work of the mission given him by the Church, Newman identifies the call to the celibate state with the pain of sacrificing the possibility of the bond of love's intimacy with another human being, the very renunciation of which might inspire in the heart and mind of the celibate a greater dependence and seeking of the love of God alone. In a poem of 1833, not without typical nineteenth-century pathos, he contemplates the mysterious Old Testament figure Melchizedek and sees in him a type of those who aspire to live the life of a celibate. The poem is headed by a quote from Hebrews 7:3, 'Without father, without mother, without descent; having neither beginning of days, nor end of life.'

[11] *LD* vii. 422. To F. W. Faber, 27 October 1840. Cf. *HS* ii. 55–6.
[12] *LD* xii. 235. To E. J. Phipps, 3 July 1848.
[13] *PS* vi. 187.
[14] *NO* 277.

Thrice bless'd are they, who feel their loneliness;
To whom nor voices of friends nor pleasant scene
Brings aught on which the sadden'd heart can lean;
Yea, the rich earth, garb'd in her daintiest dress
Of light and joy, doth but the more oppress,
  Claiming responsive smiles and rapture high;
  Till, sick at heart, beyond the veil they fly,
Seeking His Presence, who alone can bless.
Such, in strange days, the weapons of Heaven's grace;
When, passing o'er the high-born Hebrew line,
He moulds the vessel of His vast design;
Fatherless, homeless, reft of age and place,
Sever'd from earth, and careless of its wreck,
Born through long woe His rare Melchizedek.[15]

A further poem, written in 1834, sings of the celibate state, the
'Word of Grace' of the New Covenant compared to marriage
which is the Law of the pre-Christian era, as excelling
marriage as 'soul the body, heaven this world below,' as 'The
eternal peace of saints, life's troubled span, And the high
throne of God, the haunts of man.'[16] Thus Newman considers
that the 'unamiable' existence of those who 'make a single life
its own end'

... is not the Virginity of the Gospel – it is not a state of
independence or isolation, or dreary pride, or barren indolence, or
crushed affections; man is made for sympathy, for the interchange of
love, for self-denial for the sake of another dearer to him than
himself. The Virginity of the Christian soul is a marriage with
Christ.[17]

There is great passion in these words that obviously comes
from someone who was not merely living in his head. This is
proven further by a reflection on the purpose of his recording
his experience of serious illness during his 1833 sojourn in
Sicily – who else but he, and then rarely, would take an
interest in his words, take a real interest in him?

[15] VV 108.
[16] VV 202–3.
[17] NO 277.

The thought keeps pressing on me, while I write this, what am I writing for? For myself, I may look at it once or twice in my whole life, and what sympathy is there in *my* looking at it? Whom have I, whom can I have, who would take interest in it? I was going to say, I only have found one who ever took that sort of affectionate interest in me as to be pleased with such details – and that is H. Wilberforce and what shall I ever see of him? This is the sort of interest which a wife takes and none but she – it is a woman's interest – and that interest, so be it, shall never be taken in me. Never, so be it, will I be other than God has found me. All my habits for years, my tendencies, are towards celibacy. I could not take that interest in this world which marriage requires. I am too disgusted with this world – And, above all, call it what one will, I have a repugnance to a clergyman's marrying. I do not say it is not lawful – I cannot deny the right – but, whether a prejudice or not, it shocks me. And therefore I willingly give up possession of that sympathy, which I feel is not, cannot be, granted to me. Yet, not the less do I feel the need of it. Who will care to be told such details as I have put down above? Shall I ever have in my old age spiritual children who will take an interest such as a wife does?[18]

Given his position as Superior of the Birmingham Oratory Newman was called to discern and guide his charges in their spiritual formation with both the individual's and the community's good in mind. Writing to a lay brother of the Oratory, Newman counselled,

God's grace does all things for us, as He has promised; and those whom He has called to a single life, He enables (blessed be His Name) to lead it in all purity and honesty. This necessity is your yoke, as it is the yoke of all those around you; and what makes you dear to them, as they to you, is that you and they are all partakers in one and the same calling, and sympathise one with another;[19]

Either unable or unwilling to be so guided, Brother Frederic (Thomas Godwin) soon ceased to be a lay brother. Lay brothers were not bound by vows and this seems to have given the departing brother some confidence. Newman wrote with indignation to St John, who had care of the lay brothers, 'My

18 *AW* 137–8.
19 *LD* xvi. 153. To Thomas Godwin, 11 June 1854. Cf. *PS* v. 349–50.

Dear Ambrose, I am exceedingly displeased to find that Frederic has actually made a proposal to a young woman, *being in our house and having our habit on.* This seems to be so great an offence that I do not know what to say about it.'[20] Frederic was given strict instructions as to how to behave if he was to remain living in the house as a lay brother. Newman decided that he could stay until Christmas 'and no longer'. 'What astonishes, perhaps hurts us, is his utter absence of distress at breaking so old a tie. He is simply relieved and happy – and sings in the kitchen with astonishing compass and volume.'[21]

In later years, with all the experience of the close association that the Oratory School and the boys' families brought to Newman, he remarked to one parent,

I often think what poor creatures we, priests, are, who like 'gentlemen of England, sit at home at ease,'[22] while you, married men, have all the merit of the anxiety and toil, which the care of a family involves. Your state is in fact one of 'perfection', when compared with ours, and there is a day in prospect when the first shall be last, and the last first.[23]

Whilst, from time to time, Newman pondered the delights of real intimacy with another, it seems that, on the whole, he was naturally content to lead a celibate life, it suited his temperament. But that being said he assuredly did not 'make a single life its own end' but rather it genuinely was a precious means by which his heart was to be evermore consecrated singularly to Christ. So much for the reported facts. They are interesting but cannot convey a real sense of the heart of the man. 'Thou wooest me,' Newman would say to the Lord, gazing into eternity, 'O my only true Lover, the only Lover of my soul, Thee will I love now, that I may love Thee then.' 'O my all-sufficient Lord, Thou only sufficest'.[24]

[20] *LD* xvi. 278. To Ambrose St. John, 12 October 1854.
[21] *LD* xvi. 283. To Ambrose St. John, 27 October 1854.
[22] A line from M. Parker, 'The Valiant Sailors', *Early Naval Ballads,* Percy Society, 1841, 34.
[23] *LD* xxviii. 72–3. To John Hungerford Pollen, 28 May 1876.
[24] *MD* 373, 354 & 368.

9

Sacraments

'holy arms and defences'[1]

In truth, our Merciful Saviour has done much more for us than reveal the wonderful doctrines of the Gospel; He has enabled us to apply them. ... What an inactive useless world this would be, if the sun's light did not diffuse itself through the air and fall on all objects around us, enabling us to see earth and sky as well as the sun itself! ... Such would have been our religious state, had not our Lord applied and diversified and poured to and fro, in heat and light, those heavenly glories which are concentrated in Him. He would shine upon us from above in all His high attributes and offices, as the Prophet, Priest, and King of His elect; but how should we bring home His grace to ourselves? How indeed should we gain, and know we gain, an answer to our prayers – how secure the comfortable assurance that He loves us personally, and will change our hearts, which we feel to be so earthly, and wash away our sins, which we confess to be so manifold, unless He had given us Sacraments – means and pledges of grace – keys which open the treasure-house of mercy.[2]

From the time of his ordination as an Anglican deacon until his reception into the Catholic Church, Newman's appreciation of the Sacraments underwent a comprehensive transformation. As in so many aspects of his life, it was during the fifteen years before his conversion that he thought, prayed and wrote about the Sacraments, thus coming to the Catholic Church 'ready armed', as it were. As a Catholic priest the two Sacraments that Newman most frequently received and administered were, of course, the Eucharist and Confession. These were to sustain

[1] *LD* xii. 224. To Mrs William Froude, 16 June, 1848.
[2] *PS* iii. 290–1.

him throughout his life as an Oratorian priest and these are the subject of this chapter.

Journeying to Rome, whilst staying in Milan, Newman looked back, briefly, on the first anniversary of his conversion:

This day I have been a year in the Catholic Church – and every day I bless Him who led me into it more and more. I have come from clouds and darkness into light, and cannot look back on my former state without the dreary feeling which one has on looking back upon a wearisome miserable journey. When I was happy in the English Church, it was then most when it was *not* English – I mean in those respects in which I could innovate upon the received custom of the English Church, as in the early communion at St Mary's.[3]

Perhaps the proximity of the last stages of that 'miserable journey' were still too distressing for Newman as, in later years, he was able to identify much happiness and blessing in the years before he became a Catholic. But at the time when he was most distressed by his past journey it is interesting to note that he immediately cites the communion services at St Mary's as a clear instance of when he was happy as an Anglican. Evidently it was no mere emotional exhilaration that he experienced at the altar of St Mary's as some lines of a Christmas sermon that he delivered there demonstrate. The very mystery of the Incarnation and the Passion, Death and Resurrection of Christ is the Mass in which we are now able to partake:

Christ then took our nature, when He would redeem it; He redeemed it by making it suffer in His own Person; He purified it, by making it pure in His own Person. He first sanctified it in Himself, made it righteous, made it acceptable to God, submitted it to an expiatory passion, and then He imparted it to us. He took it, consecrated it, broke it, and said, "Take, and divide it among yourselves."[4]

In consequence of this, in the Old Covenant,

There were mediators many, and prophets many, and atonements many. But now all is superseded by One, in whom all offices merge,

---

[3] *LD* xi. 257. To Miss Parker, 9 October 1846.
[4] *PS* v. 117–18.

who has absorbed into Himself all principality, power, might, and
dominion, and every name that is named; who has put His holy and
fearful Name upon all, who is in and through all things, and without
whom nothing is good. He is the sole self-existing principle in the
Christian Church, and everything else is but a portion or declaration
of Him. Not that now, as then, we may not speak of prophets, and
rulers, and priests, and sacrifices, and altars, and saints, and that in
a far higher and more spiritual sense than before, but that they are
not any of them such of themselves; it is not they, but the grace of
God that is in them. There is under the Gospel but One proper Priest,
Prophet, and King, Altar, Sacrifice, and House of God.[5] Unity is its
characteristic sacrament; all grace flows from One Head, and all life
circulates in the members of One Body. And what is true of priests
and sacrifices, is true of righteous and holy men. It is their very
privilege thus to be taken into Christ, to exist in Christ, as already in
their mortal life they "have their being" in God.[6]

United with Christ the High Priest as ordained members of his
Body the Church, Newman taught that

Christian Ministers also offer sacrifices, but it is their privilege to
know that those sacrifices are not independent of Christ ... but
continuations, as it were, of His Sacrifice ... and that though distinct
as visible and literal acts, yet, as being instinct with that which they
commemorate, they are absorbed and vivified in it.[7]

Undoubtedly Newman was happy at the altar of St Mary's
but happier still in full communion with the Church at the Holy
Sacrifice of the Mass and in receiving and celebrating the
Sacraments and in adoration before the Eucharist, the
Sacrament of Sacraments. One can hear Newman's authentic
voice in one of the characters from his novel, *Loss and Gain*:

---

[5]   In the 1874 edition of these lectures Newman added the following note for
      clarification: '[It is true that there is but one Priest and one Sacrifice
      under the Gospel, but this is because the Priests of the Gospel are *one*
      with Christ, not because they are only *improperly* called Priests.
      "Christus et Sacerdotes sunt *unus Sacerdos*." – *Catech. Roman*. ii. 84.
      "Profiteor in Missa offerri Deo verum, *proprium*, et propitiatorium
      sacrificium pro vivis at defunctis." – *Profess. Fid. Trident*.]'

[6]   *Jfc*. 198.

[7]   *Jfc*. 199.

"to me nothing is so consoling, so piercing, so thrilling, so overcoming, as the Mass, said as it is among us. I could attend Masses for ever and not be tired. It is not a mere form of words, – it is a great action, the greatest action that can be on earth. It is, not the invocation merely, but, if I dare use the word, the evocation of the Eternal. He becomes present on the altar in flesh and blood, before whom angels bow and devils tremble. This is that awful event which is the scope, and is the interpretation, of every part of the solemnity. Words are necessary, but as means, not as ends; they are not mere addresses to the throne of grace, they are instruments of what is far higher, of consecration, of sacrifice. They hurry on as if impatient to fulfil their mission. Quickly they go, the whole is quick; for they are all parts of one integral action. Quickly they go; for they are awful words of sacrifice, they are a work too great to delay upon; as when it was said in the beginning: 'What thou doest, do quickly'. Quickly they pass; for the Lord Jesus goes with them, as He passed along the lake in the days of His flesh, quickly calling first one and then another. Quickly they pass; because as the lightning which shineth from one part of heaven unto the other, so is the coming of the Son of Man. Quickly they pass; for they are as the words of Moses, when the Lord came down in the cloud, calling on the Name of the Lord as He passed by, 'the Lord, the Lord God, merciful and gracious, long-suffering, and abundant in goodness and truth'. And as Moses on the mountain, so we too 'make haste and bow our heads to the earth, and adore'. So we, all around, each in his place, look out for the great Advent, 'waiting for the moving of the water'. Each in his place, with his own heart, with his own wants, with his own thoughts, with his own intention, with his own prayers, separate but concordant, watching what is going on, watching its progress, uniting in its consummation; – not painfully and hopelessly following a hard form of prayer from beginning to end, but, like a concert of musical instruments, each different, but concurring in a sweet harmony, we take our part with God's priest, supporting him, yet guided by him. There are little children there, and old men, and simple labourers, and students in seminaries, priests preparing for Mass, priests making their thanksgiving; there are innocent maidens, and there are penitent sinners; but out of these many minds rises one eucharistic hymn, and the great Action is the measure and scope of it. And oh, my dear Bateman," he added, turning to him, "you ask me whether this is not a formal, unreasonable service – it is wonderful!" he cried, rising up, "quite wonderful. When will these dear good people be enlightened?"[8]

[8]   *LG* 327–9.

Indeed it does seem that, when offering up his daily Mass, Newman himself lived out literally the words 'They hurry on as if impatient to fulfil their mission', noting once that 'The Catholic Priest says his Mass as quickly as possible; the Protestant clergyman is slow and distinct, perhaps pompous or mouthing.'[9] It seems likely that Newman really did believe in celebrating Mass with alacrity, and at 'seven o'clock sharp,'[10] each morning. Nevertheless, he evidently said Mass with sincere devotion. His desire to offer Mass in his last months is clear:

According to the custom of Cardinals he said his own private Mass in a private chapel, and always as early as convenient to others; for the last time, the Christmas Day before he died, after which Feast he always declined to say Mass himself from fear of an accident. Sight and strength had already very greatly failed him, and he feared lest he should overbalance in taking the chalice. Reverence forbade such a risk. Nevertheless he learnt by heart a Mass of the Blessed Virgin and a Mass of the Dead. One or other of these Masses he repeated daily, whole or part, and with the due ceremonies, for the chance that he hoped for, since his sight and strength varied, that with the brighter sunlight of the spring he might some day find himself in condition to say Mass once again. He was determined, he said, that no want of readiness on his part should cause him to miss the opportunity should it occur. ... The hoped-for opportunity to say Mass never came.[11]

The awe of Newman for the mystery of the presence of Christ during the offering of Mass is tangible in the words of a sermon that he preached in Dublin on the first Sunday after Epiphany, 1857. The sermon is entitled 'Omnipotence in Bonds':[12]

He took bread, and blessed, and made it His Body; He took wine, and gave thanks, and made it His Blood; and He gave His priests the

[9] *LD* xii. 235. To E. J. Phipps, 3 July 1848.
[10] *LD* xvii. 66. To John Hardman, Junior, 26 May 1874.
[11] *Ward* ii. 532–3. Extract from Fr Neville's account of Newman's last two years.
[12] This sermon takes as its text Luke 2:51: "And He went down with them, and came to Nazareth; and was subject to them."

power to do what He had done. Henceforth, He is in the hands of sinners once more. Frail, ignorant, sinful man, by the sacerdotal power given to him, compels the presence of the Highest; he lays Him up in a small tabernacle; he dispenses Him to a sinful people.[13]

And in one of his Meditations, Newman ponders that

In the Holy Mass that One Sacrifice on the Cross once offered is renewed, continued, applied to our benefit. He seems to say, My Cross was raised up 1800 years ago, and only for a few hours – and very few of my servants were present there – but I intend to bring millions into my Church. For their sakes then I will perpetuate my Sacrifice, that each of them may be as though they had severally been present on Calvary. I will offer Myself up day by day to the Father, that every one of my followers may have the opportunity to offer his petitions to Him, sanctified and recommended by the all-meritorious virtue of my Passion. Thus I will be a Priest for ever, after the order of Melchisedech – My priests shall stand at the Altar – but not they, but I rather, will offer. I will not let them offer mere bread and wine, but I myself will be present upon the Altar instead, and I will offer up myself invisibly, while they perform the outward rite. And thus the Lamb that was slain once for all, though He is ascended on high, ever remains a victim from His miraculous presence in Holy Mass under the figure and appearance of mere earthly and visible symbols.[14]

Whilst still an Anglican minister, in the introduction to *An Essay on the Development of Christian Doctrine,* Newman speaks of the gift of the Eucharist:

I have learned it from the Fathers: I believe the Real Presence because they bear witness to it. St. Ignatius calls it "the medicine of immortality": St. Irenæus says that "our flesh becomes incorrupt, and partakes of life, and has the hope of the resurrection," as "being nourished from the Lord's Body and Blood"; that the Eucharist "is made up of two things, an earthly and an heavenly":[15] perhaps Origen and perhaps Magnes, after him, say that It is not a type of our

---

[13] *OS* 87.
[14] *MD* 203.
[15] Hær. iv. 18, § 5.

Lord's Body, but His Body: and St Cyprian uses language as awful as can be spoken of those who profane it. I cast my lot in with them, I believe as they.[16]

It is thus no surprise to read in his first letter from his new home at Maryvale, how Newman delights in the closeness of the Blessed Sacrament and that as a Catholic, prayer before the Blessed Sacrament was a vital privilege:

I am writing next room to the Chapel – It is such an incomprehensible blessing to have Christ in bodily presence in one's house, within one's walls, as swallows up all other privileges and destroys, or should destroy, every pain. To know that He is close by – to be able again and again through the day to go in to Him; and be sure, My dearest W[ilberforce], when I am thus in His Presence you are not forgotten. It is *the* place for intercession surely, where the Blessed Sacrament is. Thus Abraham, our father, pleaded before his hidden Lord and God.[17]

Indeed, 'It is an inexpressible blessing to be under the same roof with the Blessed Sacrament.'[18] 'It is well to be a pilgrim – and with the Blessed Sacrament ever upon one's footsteps, as it now dwells under our very roof, one cannot be much of an exile any where.'[19]

Writing from Milan, where Newman paused for five weeks on his journey to Rome, he wrote,

And then too, it is not a mere imagination, as it might be in a ruined city, or in a desolate place where Saints once dwelt – but here a score of Churches which are open to the passer by, and in each of which are found their relics, and the Blessed Sacrament ready for the worshipper even before he enters. There is nothing which has brought home to me so much the Unity of the Church, as the Presence of its Divine Founder and Life wherever I go – All places are, as it were, one – while the friends I have left enjoy His Presence and adore Him at Mary Vale, He is here also.[20]

16 *Dev.* 23.
17 *LD* xi. 129. To Henry Wilberforce, 26 February 1846.
18 *LD* xi. 132. To Miss M. R. Giberne, 9 March 1846.
19 *LD* xi. 133. To W. J. Copeland, 10 March 1846.
20 *LD* xi. 254. To Mrs J. R. Bowden, 4 October 1846.

In Milan Newman found a particularly calm and beautiful church where,

> Nothing moves there but the distant glittering Lamp which betokens the Presence of our Undying Life, hidden but ever working, [[for us]], though [[He has]] entered into His rest.
>
> It is really most wonderful to see the Divine Presence looking out almost into the open streets from the various churches.[21]

Here was Christ's 'Presence in the sacred Tabernacle, not as a form of words, or as a notion, but as an Object as real as we are real'.[22]

Writing in his first novel, *Loss and Gain: The Story of a Convert,* published in 1848, the impressions of the hero, Charles Reading, are surely also the sentiments of Newman himself. As Charles is drawn ever closer to converting to Catholicism he is encouraged to attend Mass which is described to him as 'not a mere form of words, – it is a great action, the greatest action that can be on earth'.[23] And at that Mass in that church, Charles, for the first time, encounters 'the Great Presence, which makes a Catholic Church different from every other place in the world'.[24]

That 'Great Presence' Newman presented to those he hoped would enter into full Communion with the Church. To one such he wrote,

> I was thinking of you this morning, when I said Mass – Oh that you were safe in the True Fold! – I think you will be one day. You will then have the blessedness of seeing God face to face. You will have the blessedness of finding, when you enter a Church, a Treasure Unutterable – the Presence of the Eternal Word Incarnate – the Wisdom of the Father who, even when He had done His work, would not leave us, but rejoices still to humble Himself by abiding in mean places on earth for our sakes, while He reigns not the less on the right hand of God.[25]

[21] *LD* xi. 252. To Henry Wilberforce, 24 September 1846.
[22] *DA* 388.
[23] *LG* 327–8.
[24] *LG* 427.
[25] *LD* xii. 224. To Mrs William Froude, 16 June 1848.

Just under eighteen years later, with all the assurance of one who has lived his words, the aging Newman encouraged a correspondent who was 'suffering so much' to find solace in the sanctuary:

Why, what exercise of devotion is there, which equals that of going before the Blessed Sacrament, before our Lord Jesus really present, though unseen? To kneel before Him, to put oneself into His hands, to ask His grace, and to rejoice in the hope of seeing Him in heaven! In the Catholic Church alone is the great gift to be found. You may go the length and breadth of England, and see beautiful prospects enough, such as you speak of, the work of the God of nature, but there is no benediction from earth or sky which falls upon us like that which comes to us from the Blessed Sacrament, which is Himself.[26]

Unsurprisingly Newman also found that for himself, 'it is the Presence of our Lord in the Blessed Sacrament which is the relief and consolation for all the troubles of ecclesiastical affairs'[27] and that this was a form of prayer which he was most attracted to. Fr Neville left an account of Newman in prayer before the Blessed Sacrament:

he would rest upon what was before him, with his face in his hands, or with his hands clasped against the back of his head. But when engaged in a religious act, whether private or public, his whole mien was that of a person most reverently and absolutely absorbed in what he was about; this, however, did not hinder him in any act proper for the time and place, nor did he need to have his attention drawn to it. If he knelt upright without support, it would be at times when it was proper or becoming; and whatever his attitude might be, it was always natural and free from appearance of strain. Even on occasion such as the procession of the Blessed Sacrament on Corpus Christi, there would not be anything noteworthy in him to strike an ordinary observer, yet some at least of his assistants, when he carried the Blessed Sacrament, have a still lasting impression of him that had been made on them from his ready exactness in his recitation of the Psalms, and the reverence that accompanied all he said and did. It was the accumulation in the memory of these passing views of him,

---

[26] *LD* xxii. 194. To Lady Chatterton, Holy Thursday 1866.
[27] *LD* xxv. 156. To Mrs Wilson, 3 July 1870.

each year adding its own – whether differing or the same – that so impressed them with the reality and the meaning of this act of devotion, and of his own faith.

All this can, no doubt, be said of many another; but here it answers questions about J. H. Newman in particular. To the last, he himself gave much attention to the externals of this devotion in honour of Our Lord; the singing, the orderliness, etc., of all the proceedings, each had his interest in them beforehand, nor did they escape him at the time. Moreover, at all times, when he genuflected to the Blessed Sacrament, he was invariable in touching the ground, or all but so, with his knee – occasionally on seeing those to whom he could speak getting into a careless habit in this respect, he would draw their attention to it. This was always done quietly, gently, almost imperceptibly.[28]

Of the strength and stay that is the Eucharistic Presence of Christ, Newman penned a new translation of an old text, the *Anima Christi*:

> Soul of Christ, be my sanctification;
> Body of Christ, be my salvation;
> Blood of Christ, fill all my veins;
> Water of Christ's side, wash out my stains;
> Passion of Christ, my comfort be;
> O good Jesu, listen to me;
> In thy wounds I fain would hide,
> Ne'er to be parted from Thy side;
> Guard me, should the foe assail me;
> Call me when my life shall fail me;
> Bid me come to Thee above,
> With Thy saints to sing Thy love,
> World without end. Amen.

As well as the offering of the Holy Sacrifice of the Mass and adoring the Lord in the tabernacle, Newman encouraged the practice of Benediction:

I need hardly observe to you, my Brothers, that the Benediction of the Blessed Sacrament is one of the simplest rites of the Church. The

---

[28] *Ward* 359–60.

priests enter and kneel down; one of them unlocks the Tabernacle, takes out the Blessed Sacrament, inserts it upright in a Monstrance of precious metal, and sets it in a conspicuous place above the altar, in the midst of lights, for all to see. The people then begin to sing; meanwhile the Priest twice offers incense to the King of heaven, before whom he is kneeling. Then he takes the Monstrance in his hands, and turning to the people, blesses them with the Most Holy, in the form of a cross, while the bell is sounded by one of the attendants to call attention to the ceremony. It is our Lord's solemn benediction of His people, as when He lifted up His hands over the children, or when He blessed His chosen ones when He ascended up from Mount Olivet. As sons might come before a parent before going to bed at night, so, once or twice a week the great Catholic family comes before the Eternal Father, after the bustle or toil of the day, and He smiles upon them, and sheds upon them the light of His countenance. It is a full accomplishment of what the Priest invoked upon the Israelites, "The Lord bless thee and keep thee; the Lord show His face to thee and have mercy on thee; the Lord turn His countenance to thee and give thee peace." Can there be a more touching rite, even in the judgment of those who do not believe in it? How many a man, not a Catholic, is moved, on seeing it, to say "Oh, that I did but believe it!" when he sees the Priest take up the Fount of Mercy, and the people bent low in adoration! It is one of the most beautiful, natural, and soothing actions of the Church.[29]

In union with his devotion to the Eucharist it is clear that he held as essential his frequent presence as a penitent in the confessional. In poetry Newman declared,

> O Father, list a sinner's call!
> Fain would I hide from man my fall –
>   But I must speak, or faint –
> I cannot wear guilt's silent thrall:
>   Cleanse me, kind Saint!
>
> "Sinner ne'er blunted yet sin's goad;
> Speed thee, my son, a safer road,
>   And sue His pardoning smile
> Who walk'd woe's depths, bearing man's load
>   Of guilt the while."

[29] *Prepos.* 255–6.

Yet raise a mitigating hand,
And minister some potion bland,
    Some present fever-stay!
Lest one for whom His work was plann'd
    Die from dismay.

"Look not to me – no grace is mine;
But I can lift the Mercy-sign.
    This wouldst thou? Let it be!
Kneel down, and take the word divine,
    Absolvo te."[30]

Whilst in prose, Newman said,

No state of things comes amiss to a Catholic priest; he has always a work to do, and a harvest to reap.

Were it otherwise, had he not confidence in the darkest day, and the most hostile district, he would be relinquishing a principal note, as it is called, of the Church. She is Catholic, because she brings a universal remedy for a universal disease. The disease is sin; all men have sinned; all men need a recovery in Christ; to all must that recovery be preached and dispensed. If then there be a preacher and dispenser of recovery, sent from God, that messenger must speak, not to one, but to all;[31]

'We, Oratorians, by our Rule, go to confession three times a week',[32] he wrote. As an Anglican, Newman became convinced of the need of such a Sacrament as Confession:

As to reminding my People about Confession, it is the most dreary and dismal thought which I have about my Parish that I dare do so little, or rather nothing. I have long thought it would hinder me ever taking another cure. Confession is the life of the Parochial charge – without it all is hollow – and yet I do not see my way to say that I should not do more harm than good by more than the more distant mention of it.[33]

[30] *VV* 83–4.
[31] *Mix.* 246.
[32] *LD* xxvii. 16. To H. A. Woodgate, 13 February 1874. Apparently this practice was altered a century later.
[33] *LD* ix. 175. To J. Keble, 20 December 1842. According to his detailed account of 18 March 1838, *AW* 214–15, Newman had heard his first confession as an Anglican on 17 March 1838.

Indeed he would write a year later that

> If there were no other reason in the world, why I should not undertake a parochial cure in our Church, this alone would suffice for the future that there is no confession. I cannot understand how a clergyman can be answerable for souls, if souls are not submitted to him. There is *no real* cure of *souls* in our Church.[34]

And so as a Catholic he reflected on his Anglican years, writing, 'In my dealings with my people I so keenly felt the want of ecclesiastical authority over them, the need of obligatory confession to know their state, that the cure of souls was always a dreadful burden. I had the responsibility without the means to fulfil it.'[35] Once settled in Birmingham as a Catholic priest he wrote to a friend, 'Your ideas about confession are most unreal and romantic. The Priest is nothing – God is everything. They are the greatest friends who know each other most intimately. The Confessor's sympathy so flows out upon a penitent that it is as if he were making, not hearing a Confession.'[36] In this as in so much, Newman held before himself the example of St Philip Neri who 'At confession he used to say, "I have never done one good action." He often said, "I am past hope." To a penitent he said, "Be sure of this, I am a man like my neighbours, and nothing more."'[37]

Yet the man who is a priest is empowered by Christ to be an instrument in His redeeming work:

> Christ is a Priest, as forgiving sin, and imparting other needful divine gifts. The Apostles, too, had this power; "Whose soever sins ye remit, they are remitted unto them; and whose soever sins ye retain, they are retained." "Let a man so account of us as . . . Stewards of the Mysteries of God.". . .
> His Death upon the Cross is the sole Meritorious Cause, the sole Source of spiritual blessing to our guilty race; but as to those offices and gifts which flow from this Atonement, preaching, teaching, reconciling, absolving, censuring, dispensing grace, ruling, ordaining,

---

[34] *LD* ix. 523. To Mrs J. Mozley, 15 September 1843.
[35] *LD* xi. 258. To Miss Parker, 9 October 1846.
[36] *LD* xiv. 329. To William Froude, 11 August 1851.
[37] *OS* 96.

these all are included in the Apostolic Commission, which is instrumental and representative in His absence. "As My Father hath sent Me, so send I you." His gifts are not confined to Himself. "The whole house is filled with the odour of the ointment." ...

By a Priest, in a Christian sense, is meant an appointed channel by which the peculiar Gospel blessings are conveyed to mankind, one who has power to apply to individuals those gifts which Christ has promised us generally as the fruit of His mediation. ...

And it will be observed, that the only real antecedent difficulty which attaches to the doctrine of the Christian Priesthood, is obviated by Scripture itself. It might be thought that the power of remitting and retaining sins was too great to be given to sinful man over his fellows; but in matter of fact it was committed to the Apostles without restriction, though they were not infallible in what they did. "*Whose soever* sins ye remit they are remitted unto them; and *whose soever* sins ye retain, they are retained." The grant was in the very form of it unconditional, and left to their Christian discretion. What has once been given, may be continued.[38]

Whilst encouraging those who sought spiritual counsel from him to regularly receive Sacramental absolution, Newman could also be dismayed at the reception that his correspondents occasionally received once inside the confessional box. At the time of the promulgation of the dogma of Papal Infallibility there were widely differing ways in which this particular truth was brought home to the Faithful. Newman distinctly disapproved of the manner of some. He had received a letter from a troubled soul who had attended the Redemptorist church in Clapham. She had written, 'I have now returned to England and the first thing I am told is that the Fathers here will not give the Sacraments to any one who does not receive the new Dogma of the Infallibility[.] In Milan I have never heard it mentioned in the pulpits.'[39] Newman replied,

I think there are some Bishops and Priests, who act as if they did not care at all whether souls were lost or not – and only wish to save souls on their own measure. If you directly asked your Confessor, whether you were obliged to receive the Pope's Infallibility, you

[38] *PS* ii. 304–7.
[39] *LD* xxv. 216. From Mrs Wilson, October 1870.

acted imprudently – if he asked you, he was not only imprudent but cruel.[40]

According to the practice of the day, Newman desired that in the Birmingham Oratory there should be 'an effective crucifix for *devotion* near the Confessionals',[41] confessionals that he would use until the time he was made a Cardinal for the relief of thousands of souls.

How many are the souls, in distress, anxiety or loneliness, whose one need is to find a being to whom they can pour out their feelings unheard by the world? Tell them out they must; they cannot tell them out to those whom they see every hour. They want to tell them and not to tell them; and they want to tell them out, yet be as if they be not told; they wish to tell them to one who is strong enough to bear them, yet not too strong to despise them; they wish to tell them to one who can at once advise and can sympathize with them; they wish to relieve themselves of a load, to gain a solace ... If there is a heavenly idea in the Catholic Church, looking at it simply as an idea, surely, next after the Blessed Sacrament, Confession is such.[42]

So essential to the ministry of the priest is the Sacrament of Reconciliation that Newman not only identifies this particular role with the priestly office, but characterizes the office in this sense:

> In service o'er the Mystic Feast I stand;
>   I cleanse Thy victim-flock, and bring them near
>   In holiest wise, and by a bloodless rite.
>   O fire of Love! O gushing Fount of Light!
> (As best I know, who need Thy pitying Hand)
>   Dread office this, bemired souls to clear
>   Of their defilement, and again made bright.[43]

---

[40] *LD* xxv. 216. To Mrs Wilson, 20 October 1870.
[41] *LD* xv. 344. To Antony Hutchinson, 11 April 1853.
[42] *Prepos.* 351.
[43] *VV* 197.

The priest is a minister of the grace of God, the very divine life that God wills to share with His creatures by means of the Sacraments administered by priests:

has not the Gospel Sacraments? and have not Sacraments, as pledges and means of grace, a priestly nature? If so, the question of the existence of a Christian Priesthood is narrowed at once to the simple question whether it is or is not probable that so precious an ordinance as a channel of grace would be committed by Providence to the custody of certain guardians. The tendency of opinions at this day is to believe that nothing more is necessary for acceptance than faith in God's promise of mercy; whereas it is certain from Scripture, that the gift of reconciliation is not conveyed to individuals except through appointed ordinances. Christ has interposed something between Himself and the soul; and if it is not inconsistent with the liberty of the Gospel that a Sacrament should interfere, there is no antecedent inconsistency in a keeper of the Sacrament attending upon it. Moreover, the very circumstance that a standing Ministry has existed from the first, leads on to the inference that that Ministry was intended to take charge of the Sacraments; and thus the facts of the case suggest an interpretation of our Lord's memorable words, when He committed to St. Peter "the *keys* of the Kingdom of Heaven."[44]

Thus in all the Seven Sacraments, Newman witnessed that

the Atonement of Christ is not a thing at a distance, or like the sun standing over against us and separated off from us, but that we are surrounded by an *atmosphere* and are in a medium, through which his warmth and light flow in upon us on every side, what can one ask, what can one desire, more than this?[45]

And in all the Seven Sacraments he anticipated the divine touch on earth of the life of heaven:

At times we seem to catch a glimpse of a Form which we shall hereafter see face to face. We approach, and in spite of the darkness, our hands, or our head, or our brow, or our lips become, as it were, sensible of the contact of something more than earthly. We know not

---

[44] *PS* ii. 309–10.
[45] *LD* xii. 224. To Mrs William Froude, 16 June, 1848.

where we are, but we have been bathing in water, and a voice tells us that it is blood. Or we have a mark signed upon our foreheads, and it spake of Calvary. Or we recollect a hand laid upon our heads, and surely it had the print of nails in it, and resembled His who with a touch gave sight to the blind and raised the dead. Or we have been eating and drinking; and it was not a dream surely, that One fed us from His wounded side, and renewed our nature by the heavenly meat He gave. Thus in many ways He, who is Judge to us, prepares us to be judged, – He, who is to glorify us, prepares us to be glorified, that He may not take us unawares; but that when the voice of the Archangel sounds, and we are called to meet the Bridegroom, we may be ready.[46]

[46] *PS* v. 10–11. Sermon 1, 'Worship, a Preparation for Christ's Coming.'

10

Mary, Mother of God

No one has access to the Almighty as His Mother has[1]

The Blessed Sacrament was Newman's greatest love and, accordingly, he grew in love and respect for the Mother of God – for to honour the mother is to honour the Son – and he valued the various devotions to her not least because, 'The Blessed Virgin is the great pattern of prayers, especially intercessory. ... If she is the Intercessor, and the effectual intercessor, she is so as regards earth, as regards Purgatory, as regards the whole created Universe.'[2] As a Catholic priest, Newman was personally devoted to the Blessed Virgin Mary and encouraged devotion in others.

Newman came to understand the critical importance in matters Marian of 'making a distinction ... the distinction between faith and devotion.'[3] Not nurtured in his early years with either faith or devotion to the Mother of God, Newman was to learn of the mysteries of Mary and develop a profound love and respect for her under the influence of friends and of the Fathers of the Church.

Perhaps the first great influence on the future Cardinal with respect to Our Lady was a friend, Hurrell Froude, with whom Newman first was acquainted in 1826, the year in which he was appointed a tutor at Oriel College, Oxford, Froude being appointed a Fellow of the same college that year. Froude's friendship was to be highly influential and it was from Froude that Newman learned of the respect due to the Mother of God.

---

[1] *MD* 71.
[2] *LD* xxi. 401–2. To E. B. Pusey, 3 February 1865.
[3] *Diff.* ii. 26.

His faith regarding her is clear in a sermon given on the Feast of the Annunciation, 1832:

In her was now to be fulfilled that promise which the world had been looking out for during thousands of years. The Seed of the woman, announced to guilty Eve, after long delay, was at length appearing upon earth, and was to be born of her. In her the destinies of the world were to be reversed, and the serpent's head bruised. On her was bestowed the greatest honour ever put upon any individual of our fallen race. God was taking upon Him her flesh, and humbling Himself to be called her offspring; – such is the deep mystery! ... But further, she is doubtless to be accounted blessed and favoured in herself, as well as in the benefits she has done us. Who can estimate the holiness and perfection of her, who was chosen to be the Mother of Christ? If to him that hath, more is given, and holiness and Divine favour go together (and this we are expressly told), what must have been the transcendent purity of her, whom the Creator Spirit condescended to overshadow with His miraculous presence? What must have been her gifts, who was chosen to be the only near earthly relative of the Son of God, the only one whom He was bound by nature to revere and look up to; the one appointed to train and educate Him, to instruct Him day by day, as He grew in wisdom and in stature? This contemplation runs to a higher subject, did we dare follow it; for what, think you, was the sanctified state of that human nature, of which God formed His sinless Son; knowing as we do, "that which is born of the flesh is flesh," and that "none can bring a clean thing out of an unclean"? [1 John iii. 6. Job xiv. 4.][4]

Faith was not, however, immediately followed by devotion. On Froude's death in 1836 Newman was given Froude's Roman Breviary. The Breviary was a decisive discovery for Newman and whilst he liked to follow it, increasingly on a daily basis, he could not bring himself to recite the prayers that invoked Our Lady and the saints. As a Catholic, Newman quickly absorbed the doctrine and discerned the nature of devotions to Our Lady. In 1865 he responded to a book of Pusey's that he felt was not only inaccurate in its portrayal

---

[4] *PS* ii. 128, 131–2.

of Catholic Marian beliefs but also offensive to both the Mother of God and to those who had recourse to her:

Religion acts on the affections; who is to hinder these, when once roused, from gathering in their strength and running wild? They are not gifted with any connatural principle within them, which renders them self-governing, and self-adjusting. They hurry right on to their object, and often in their case it is, the more haste, the worse speed. Their object engrosses them, and they see nothing else. And of all passions love is the most unmanageable; nay more, I would not give much for that love which is never extravagant, which always observes the proprieties, and can move about in perfect good taste, under all emergencies. What mother, what husband or wife, what youth or maiden in love, but says a thousand foolish things, in the way of endearment, which the speaker would be sorry for strangers to hear; yet they are not on that account unwelcome to the parties to whom they are addressed. Sometimes by bad luck they are written down, sometimes they get into the newspapers; and what might be even graceful, when it was fresh from the heart, and interpreted by the voice and the countenance, presents but a melancholy exhibition when served up cold for the public eye. So it is with devotional feelings. Burning thoughts and words are as open to criticism as they are beyond it. What is abstractedly extravagant, may in particular persons be becoming and beautiful, and only fall under blame when it is found in others who imitate them. When it is formalized into meditations or exercises, it is as repulsive as love-letters in a police report.[5]

Thus whilst Newman recognized the concerns of ministers like his friend Pusey and could easily recognize 'the extravagances in the devotions practised by some Catholics to the Blessed Virgin – nay, for what I know, by many',[6] he gently yet firmly warns against the bludgeoning of the devotions of others as this too damages true doctrine:

Have you not been touching us on a very tender point in a very rude way? Is it not the effect of what you have said to expose her to scorn and obloquy, who is dearer to us than any other creature? Have you

---

[5] *Diff.* ii. 79–80.
[6] *LD* xxviii. 149. To Robert E. Forsaith, 25 December 1876.

even hinted that our love for her is anything else than an abuse? Have you thrown her one kind word yourself all through your book? I trust so, but I have not lighted upon one.[7]

From correct faith, due devotion develops, growing, according to Newman in a kind of 'rivalry' together, 'not one overshadowing the other, but each in its due place confronting each.'[8] Whilst devotions to the Blessed Virgin Mary 'have been surprisingly developed' Newman held that 'the devotion to the Blessed Sacrament, our Lord Himself Present and Unseen, has acted as a sufficient balance to keep the whole system of doctrine and worship in aequilibrio',[9] as he demonstrates to one inquirer:

A Protestant visitor of a dear Catholic friend of mine, a convert, who was on her deathbed, spoke with great feeling to her on the danger of letting any creature, however holy, as the Blessed Virgin, come between her soul and her Lord and leading her to forget Him. My friend opened her eyes wide, and said 'Forget Him? why He was with me just now in this room' – she had just communicated. There was nothing in her devotion to our Lady to obscure the incommunicable claim of her Maker upon her love and loyalty.[10]

This balance was but a faithful reflection of the humility of Mary herself:

You know, when first He went out to preach, she kept apart from Him; she interfered not with His work; and, even when He was gone up on high, yet she, a woman, went not out to preach or teach, she seated not herself in the Apostolic chair, she took no part in the Priest's office; she did but humbly seek her Son in the daily Mass of those, who, though her ministers in heaven, were her superiors in the Church on earth.[11]

From the early years of his Catholic ministry Newman encouraged devotion to Our Lady and was himself nourished

---

[7] *Diff.* ii. 116.
[8] *LD* xx. 307. To David Radford, 15 October 1862.
[9] Ibid.
[10] Ibid.
[11] *Mix.* 356.

by it, noting in 1868 that 'I have now been 46 years under the shadow of Maria Purificans.'[12] To one correspondent he wrote, 'I certainly think you *should* get into the Catholic ways of devotion by degrees', suggesting that it might help him to say the Rosary if he said it with others or at least fixed a time when the prayer was to be said.[13]

Try it thus . . . viz before each mystery, set before you a picture of it, and fix your mind upon that picture, (e.g. the Annunciation, the Agony, etc.) *while* you say the Pater and 10 Aves, not thinking of the words, only saying them correctly. Let the exercise be hardly more than a meditation. Perhaps this will overcome any sense of tedium.[14]

The fullest account that we have of the importance of Newman's devotion to the Blessed Virgin Mary as practically enacted in the Oratory house and parish comes from a letter of Bishop Ullathorne to the editor of *The Tablet* defending Newman from a charge of lacking in true Catholic spirit with regard to praise and petition to the Mother of God. 'For myself,' Ullathorne wrote, 'I prefer solid facts to lightly flying assertions, and so I proceed to give them in historic order.' Having noted that Newman had chosen the name Mary as his Confirmation name, Ullathorne continues to comprehensively record the Marian devotion of his most celebrated priest:

He selected the feast of the Purification for the commencing the Oratory at Mary Vale. He chose the same festival of Our Lady, in the following year, for commencing the Oratory at Birmingham. He dedicated the house and church at Edgbaston to the Mystery of the Immaculate Conception. When sent by the Sovereign Pontiff to found the University in Dublin, he at once placed the University under the patronage of Mary as the Sedes Sapientiæ, and dedicated the church which he there built with his own funds to SS. Peter and Paul.

When you enter the Oratory, the first thing that meets your eye in the entrance hall, is a statue of the Blessed Virgin, raised upon an altar, as a sign of the patronage under which you enter. And on

[12] *LD* xxiv. 25. To Sir Frederic Rogers 2 February 1868.
[13] *LD* xii. 263. To George Ryder, 19 September 1848.
[14] Ibid.

proceeding further into the church, you find it a complete representation of a fervid Roman church. The altars everywhere exhibit the cultus of the Blessed Virgin or of the Saints, and of their relics, where you have not immediately the representation of Our Lord's Passion and Crucifixion. I repeat, that no other Church in England that I have ever seen, is so complete a representation, in all its appointments, of a fervid Roman church.

At this point Ullathorne turns to enumerate the devotions practised at the Birmingham Oratory towards Our Lady, pointing out that before their school became a further demand upon their time, yet more devotions were made.

1. Every day in the year the Rosary is publicly said in the church.
2. Every Sunday the Rosary is said twice; once for the students, and once for the people.
3. A large number of the students meet their tutors daily to say the Rosary as an act of free devotion.
4. The Angelus is, of course, three times a day.
5. On Sundays, the children of the poor schools at mass and catechism, sing hymns and the Litany of Loreto, in honour of the Blessed Virgin.
6. There is a Novena before the feast of the Purification, the day on which the superiors of the congregation are elected, to place their election under the protection of the Blessed Virgin.
7. A Novena is made before the feast of the Assumption, and another before that of the Immaculate Conception, the patroness of the Church, and principal feast of the congregation, followed, as in all the churches of Birmingham, by the forty hours' adoration, when all that art and resources can do is expended on the adornment of the altar and sanctuary.
8. The month of Mary is celebrated with all the Roman devotions; and a picture of Mary Immaculate, painted at Rome, and framed in a costly manner by the devotion of the students, is set up in the middle of the church, with flowers and lights. There are two celebrations of the devotion each day of the month; one for the students, and one for the people.
9. The statue of the Blessed Virgin at her altar is always adorned with flowers and lights, and has ever attracted much devotion from the people.
10. There is a Holy Guild of the Immaculate Heart of Mary, which

meets monthly in the chapel of the Sacred Heart for instruction, and whose communion days are the feasts of the Blessed Virgin. 11. Dr. Newman was the first to introduce this cycle of devotions to the Blessed Virgin, and from Birmingham they went with his disciples to London.

Of course I am limiting myself to an account of devotions to the Blessed Virgin exclusively, and every one will understand that other devotions are observed in due proportion.

Ullathorne continues by mentioning the writings of the Oratory Fathers written in honour of the Blessed Virgin: two published sermons by Newman on the Glories of Mary; a book of hymns of which Newman himself had contributed three in honour of Our Lady; Fr Caswell had made a translation of the Office of the Immaculate Conception as well as composing numerous Marian poems and popular hymns and Fr St John had translated the *Racoltà*, a work that included all the indulgenced prayers and Novenas used at Rome in honour of Our Lady. In conclusion Ullathorne noted that

[Newman] brought from Rome what he found in Rome, and I well recollect the pregnant answer which he wrote when it became my duty to interrogate each priest having cure of souls in this diocese, prior to the definition of the Immaculate Conception. The question sent to each asked the sense of the priest, and the traditional sense entertained in his congregation with respect to that mystery. And he wrote in substance: 'We are too young to have a tradition of our own, but we brought the doctrine of the Immaculate Conception of the Mother of God from Rome, where we imbibed it with our other teaching.'

What more exquisite, or more ample proof could we have of the depth to which the singular privileges and glories of the Mother of our Lord have been imbibed into the mind and heart of the person in question, than the exposition of the Mystery of the Immaculate Conception in the letter to Dr. Pusey; an exposition which, I have reason to know, has cleared away the difficulties that obscured the minds of several earnest inquirers with respect to the whole subject of the Blessed Virgin.[15]

---

[15] *LD* xxii. 341.

The public practice of the Oratory is amply borne out in Newman's private correspondence such as a letter written on Holy Thursday, 1866:

And so far from the teaching of the Church concerning the Blessed Virgin being a burden, it seems to me the greatest of privileges and honours to be admitted into the very family of God. So we think on earth, when great people ask us into their most intimate circle. This it is, and nothing short of it, to be allowed to hold intercourse with Mary and Joseph; and, so far from its hindering our communion with our Lord, and our faith in Him, it is all that we should have had without it, and so much more over and above. As He comes near us in His Sacrament of love, so does He bring us near to Him by giving us an introduction (as I may say) to His Mother. In speaking to her, we are honouring Him; as He likes to be petitioned by His chosen ones, so does He especially love the petitions which she offers Him; and in asking her to intercede for us, we are pleasing both her and Him.[16]

And in a letter to Pusey written the following year, Newman tells him that since August 1845 'I saw my way clear to put a miraculous medal round my neck.'[17] In fact Newman's diary entry of Friday 11 September 1846 records his being introduced to the Abbé Degenettes, the curé of N. D. des Victoires, who had founded the Archconfraternity of the Immaculate Heart of Mary, which had the miraculous medal as its badge.[18] Newman was in Paris at the time. The Confraternity had only been established, under a special inspiration, in 1836. Newman's devotion led him to have a replica of the statue of Our Lady of Victories carved for the Birmingham Oratory, a statue which is venerated there to this day.

Among the shrines of Our Lady that were centres of devotion, the thought of the shrine at Loreto was the most dear to him and he composed a series of meditations for the month of May upon the Litany of Loreto. Indeed Newman

---

[16] *LD* xxii. 194. To Lady Chatterton, Holy Thursday 1866.
[17] *LD* xxiii. 318. To E. B. Pusey, 22 August 1867.
[18] *LD* xi. 245.

was hurt at the suggestion that for him to go to Lourdes would be beneficial and "tell well": his notion seems to have been this. He did not deem it likely that with his life-long deep attachment and devotion to the Blessed Virgin under one invocation, she would be more powerful in his regard elsewhere under another.[19]

Newman considered that 'as Eve had a secondary part in the fall, so had the Blessed Mary in the redemption' and that 'knowing the Will of Our Lord most intimately, she prays *according* to His will, or thus is the ordained means or channel by which that will is carried out. Therefore "every thing goes through the hands of Mary" – and this is a great reason for our asking her prayers.'[20]

Newman united his prayer with that of the saints and angels, entrusting himself and his petitions to their familial care: 'We believe in a family of God, of which the Saints are the heavenly members and we the earthly – yet one family embracing earth and heaven.'[21] The Saints are 'the glad and complete specimens of the new creation', 'the most complete and logical evidence while the most popular' of Christianity and books and articles on their lives 'the main and special instruments, to which, under God, we may look for the conversion of our countrymen at this time.'[22]

Blessed shall you and I be, my dear Fathers, if we learn to live now in the presence of Saints and Angels, who are to be our everlasting companions hereafter. Blessed are we, if we converse habitually with Jesus, Mary, and Joseph, – with the Apostles, Martyrs, and great Fathers of the early Church, – with Sebastian, Laurence, and Cecilia, – with Athanasius, Ambrose, and Augustine, with Philip, whose children we are, – with our guardian angels and our patron saints, careless what men think about us, so that their scorn of us involves no injury to our community, and their misconception of us is no hindrance to their own conversion.[23]

---

[19] E. Bellasis, *Coram Cardinali*, 79–80.
[20] *LD* xxii. 68. To John Keble, 8 October 1865.
[21] *LD* xxii. 64. To Edward Berdoe, 2 October 1865.
[22] *LD* xii. 399–400. Draft of an unpublished Preface for Faber's *Lives of the Saints* probably written in the Autumn of 1848.
[23] *OS* 242.

The intercessory role of Our Lady and the Saints was both an inspiration to Newman and a comfort. Regarding a drawing given him by Miss M. R. Giberne, Newman reflected,

Every time I look at it, there is something more and more taking in it. There is something so striking in their all being in the attitude of praying – and when I go in again, I am tempted to say 'What?' you are all at it still?' if that were a reverent and proper speech. It seems an impressive emblem of the perpetual intercession of the Saints perfected waiting for Christ's coming.[24]

'We have access to heavenly members [of the Church], and are at liberty to converse with them,' Newman wrote, 'we can ask them for benefits and they can gain them for us.'[25] Through membership of the Church and living her sacramental life it is a reality of Faith,

To know too that you are in the Communion of Saints – to know that you have cast your lot among all those Blessed Servants of God who are the choice fruit of His Passion – that you have their intercessions on high – that you may address them – and above all the Glorious Mother of God, what thoughts are greater than these?[26]

To this bright vision of the role of saints, Newman surely never lost a darker one, a role perfected in Christ yet still a necessity for His priests. At an earlier time he expressed himself in verse:

> While Moses on the Mountain lay,
> Night after night, and day by day,
>   Till forty suns were gone,
> Unconscious, in the Presence bright,
> Of lustrous day and starry night,
> As though his soul had flitted quite
>   From earth, and Eden won;

---

[24] *LD* vi. 28. To Miss M. R. Giberne, 14 February 1837.
[25] *LD* xxii. 64. To Edward Berdoe, 2 October 1865.
[26] *LD* xii. 224. To Mrs William Froude, 16 June 1848.

The pageant of a kingdom vast,
And things unutterable, pass'd
 Before the Prophet's eye;
Dread shadows of th' Eternal Throne,
The fount of Life, and Altar-stone.
Pavement, and them that tread thereon,
 And those who worship nigh.

But lest he should his own forget,
Who in the vale were struggling yet,
 A sadder vision came,
Announcing all that guilty deed
Of idol rite, that in their need
He for his flock might intercede,
 And stay Heaven's rising flame.[27]

Having spent such a length of time studying the writings of St Athanasius, it is not surprising that Newman held a great devotion to this Father of the Church. Edward Bellasis records how, on his way to Rome in 1856, Newman went to Venice to pray before the saint's relics, what he would have considered one of the 'heavenly shrines'[28]:

The detour was made at great inconvenience. His time was limited, "his strength worn out by the day and night diligence". Fr. St. John's impression was of the Father Superior [Newman] being "extraordinarily" wrapt in prayer. It "was a lasting happiness to him that this act of homage to St. Athanasius had been within his reach, so absorbed did he seem in prayer ... that 'all surroundings,' as he put it, had been lost to him, and when questioned on his return home, he could only say that the relics (so he was told) were about the altar."[29]

More popular saints also won Newman's devotion: 'His trust in St. Anthony of Padua was "downright". As to the finding of witnesses in 1852 for the trial of the following year, he said: "We had a Novena to St. Anthony, and St. Anthony kept for

[27] *VV* 208–9.
[28] *VV* 138.
[29] E. Bellasis, *Coram Cardinali*, 79.

us what he had found". Repeatedly he fell back on St. Anthony after a fruitless search.'[30] St Francis de Sales was another popular saint for whom Newman had an affection, and he dedicated his new private chapel to this saint upon being raised to the Cardinalate. And, of course, St Philip Neri was a continual inspiration and intercessor for Newman throughout his Catholic life. That great saint's mission in Rome was well reflected by Newman's in Birmingham:

St. Philip Neri bears the title of the "Apostle of Rome." Why? Was he a great divine? No; he never professed any theological learning, sufficiently as he was versed in it; and it is remarkable that, great as has been the learning of many Fathers of his Congregation after him, not one of them, as far as I know, has written on a dogmatic subject, or is an authority in the sacred sciences. Did he undertake to form great saints? not so; for, leaving (as is commonly said of him) that high office for others, he turned himself in his humility to the sanctification of ordinary men. He was *not* a theologian, *not* an ascetical writer; but in a familiar way, by precept and maxim, by biographical specimens, by the lessons of history, he addressed himself to the whole community, with a view of converting all men, high and low, to God, and forming them upon the great principles, and fixing in their hearts the substance and solidity, of religious duty. He lived in an age, too, when literature and art were receiving their fullest development, and commencing their benign reign over the populations of Europe, and his work was not to destroy or supersede these good gifts of God, but, in the spirit, I may say, of a Catholic University, to sanctify poetry, and history, and painting, and music, to the glory of the Giver.[31]

'Mary is exalted for the sake of Jesus'[32] as indeed are the saints of God. Their glory was their humility, and this is seen in none more than Mary. Unselfconsciously Newman demonstrated this same gift writing once to one whom he felt to have had an exalted impression of him that, 'I have no tendency to be a saint – it is a sad thing to say. Saints are not literary men, they do not love the classics, they do not write

[30]   Ibid. 80.
[31]   *OS* 118–19.
[32]   *Mix.* 348.

Tales. I may be well enough in my way, but it is not the "high line". It is enough for me to black the saints' shoes – if St. Philip uses blacking, in heaven.'[33] Yet whilst the saints set 'a standard before us of truth, of magnanimity, of holiness, of love' it is vital to notice that 'They are not always our examples, we are not always bound to follow them.'[34] This is because

God beholds thee individually, whoever thou art He 'calls thee by name.' He sees thee, and understands thee, as He made thee. He knows what is in thee, all thy own peculiar feelings and thoughts, thy dispositions and likings, thy strength and thy weakness. He views thee in thy day of rejoicing, and thy day of sorrow. He sympathizes in thy hopes and thy temptations. He interests Himself in all thy anxieties and remembrances, all the risings and fallings of thy spirit. He has numbered the very hairs of thy head and the cubits of thy stature. He compasses thee round and bears thee in His arms; He takes thee up and sets thee down. He notes thy very countenance, whether smiling or in tears, whether healthful or sickly. He looks tenderly upon thy hands and thy feet; He hears thy voice, the beating of thy heart, and thy very breathing. Thou dost not love thyself better than He loves thee. Thou canst not shrink from pain more than He dislikes thy bearing it; and if He puts it on thee, it is as thou wilt put it on thyself, if thou art wise, for a greater good afterwards. Thou art not only His creature (though for the very sparrows He has a care, and pitied the 'much cattle' of Nineveh), thou art man redeemed and sanctified, His adopted son, favoured with a portion of that glory and blessedness which flows from Him everlastingly unto the Only-begotten. Thou art chosen to be His, even above thy fellows who dwell in the East and South. Thou wast one of those for whom Christ offered up His last prayer, and sealed it with His precious blood.[35]

And so Newman would have us turn to Mary, Queen of All Saints, to intercede with her Son and bring us to Him:

In thee, O Mary, is fulfilled, as we can bear it, an original purpose of the Most High. He once had meant to come on earth in heavenly

---

[33] *LD* xiii. 419. To Miss Munro, 11 February 1850.
[34] *Mix.* 101.
[35] *PS* iii. 124–5.

glory, but we sinned; and then He could not safely visit us, except with a shrouded radiance and a bedimmed Majesty, for He was God. So He came Himself in weakness, not in power; and He sent thee, a creature, in His stead, with a creature's comeliness and lustre suited to our state. And now thy very face and form, dear Mother, speak to us of the Eternal; not like earthly beauty, dangerous to look upon, but like the morning star, which is thy emblem, bright and musical, breathing purity, telling of heaven, and infusing peace. O harbinger of day! O hope of the pilgrim! lead us still as thou hast led; in the dark night, across the bleak wilderness, guide us on to our Lord Jesus, guide us home.

> Maria, mater gratiæ,
> Dulcis parens clementiæ,
> Tu nos ab hoste protégé
> Et mortis horâ suscipe.[36]

---

[36] *Mix.* 358–9. 'Mary, Mother of Grace,/ Mother of mercy,/ Shield me from the enemy/ And receive me at the hour of my death.'

11

Preaching

Preparing the way for the Gospel.[1]

At a little church dedicated to the Holy Trinity in Over Worton, near Banbury, on 23 June 1824, John Henry Newman preached his first sermon. In the following nineteen years of Anglican ministry he wrote over six hundred sermons, his last, entitled 'The Parting of Friends', is numbered by him as 604. He preached many more times than this, using previously given sermons on other occasions, sometimes delivering a sermon up to eight times throughout this period of his life, reworking the original sermon each time. He had done some early work in the direction of preaching, recording that in 1817, as a sixteen-year-old, 'he employed himself in writing sermons and sermonets as an exercise'.[2]

Newman's legendary reputation as a preacher built steadily throughout his years of ministry in the Anglican Communion, especially during his tenure as University chaplain at St Mary's, the University Church of Oxford.[3] From those days comes the perhaps most oft-quoted and impressionistic account of Newman's preaching:

Who could resist the charm of that spiritual apparition, gliding in the dim afternoon light through the aisles of St Mary's, rising into the

---

[1] *LD* v. 21. To Samuel Wilberforce, 4 February 1835.

[2] *AW* 45.

[3] For a more detailed account of the context and techniques employed by Newman in his preaching see Ian Ker's *The Achievement of John Henry Newman*, 74–95 and Denis Robinson's 'Preaching' in *The Cambridge Companion to John Henry Newman*, edited by Ian Ker and Terrence Merrigan, 241–54.

pulpit, and then in the most entrancing of voices, breaking the silence with words and thoughts which were religious music – subtle, sweet, mournful?[4]

Yet it was not only his preaching that stirred his listeners' hearts but also the manner in which he read from the Scriptures. Another great convert of the nineteenth century noted that

His delivery of scripture was a sermon in which you forgot the human preacher; a drama in which the vividness of the representation was marred by no effort and degraded by no art. He stood before the sacred volume as if penetrating its contents to their very centre, so that his manner alone, his pathetic changes of voice, or his thrilling pauses, seemed to convey the commentary in the simple enunciation of the text. He brought out meanings where none had been suspected. ...[5]

It seemed to those who heard him that Newman's veneration for the Scriptures was clearly audible when he proclaimed them during the liturgy, one hearer reminiscing that 'His reading was a commentary.'[6] One of the Fathers of the Oratory, Fr Joseph Bacchus, recorded how at the Sunday High Mass the church notices would be read by one of the Fathers and then

When these were disposed of, [Newman's] voice was heard like a soft piece of music from a distance reading the Epistle. He read it, so far as can be remembered, with very little variation in his voice, except perhaps a barely perceptible lingering over the last words, in which he seemed to die away. His manner of reading the Gospel was different. There were of course the pauses required to mark off the

---

4   Matthew Arnold, *Discourses in America*, 139–40.
5   Frederick Oakley, *Historical Notes on the Tractarian Movement 1833–1845*, 25–6.
6   *LD* xxxii. 558. Personal reminiscences of Canon Charles Wellington Furse about John Henry Newman. The whole passage reads, 'His reading was a commentary: and in later studies and expositions of the Corinthians and other Epistles I have often wondered with delight how much I owe to Newman's reading for the enjoyment I have in following St Paul's autobiography in those wonderful letters.'

purely narrative portions from the words of different speakers, accompanied by slight changes in the voice. But the marked thing, which cannot be described, was the increased reverence in the reader's voice which culminated when he came to the words of our Saviour. Before and after these there was a kind of hush. A most wonderful thing about it all was the complete elimination of the personality of the reader. He seemed to be listening as much as reading. The words were the living agent, he but their instrument.[7]

In a sermon delivered in 1831, 'On the objects and effects of Preaching', Newman wrote, 'In Scripture to preach, is to do the work of an evangelist, is to teach, instruct, advise, encourage in all things pertaining to religion, in any way whatever.'[8] Newman's letters also address this subject: 'the Christian preacher using his own words cannot dare hope to be more than a Baptist preparing the way for the Gospel.'[9] The person of Christ was to be presented to congregations not in an 'unreal way – as a mere idea or vision', but as 'Scripture has set Him before us in His actual sojourn on earth, in His gestures, words and deeds'.[10] And yet, as important the task of preaching was, Newman also felt that its role was exaggerated:

And here I will notice a further evil which may and often does arise. Preaching being almost the only mode of intercourse between the Minister and his flock, is in consequence unduly exalted in the scale of importance, – or at least erroneously viewed in relation to the general system of Christian ministration – Men are tempted to come to their Church, not to pray, but to hear – nay they often feel < are > impatient of the length of the prayers, if they feel any especial interest in the preacher.[11]

This was a theme that concerned Newman much in his first years at St Mary's. Newman quotes, approvingly, the great Anglican writer Richard Hooker in his saying that 'Sermons are not the only preaching which doth save our souls.' 'This,'

---

[7] *SN* xi–xii.
[8] *Sermons* i. 25.
[9] *LD* v. 21. To Samuel Wilberforce, 4 February 1835.
[10] *PS* iii. 130.
[11] *Sermons* i. 6–7.

comments Newman, 'were to shut up the use and sense of this word preaching in a close prison.'[12]

The public exposition and application of the word of God is doubtless a material *part* of ministerial instruction, yet not the principal part, and much less the whole – We meet together here for a distinct and superior purpose from that of hearing any human instructor ... we meet principally to claim the promises by united prayer. ... And as one mode of the Christian minister's universal preaching consists in sermons, so another consists in catechising the young, another in visiting the sick, nay another and the most solemn in that reading Scripture and the services of prayer in church which I have been all along exalting – The prayers, the services of the Liturgy are a chief part of his preaching.[13]

'Would that [the ministers of Christ's] whole lives could be one unceasing witness of Him who has chosen them for Himself', wrote Newman. If only each would be

a witness in all things in season and *out* of season, as the ministers of God, preaching Christ 'by much patience, by afflictions, by necessities, by distresses, ... by pureness, by knowledge, by longsuffering, by kindness, by the Holy Ghost, by love unfeigned, by the word of truth, by the power of God, by the armour of righteousness on the right hand and on the left, by honour and dishonour, by evil report and good report' <2 Cor 6>. So, they *should* preach Him whether by life or death.[14]

This was considered by Newman as a 'continual life-preaching'[15] that gave flesh to any words that the preacher might utter and, he believed, that such 'life-preaching' would be perceptible to the hearer of the preacher's words. It would seem that such a complete mode of communication, a heartfelt

---

[12] From Sermon 214, 'On Preaching', probably first delivered on 1 November 1829 at St Mary's, Oxford. The second preachment, which forms the body of the published sermon, being given on 18 October 1839: *Sermons* i. 21, quoting *The Works of . . . Richard Hooker, A New Edition,* Oxford 1820, ii. 76. Cf. Sermon No. 290, 'On the object and effects of preaching – (on the anniversary of my entering on my living): *Sermons* i. 23–31.

[13] *Sermons* i. 21–2.

[14] *Sermons* i. 21.

[15] Ibid.

knowledge of self and a keenly perceptive and patient sense of others, was tangible to those who heard Newman preach. The necessity of the integrity of the preacher was a theme that he returned to as a Catholic:

Nature itself witnesses to this connexion between sanctity and truth. It anticipates that the fountain from which doctrine comes should itself be pure; that the seat of Divine teaching, and the oracle of faith should be the abode of angels; that the consecrated home, in which the word of God is elaborated, and whence it issues forth for the salvation of the many, should be holy, as that word itself is holy. Here you see the difference of the office of a prophet and a mere gift, such as that of miracles. Miracles are the simple and direct work of God; the worker of them is but an instrument or organ. And in consequence he need not be holy, because he has not, strictly speaking, a share in the work. So again the power of administering the Sacraments, which also is supernatural and miraculous, does not imply personal holiness; nor is there anything surprising in God's giving to a bad man this gift, or the gift of miracles, any more than in His giving him any natural talent or gift, strength or agility of frame, eloquence, or medical skill. It is otherwise with the office of preaching and prophesying, and to this I have been referring; for the truth first goes into the minds of the speakers, and is apprehended and fashioned there, and then comes out from them as, in one sense, its source and its parent. The Divine word is begotten in them, and the offspring has their features and tells of them. They are not like "the dumb animal, speaking with man's voice," on which Balaam rode, a mere instrument of God's word, but they have "received an unction from the Holy One, and they know all things," and "where the Spirit of the Lord is, there is liberty"; and while they deliver what they have received, they enforce what they feel and know. "We have *known and believed*," says St. John, "the charity which God hath to us."[16]

Newman insists on this point:

If one drop of corruption makes the purest water worthless, as the slightest savour of bitterness spoils the most delicate viands, how can it be that the word of truth and holiness can proceed profitably from

[16] *Mix.* 366–7.

impure lips and an earthly heart? No; as is the tree, so is the fruit; "beware of false prophets," says our Lord; and then He adds, "from their fruits ye shall know them. Do men gather grapes of thorns, or figs of thistles?" Is it not so, my brethren? which of you would go to ask counsel of another, however learned, however gifted, however aged, if you thought him unholy? nay, though you feel and are sure, as far as absolution goes, that a bad priest could give it as really as a holy priest, yet for advice, for comfort, for instruction, you would not go to one whom you did not respect. "Out of the abundance of the heart, the mouth speaketh;" "a good man out of the good treasure of his heart bringeth forth good, and an evil man out of the evil treasure bringeth forth evil".[17]

James Anthony Froude was one of the many admirers of Newman who evidently were completely convinced of the 'good treasure' of Newman's heart, being able to perceive both the incisive psychological insight and the attractive practical wisdom of his words:

I had then never seen so impressive a person . . . He told us what he believed to be true . . . No one who heard his sermons in those days can ever forget them. Newman, taking some Scripture character for a text spoke to us about ourselves, our temptations, our experiences. His illustrations were inexhaustible. He seemed to be addressing the most secret consciousness of each of us, as the eyes of a portrait appear to look at every person in a room. He never exaggerated; he was never unreal. A sermon from him was a poem, formed on a distinct idea, fascinating by its subtlety, welcome – how welcome! – from its sincerity, interesting from its originality, even to those who were careless of religion: and to others who wished to be religious, but had found religion dry and wearisome, it was like the springing of a fountain out of the rock.[18]

Newman would have been grateful for such an appreciation as Froude's as throughout his life Newman held that 'the way to refute error is to preach truth',[19] which itself Newman understood as being 'neither light nor darkness, but both

---

[17] *Mix.* 368.
[18] Froude, *Short Studies*, vol. iv, 278–84.
[19] *PS* vi. 203.

together'.[20] It was thus 'not enough to expose the wrong meaning [of Holy Scripture], unless we expound the right also'.[21] The essential need for preaching the whole of the Gospel message, even those parts which the preacher will know to be difficult for him or his listeners, is conveyed by Newman's assertion that 'how much more powerful even a false interpretation of the sacred text is than none at all.'[22] Yet he recognizes that it will not be possible for someone to adequately grasp an understanding of Scripture 'without express trouble on [our] part',[23] having consulted commentaries and noted writers, and making use of the disciplines such as history and archaeology.

But before all else a specific virtue is required if one is to be able to understand at its deepest level the riches of the inspired words of Scripture: 'humility and teachableness are qualities of mind necessary for arriving at the truth in any subject, and in religious matters as well as others.'[24] Indeed we must 'read the Gospels with a serious and humble mind, and as in God's presence',[25] or as Newman expressed this poetically,

> Christ bade His followers take the sword;
> And yet He chid the deed,
> When Peter seized upon His word,
> And made a foe to bleed.

> The gospel Creed, a sword of strife,
> Meek hands alone may rear;
> And ever Zeal begins its life
> In silent thought and fear.

> Ye, who would weed the Vineyard's soil,
> Treasure the lesson given;
> Lest in the judgement-books ye toil
> For Satan, not for heaven.[26]

[20] *Essays* i. 41.
[21] *PS* vi. 203.
[22] *Apo.* 11.
[23] *PS* viii. 192.
[24] *PS* viii. 113.
[25] *PS* iii. 77.
[26] *VV* 170.

And so, 'A preacher should be quite sure that he understands the persons he is addressing before he ventures to aim at what he considers to be their ethical condition; for, if he mistakes, he will probably be doing harm rather than good.'[27]

Unlike many of his contemporaries for Newman, 'preaching was not the way to convert people, but the way to prepare them for conversion'.[28] As an Anglican Newman's sermons were sometimes criticized for being 'cold and uninfluential' yet his aim was far from that of the fiery Evangelical preachers whom he felt produced only emotion without any positive lasting effects.[29] By this point in his Anglican ministry, Newman strongly held that many preachers were having to attempt too much by means of the sermon simply because the Anglican liturgical rites were so impoverished and were denuded of

the idea which had actually been the rule of the Primitive Church, of teaching the more sacred truths ordinarily by rites and ceremonies. No mode of teaching can be imagined so public, constant, impressive, permanent, and at the same time reverential than that which makes the forms of devotion the memorial and declaration of doctrine – reverential, because the very posture of the mind in worship is necessarily such. In this way Christians receive the Gospel literally on their knees, and in a temper altogether different from that critical and argumentative spirit which sitting and listening engender.[30]

To the same correspondent, James Stephen, Newman had written some weeks earlier,

Certainly in my judgement Preaching is not the means of conversion – but a subsidiary, as rousing, convincing, interesting, and altogether preparing the way; a work especially necessary now, when Christians need the exhibition of (what is called) the Law, as much perhaps as when St James wrote his (uninfluential) Epistle. The Church with the Sacraments etc, and the life of good men seem to me the great

---

[27] *Idea* 418.
[28] Ker, *John Henry Newman*, 113.
[29] *LD* v. 32. To James Stephen, 27 February 1835.
[30] *LD* v. 46. To James Stephen, 16 March 1835. Cf. *LD* v. 21. To Samuel Wilberforce, 4 February 1835.

persuasives of the Gospel, as being visible witnesses and substitutes for Him who is Persuasion itself. Yet surely He in His day had so little success, that even the Church His representative, much more a mere preacher, may well acquiesce in failure. As far as *impressing* persons, I think my way does as well as another; not so, as regards warming, melting, subduing, capturing etc, doubtless. This latter way seems indeed to do great things – but, though I am willing to have the contrary proved, at first sight I confess my fear that it is but a blaze among the stubble.[31]

The Sacraments were the 'means of persuasion' precisely because they 'are the embodied forms of the Spirit of Christ.'[32] The different effect desired by Newman in his preaching is both defined and delivered at the end of his very last sermon as an Anglican, *The Parting of Friends*:

And, O my brethren, O kind and affectionate hearts, O loving friends, should you know any one whose lot it has been, by writing or by word of mouth, in some degree to help you thus to act; if he has ever told you what you knew about yourselves, or what you did not know; has read to you your wants or feelings, and comforted you by the very reading; has made you feel that there was a higher life than this daily one, and a brighter world than that you see; or encouraged you, or sobered you, or opened a way to the inquiring, or soothed the perplexed; if what he has said or done has ever made you take interest in him, and feel well inclined towards him; remember such a one in time to come, though you hear him not, and pray for him, that in all things he may know God's will, and at all times he may be ready to fulfil it.[33]

The key to Newman's method of preaching lies in the words, 'if he has ever told you what you knew about yourselves, or what you did not know,' that is the ability to enter incisively into the very personal thoughts of his listeners.

Merely I would say the *general object* of preaching is to enlighten the mind as to its real state – to dig round about the Truth – to make men

---

[31] *LD* v. 32. To James Stephen, 27 February 1835.
[32] *LD* v. 39. To Samuel Wilberforce, 10 March 1835.
[33] *SD* 409. 'The Parting of Friends' was preached on the anniversary of the consecration of the chapel that Newman had built at Littlemore, 25 September 1843.

feel they are sinners and lost – to make them understand their need of pardon and sanctification – and the difficulty of the latter, to hinder them for mistaking words for ideas, and going on in a *formal* way, . . . – and if I effect this great object in preaching, I am little solicitous to inquire whether I have every where brought forward in the front those simple Truths – towards which I labour, and which the Sacraments secure, or whether I have gone through the full series of Christian doctrines in detail, which is the business of the Catechist. Services and Catechising are both essential, and I do not see how Sermons can supply their place.[34]

At the height of his powers preaching at St Mary's, Newman was regularly giving sermons that had been scrupulously prepared and written out over, on average, fourteen pages. Many of these sermons were published yet many more are only now being set in print. These sermons took about forty-five minutes to deliver. After giving his last sermon as an Anglican minister it was to be over three years before Newman preached again. The occasion was the giving of a funeral oration at St Isidore's, the Irish Franciscan Church in Rome, on 4 December 1846 for a niece of the Countess of Shrewsbury, and Newman was given just a few hours' notice that he was to speak. Newman was in minor orders and resident in Rome at the College of Propaganda. He preached without a text and afterwards commented to a friend, 'I assure you I did not like it at all.'[35]

On Sunday 31 October 1847 Newman preached his first sermon in the chapel at Collegio di Propaganda. Whilst in Rome he is also known to have preached at the English College, an account of which is given in a collection entitled, *Good Words* edited by Donald Macleod, who was to become Moderator of the Church of Scotland (1895–6), and published in 1883.[36] On his return to England, Newman once again took up the responsibility of preaching and very quickly adapted to the Catholic custom of not actually reading his sermons.

The Catholic Newman further accommodated himself to

---

[34] *LD* v. 47. To James Stephen, 16 March 1835.
[35] *LD* xi. 290. To J. D. Dalgairns, 8 December 1846.
[36] *LD* xii. 128, n.1. See 'Some Italian Memories', in *Good Words*, 1883, 424.

those who now heard him preach by speaking in a simpler fashion well suited to the populace of such a large industrial town as Birmingham. Thus there are very few complete sermons extant from Newman's Catholic years. Those sermons prepared for special occasions, however, give ample evidence that he never lost his ability to skilfully, if seemingly artlessly, compose sermons of the utmost power and beauty.

As a Catholic, Newman adhered to the same foundational principles with regard to the preparation of sermons as he had as an Anglican. Advice given to a student of Maynooth in 1868 is entirely consistent with precepts given in his younger days as in later years. Preparing to preach, the seminarian was 'to have your subject distinctly before you; to think over it till you have got it perfectly in your head.'[37] He should make notes to help him learn the sermon by heart and

... humility, which is a great Christian virtue, has a place in literary composition – he who is ambitious will never write well. But he who tries to say simply and exactly what he feels or thinks, what religion demands, what Faith teaches, what the Gospel promises, will be eloquent without intending it, and will write better English than if he made a study of English literature.[38]

Humility was ever in Newman's mind with regard to preaching. 'I feel (I can say this without affectation) that I am not worthy to suggest any thing to any one – What am I among the thousands in Israel? arises in my mind continually,'[39] he wrote to a friend, 'and if it is any comfort to you so to say, I have before now felt in my own mind the distress you speak of about the right mode of preaching – at one time (as you may have heard me say) so sorely that I thought I must have given up my curacy, nay have left the Church.'[40]

In Chapter 6 of *The Idea of a University,* Newman summarizes three qualities that he considered made a good sermon. In the first place those listening to the preacher must

---

[37] *LD* xxiv, 44. To a Student at Maynooth, 2 March 1868.
[38] Ibid. 45.
[39] *LD* ii. 84. To Robert Isaac Wilberforce, 29 July 1828.
[40] Ibid.

sense an earnestness which Newman believed was the result of 'personal traits of an ethical nature evident in the orator'.[41] Secondly, 'As a marksman aims at the target and its bull's-eye, and at nothing else, so the preacher must have a definite point before him, which he has to hit.'[42] Thus, as Newman had written many years earlier, this necessarily would preclude the temptation 'to bring in every doctrine every where' and 'that a Sermon to be effective must be imperfect.'[43] Thirdly, the sermon had to be conceived with the specific listeners to it in mind – as he wrote in another work, 'personal influence requires personal acquaintance, and the minute labour a discretionary rule'.[44] The lack of 'personal acquaintance' was a major part in Newman's repeatedly declining frequent invitations to preach at great celebrations up and down the country let alone the fact that, 'To preach outside the Oratory does not enter our vocation, for we are a home people.'[45] Thus he was speaking according to his natural pattern, even if mixed with ulterior motives, when he wrote to Mgr George Talbot, who had employed some strong-arm tactics to attempt to coerce Newman to preach a series of sermons in Rome 'for the greater glory of God, and the Salvation of Souls'.[46] 'Birmingham people have souls',[47] Newman replied: he was not to be so easily prised from what he had ever hoped as a Catholic would have consistently been the main work of his life, the saving of the souls entrusted to him in Birmingham.

An earlier outline of what Newman considered a sermon's purpose to be, and the manner of achieving this end, was given by him in a letter preparing for a short series of sermons to be given in London in 1848:

NB. *The* object of the Sermons is to *bring the minds of our listeners into a state fitting the coming Season.*

---

[41] *Idea* 408.
[42] *Idea* 406.
[43] *LD* v. 38. To Samuel Wilberforce, 10 March 1835.
[44] *Campaign* 37.
[45] *LD* xxiii. 257. To Lady Herbert of Lea, 29 June 1867.
[46] *LD* xxi. 166. From Mgr George Talbot, 24 July 1864.
[47] *LD* xxi. 165–7. To Mgr George Talbot, 25 July 1864.

This must be kept in mind. If we keep it in mind as we write and preach it will give a character to each sermon, and prevent us from aiming too much at a course, or at a system – or from being methodical – or wishing to introduce new thoughts or views. It will keep us earnest and natural. And when we speak of doctrine, it will direct the Doctrine to an immediate practical end.[48]

Each sermon was to be on one subject and to include edifying stories, 'not such as are likely to surprise or offend people, as some miraculous accounts would do.' 'We must avoid every thing extreme.'[49]

Already as a famous Anglican preacher, Newman considered the dangers of the preacher's life being estranged from those to whom he was called upon to preach to:

As to Town-preacherships, they seem to me dangerous to the holder, as corrupting the minister into the orator. The *realities* of our profession are in parochial and such-like engagements – the sickbed, the schoolroom, the accidental intercourse of the week – but a pulpit makes one *un*real, rhetorical – conceited – it hardens the heart, while it effeminates it. ... Are you to preach *before* trustees etc., before you are elected, as a spectacle and a sort of examination? This no clergyman can consent to. Is there any means of parochial duty or quasi-parochial during the week? workhouse, infirmary or school? – these should be something to humble and sober one. On the other hand a pulpit in London to a truly serious *manly* servant of Christ is a means of great usefulness. But a station of exceeding difficulty and over-much vexation. – It is to have a part of that Saint whose day we are approaching[50] – to be charged to rebuke vice in high places – to over throw the luxurious wantonness of mind, the pride, the especial cold-heartedness of this age – and to do this faithfully requires a firmness, a wisdom, and a clear calm steady-sightedness, which Apostles scarcely possess, and *ensures a persecution* – One out of many dilemmas in which a London-preacher finds himself, is the following – let *him withstand* the popular love of novelty and desire of excitement, he must preach (what will be called) *dully* and if so, he will *empty his chapel* – let him try to keep his congregation together, he will be pampering their bad tempers and habits. –

---

[48] *LD* xii. 197. To Anthony Hutchinson, 2 April 1848.
[49] Ibid.
[50] St John the Baptist on 24 June.

Yet, after all, I am by no means against your undertaking it – as far as I can judge without knowledge of particulars. But if you undertake it, 'Think not of peace – tho' dreams be sweet', 'Start up and ply your heaven-bound feet –'[51] You will have a most dry and melancholy work – unless, i.e., you go out of the narrow ways and turn popular preacher, which I am sure you will not do.[52]

Knowing his congregation, Newman issued a cautionary sanction before he delivered one of his most important sermons, 'The Theory of Developments in Religious Doctrine' on Thursday 2 February 1843: 'If any one values his Luncheon on Thursday, he must not go to hear me at St Mary's, for my sermon is of portentous length – and my only satisfaction is that, if any persons go out of curiosity, they will be punished.'[53] Of this sermon John William Burgon, then a student at Worcester College, Oxford, and later Dean of Chichester, recounted that it was

... the most remarkable production *of its class* I ever heard. So extremely universal in its scope, that it was impossible, from hearing it once, to grasp its meaning as a whole, and so exceedingly subtle and often metaphysical, that it was no less difficult to understand its several parts. Still the general *impression* was clear enough, and such as I shall not easily forget ... I thought him singularly *effective*, – yet could not but feel how completely his very weakness (so to speak) was his strength. His silence was eloquent, and his pauses worth a torrent of rhetoric.[54]

Ultimately, Newman writes,

On these grounds I would go on to lay down a precept, which I trust is not extravagant ... It is, that preachers should neglect everything whatever besides devotion to their one object, and earnestness in pursuing it, till they in some good measure attain to these requisites. Talent, logic, learning, words, manner, voice, action, all are

---

[51] Keble's *Christian Year*, Second Sunday in Advent, last stanza.
[52] *LD* ii. 337–8. To Simeon Lloyd Pope, 21 June 1831.
[53] *LD* ix. 217.
[54] E. M. Goulburn, *John William Burgon, Late Dean of Chichester*, i, 139–40.

required for the perfection of a preacher; but "one thing necessary," – an intense perception and appreciation of the end for which he preaches, and that is, to be the minister of some definite spiritual good to those who hear him. Who could wish to be more eloquent, more powerful, more successful than the Teacher of the Nations? yet who more earnest, who more natural, who more unstudied, who more self-forgetting than he?[55]

---

[55] *Idea*, 408.

12

Preaching the Priesthood

this unspeakable trust[1]

On Sunday 18 December 1831 Newman was invited to preach upon the occasion of the conferring of Anglican orders at Christ Church Cathedral, Oxford – the very place of both his own diaconal and priestly ordinations. Amongst the ordinands who heard Newman preach was his future brother-in-law, Thomas Mozley.

This morning's meeting is one of those rare occasions on which Christ's Kingdom, which cometh not with observation, shows its open presence among us, graciously forcing itself on our notice. Surely I may say this. Considering the circumstances under which we are now brought together, the congregation itself thus formed, the great and sacred act to be solemnized before we part, and the sacrament following it, its importance moreover to those who are to be the subjects of it, both in years past while they were preparing for it, and much more in its bearing on their future life and eternal prospects, – considering these things, surely the early times seem come again, and we stand with the Apostles on the day of Pentecost, waiting for the first and visible descent of that Divine Power which has ever since secretly rested on the Christian Church. – For a time we are as much shut out from the world, its employments and its troubles, as if we were collected in that upper chamber where the first congregation of believers assembled with one accord,

All this, I doubt not, has had its influence on *your* minds, My

---

[1] B.O.A., A. 50. 2. 19+1 This sermon, No. 323, 'On the Ministerial Order, as an existing divine institution', is unpublished at the time of writing. The copy kindly given to me is a draft of the version to be published by Oxford University Press in Volume iv of *John Henry Newman Sermons 1824 – 1843*. This quotation comes from the final preaching of this sermon.

Brethren, whom I am soon to call brethren in the Christian ministry.
– This is a day much to be remembered by you through life for the
inexpressible thoughts you have had in it.[2]

Newman gave the sermon on two subsequent occasions –
Friday 28 October 1836, the Feast of Sts Simon & Jude, and
Monday 24 August 1840, the Feast of St Bartholomew (both at
St Mary the Virgin, Oxford) – revising it each time. Given that
the final version of this sermon was delivered towards the close
of Newman's preaching life as an Anglican and the original
preachment being on such a significant occasion as an
ordination, it provides a good indication of his thought on
what, at that time, he understood to be the priesthood to which
he himself was ordained.

For it is good and pleasant to devote oneself to God's service, soul
and body – and even the momentous nature of the vows you make
and the commission you receive, and the awfulness of that peculiar
fearful gift, the ordination-grace (which we best reverence in thought
and deed, not in word) even these considerations elevate the mind.[3]

It is unsurprising that Newman always held in the highest
esteem the greatness of the ministry to which he was called, a
ministry whose 'one object' was 'to *offer souls*, (so to express
myself –) to bring men near to God, to bind them to God's
service here, and to save them in the end – and, as a means to
these great ends, to convey to them through the appointed
means sanctifying influences of divine grace.'[4] At that 1831
ordination he preached that,

At the very first view, regarded even as a mere human institution, the
ministerial body < ecclesiastical polity > has (it is plain) a venerable
character and a dignity, to which no other body can lay claim. – It is
without parallel in the world, viewed as an historical fact. – With
what feelings of reverence and interest (exultation at once and

---

[2] B.O.A., A. 50. 2. 19 + 1. – from original preaching.
[3] Ibid.
[4] From Sermon No. 224, 'The Liturgy the service of the Christian Priest':
Sermons i. 59.

conscious unworthiness) do we contemplate (our admission to) any celebrated society framed for whatever object – much more is such honour due to members incorporate of the Apostolical ministry and the people who are in communion with them – for thus we seem to enter into close fellowship with the Apostles, and to acquire a sort of personal interest in the fortunes and holy services of all the great men who have ruled the Church since their time. – Think of the multitude of Christian teachers and champions and rulers, famous in history – those especially which each of us respectively has read most about and admired most fully, these were members of our body.[5]

The difference, of course, between the preacher of 1840 and of the years from not long after the above words were spoken lies in what Newman understood by the word 'Church' and in the development of his understanding of the difference between Anglican orders and the Catholic priesthood. What he preached of as an Anglican by the late 1830s with regard to the ministry would develop into his natural thought about the Catholic priesthood. Thus he affirmed that the 'spiritual society, venerable even as a human institution,' of the ministry was 'of divine origin'; the Apostles provided for 'its continuance and made the Christian people to come from and to depend upon it.'[6] Being of divine origin, Newman deduces that the intrinsic and irreplaceable nature of the ministerial life will always prevail as it always had done:

... its continuance on the earth is an evidence of its divinity. – Amid numberless revolutions through many centuries, which have so swept the earth as to make for us at this day a new world, still the Christian ministry has survived as an institution, borne, like the ark, on top of the waters and shut in from peril by the hand of God – Surely there is no strange instance of long preservation parallel to it, but its counterpart, – the preservation of the scattered Jewish race to this day in the countries of enemies – and these each in its place carry with them the signs of Divine Power, for mercy or for judgement as truly, though with less observation, than < as > in their early history when miracles attended them.[7]

[5] B.O.A. A., 50. 2. 19+1 – from final preaching.
[6] Ibid.
[7] Ibid.

This strikingly high theology of the ministry Newman carried into his thought regarding the Catholic priesthood as he saw that the divine institution of the ministry was 'the chief (almost sole) instrument of the world's regeneration', 'the centre round which [the visible Church] is to grow' and 'to draw together in one' the people of God precisely because of the efficacy of the Sacraments of the Church which the priest is called upon to administer.[8]

We are brethren and fellows of the Apostles. – So high are we raised by this grace above all men, that (strange to say) our actual unbelief, our blindness to < dim perception of > to its great dignity, is our only security against the danger of bearing it[.] To baptize an infant, to consecrate bread and wine seem simple acts – but what are they in the sight of angels? Even in a natural world the most simple combination of means produces the most awful effects. . . . Did the kingdom of God come with observation, we could not receive it[.] Did we see what it really is to be the ministers of the New Covenant, the dispensers of those privileges which an inexpressible sacrifice has gained for man, we should either be cast down by utter despair, or exalted into a madness of pride as if we were gods. – Nothing but a correspondent strength of resignation to God's will, of obedience to the leadings of His Spirit, could induce a man to submit to the ministerial charge, who had a true view of his own nothingness and of the fearful power of the gifts lodged in < conveyed by > it. – God graciously leads us on gradually – and gives us so much of knowledge, faith and submission, as may balance < answer to > each other and may keep us in a steady way. – But surely the lowest degree of these will teach us the most profound reverence at the thought of our commission – a self-abasement which will penetrate our whole character, and make us own unfeignedly that *we* are verily (what St Paul calls) *earthen vessels* [2 Cor. 4:7], in whom the treasures of eternal life are stored – And withal, it will teach us an exceeding self-respect, such a sense of our own dignity, i.e. of His dignity who dwells in us, as may keep us clear from sin and safe from evil – shrinking from the contaminations of every bad passion and perverse temper, and rising *above* the world, above suffering, above sorrow, above the power of man's malice to harm us, or of his example to mislead us, or of his promises to seduce us from the pure faith of Christ.[9]

[8] Ibid.
[9] Ibid.

In order to enlighten the hearts and minds of the faithful
entrusted to his care, Newman taught that ideally the priest
should have 'a systematic knowledge of doctrine, a perception
of the proportions and connexion of its several parts, and a
penetrating foresight of the distant and ultimate consequences
and slight incipient deflections from the truth.' The priest must
be a well-informed guide for the faithful because the faithful
frequently do not have the leisure with which they might be
able, properly, to study the complexities of the theological
arguments that lay behind any particular proposition of the
Church. If he is not, he and the community which he is called
upon to serve risk losing 'the discipline of the Church' so that
'all are scattered each to his own way'.[10]

But it is not sufficient, in Newman's thought, for the priest
to be simply well informed. The priest has to be united with his
bishop, for it is the bishop whose 'special object' is to 'provide
for soundness and unity of doctrine.'[11] 'The rule of conscience
(as I may call it) which has ever been before me, is "Do
nothing without the Bishop", as St Ignatius lays it down.'[12]

Even in his experience as a minister of the Church of
England, Newman had determined that the principle of
Episcopal authority had 'seemed to simplify and settle all other
questions' for him, indeed he had 'a great dread of breaking
this'.[13] 'No one can accuse me of not obeying St Ignatius's
rule,' stated Newman, 'indeed the words constantly in my
mind have been "He who trifles with the Bishop, trifles with
the Bishop invisible".'[14] And, with over a year to go before

[10] Ibid. Cf. *VM* i. 141–2.
[11] *VM* ii. 70–1.
[12] *LD* ix. 116. To Thomas Mozley, 26 September 1842. Ignatius of Antioch
insisted, in his *Epistle to the Trallians*, 2.2, that 'It is necessary,
therefore, that you should do nothing without the bishop, as indeed you
do, and that you should submit yourselves to the presbytery also, as to the
Apostles of Jesus Christ, our hope, in whom we shall be found walking.'
Cf. *OS* 183–98, 'Order, The Witness and Instrument of Unity' a sermon
preached in St Chad's Cathedral, Birmingham.
[13] Ibid.
[14] 'It is therefore fitting that you should, after no hypocritical fashion, obey
[your bishop], in honour of Him who has willed us [to do so], since he
who does not do so deceives not [so much by such conduct] the bishop
who is visible, but mocks Him who is invisible.' Ignatius of Antioch,
Epistle to the Magnesians, 3.2.

Newman made his submission, as he would regard it, to Rome and the Catholic Church he was clear that

> I should, if a Roman Catholic, be, not a Gallican, but obey submissively and unreservedly the 'one Bishop' in the person of the Pope, as the representative of the Bishop unseen. In this it is that Keble and I have ever differed from Palmer, etc etc. in looking on the Episcopate as an absolute monarchy – *the right faith* being the constitution, not a presbytery – *orthodoxy* being the condition and limit of the Bishop's authority.[15]

Does this mean that at this point in his life Newman held that bishops other than the Bishop of Rome were of little account? Not at all. He is clear that St Ignatius 'always contemplates in theory *one* Bishop when he is speaking of those *under* the Bishop.'

> The Apostles are a Council to *Christ* – but singly they are each a perfect type of Christ. In like manner St Cyprian's language is, that the Episcopal power is shared by *all* Bishops *fully*. His expression is 'in solidum', which means like *joint tenure* or *partnership*, where each has full enjoyment of all the perogatives and the whole responsibility. Dioceses are unknown, – there are no local distinctions, in the *idea* of the Church. Hooker will tell you this – Bishops 'by restraint',[16] as I think the phrase is, are a *bye law* of the Church – not a part of the Episcopal theory – by which all Bishops are 'Bishops at large'.[17]

Thus Newman taught that 'When we approach the Ministry He has ordained, we approach the steps of His throne. When we

---

[15] *LD* x. 213. To Mrs John Mozley, 19 April 1844.

[16] 'Now even as pastors, so likewise bishops being principal pastors, are either at large or else with restraint: at large, when the subject of their regiment is indefinite, and not tied to any certain place; bishops with restraint are they whose regiment over the Church is contained within some definite, local compass, beyond which their jurisdiction reacheth not. Such therefore we always mean when we speak of that regiment by bishops which we hold a thing most lawful, divine, and holy in the Church of Christ.' R. Hooker, *The Laws of Ecclesiastical Polity*, Book VII, Chapter II, 3, final paragraph, *The Works of that learned and judicious divine Mr. Richard Hooker, III*, ed. J. Keble, seventh edn., Oxford 1888, 148–9.

[17] *LD* x. 213. To Mrs John Mozley, 19 April 1844.

approach the Bishops, who are the centres of that Ministry, what have we before us but the Twelve Apostles, present but invisible?'[18]

Such being Newman's belief of the relationship between bishops, an incident within the Oratory community once he was a Catholic priest illustrates his conception of the relationship between bishops and priests. Addressing a misunderstanding, Newman reminded Edward Caswell, who was acting as Rector during a period of Newman's absence, that 'The Brothers are our equals in the same sense in which a Priest is a Bishop's equal. The Bishop is above the Priest ecclesiastically – but they are both sacred ministers. The Father is above the Brother sacerdotally – but in the Oratory they are equal.'[19]

On a number of other occasions as an Anglican, Newman preached on the subject of the ministerial order. A sermon delivered on St Peter's day, 'The Christian Ministry', takes that apostle 'as the appropriate type and representative of the Christian ministry', the 'peculiar dignity' of whom consists first and foremost in that the minister 'is the representative of Christ', 'an appointed channel by which the peculiar Gospel blessings are conveyed to mankind, one who has the power to apply to individuals those gifts which Christ has promised us generally as the fruit of His mediation.'[20]

In Sermon 18, 'The Gainsaying of Korah', from the fourth volume of *Parochial and Plain Sermons*, Newman examines 'how great must be the sin of resisting the ministers of Christ, or of intruding into their office! How great a sin of presuming to administer the rites of the Church, to baptize, to celebrate the Holy Communion, or to ordain, or to bless, without a commission!'[21] Whilst there is possible the sin of presumption in taking up the ministerial order there must always be an awareness amongst the ordained that they too are fragile instruments of the Almighty's power:

---

[18] *PS* iv. 177.
[19] *LD* xvi. 267. To Edward Caswell, 4 October 1854.
[20] *PS* ii. 300–5.
[21] *PS* iv. 281.

Now, what is the Church but, as it were, a body of humiliation, almost provoking insult and profaneness, when men do not live by faith? an earthen vessel, far more so even than His body of flesh, for that was at least pure from all sin, and the Church is defiled in all her members. We know that her ministers at best are but imperfect and erring, and of like passions with their brethren; yet of them He has said, speaking not to the Apostles merely but to all the seventy disciples (to whom Christian ministers are in office surely equal), "He that heareth you, heareth Me, and he that despiseth you, despiseth Me, and he that despiseth Me, despiseth Him that sent Me."[22]

In another sermon, whilst exploring in an incisive manner the commitment of Christians generally, Newman turns a spotlight onto the ministerial order, those who, like the apostles James and John say, 'We are able.'[23]

They know not whither they are being carried; they see not the end of their course; they know no more than this, that it is right to do what they are now doing; and they hear a whisper within them, which assures them, as it did the two holy brothers, that whatever their present conduct involves in time to come, they shall, through God's grace, be equal to it.[24]

Sermons were not the only chosen method by which Newman sought to preach. It was with the intention of forming the clergy that Newman and others set about the publication of the Tracts. 'It is necessary to *wake* the clergy,' he wrote, 'if you get them even to criticize, it is no slight thing. Willingly would I (if I) be said to write in an irritating and irritated way, if in that way I *rouse* people – and I maintain (whether rightly or wrongly, but I *maintain*) that by ways such as these alone can one move them.'[25]

Happy as he was to 'rouse' the clergy, Newman was less enthusiastic that they should take up contentious issues with

[22] *PS* iv. 250. Cf. *Ari.* 382–4.
[23] Matthew xx. 22.
[24] *PS* iv. 304–5.
[25] *LD* iv. 117. To Samuel Rickards, 22 November 1833.

him personally, as he quite reasonably explained to one would-be interlocutor: 'I conceive that, if every Clergyman wrote to every other on the subject of their mutual differences, we should none of us have time for those duties which have a prior call upon our time and attention.'[26]

It is salutary to note that the number of clergy and candidates for ordination who could preach the Gospel was a concern even in 1841. To an unknown correspondent requesting assistance in procuring a curate Newman writes, 'Doubtless you are aware of the great scarcity of clergymen, or candidates for orders, which exists ... we are much inconvenienced by it here', but he promises that his 'best endeavours shall not be wanting.'[27] According to Newman, previous ages had other methods of ensuring the spread of the Gospel:

Another remarkable instance of the force which was put upon men by the early Church, will be found in the then existing usage of bringing such as had the necessary gifts to ordination, without asking their consent. The primitive Christians looked upon Ordination very differently (alas for ourselves!) from this age. Now the ministerial office is often regarded as a *profession* of this world, – a provision, a livelihood; it is associated in men's minds with a comparatively easy, or at least not a troubled life, – with respectability and comfort, a competency, a position in society. Alas for us! we feel none of those terrors about it, which made the early Christians flee from it! But in their eyes (putting aside the risk of undertaking it in times of persecution) it was so solemn a function, that the holier a man was, the less inclined he felt to undertake it. They felt that it was in some sort to incur the responsibility of other men, and to be put in trust with their salvation; they felt it was scarcely possible to engage in it, without the risk of being besprinkled with the blood of ruined souls. They understood somewhat of St. Paul's language when he said that necessity was laid upon him, and woe to him unless he preached the Gospel. In consequence they shrank from the work, as though (to use a weak similitude) they had been bid dive down for pearls at the bottom of the sea, or scale some precipitous and dizzy cliff. True, they knew that abundance of heavenly aid would be given them,

[26] *LD* v. 395. To James Henin, 19 December 1836.
[27] *LD* viii. 235. To an Unknown Correspondent, 1 August 1841.

according to their need; but they knew also, that even if any part of the work was to be their own, though they were only called to co-operate with God, that was in such a case fearful undertaking enough. So they literally fled away in many instances, when they were called to the sacred office; and the Church as literally took them by force and (after the precedent of St. Paul's own conversion) laid hands upon them.[28]

Above all a priest is a priest through his participation in the Priesthood of Jesus Christ, he is a man in the Church for the sake of the Church:

But when Christ had come, suffered, and ascended, He was henceforth ever near us, ever at hand, even though He was not actually returned, ever scarcely gone, ever all but come back. He is the only Ruler and Priest in His Church, dispensing gifts, and has appointed none to supersede Him, because He is departed only for a brief season. Aaron took the place of Christ, and had a priesthood of His own; but Christ's priests have no priesthood but His. They are merely His shadows and organs, they are His outward signs; and what they do, He does; when they baptize, He is baptizing; when they bless, He is blessing. He is in all acts of His Church, and one of its acts is not more truly His act than another, for all are His. Thus we are, in all times of the Gospel, brought close to His Cross. We stand, as it were, under it, and receive its blessings fresh from it; only that since, historically speaking, time has gone on, and the Holy One is away, certain outward forms are necessary, by way of bringing us again under His shadow; and we enjoy those blessings through a mystery, or sacramentally, in order to enjoy them really.[29]

As a Catholic, Newman doubtless preached a number of times on the calling of priests in the Church, but as so many of these sermons were delivered from notes rather than scripts, it is not usually possible to trace his line of thought. He certainly would have preached of the priesthood that he shared in terms and themes taken from the Council of Trent, the Catechism and the received piety of the day, yet clues as to the exact content of such sermons like the notes that exist for Passion

[28] *PS* iv. 60–1.
[29] *PS* vi. 242.

Sunday 1851 when Newman preached 'On The Priesthood of Christ'[30] are few and far between.

Of the published sermons, we have the reflections of Newman that were given for specific occasions, such as 'The Salvation of the Hearer the Motive of the Preacher' that was delivered at the opening of the chapel at Alcester Street, a sermon that sets out the basic mission of the priest in bringing the Gospel, through Word and Sacrament, to men and women in a particular place and at a particular time. 'We come to you in the name of God,' declared Newman, 'we ask no more of you than that you would listen to us; we ask no more than that you would judge for yourselves whether or not we speak God's words; it shall rest with you whether we be God's priests and prophets or no.'[31]

Another of Newman's Catholic sermons that concerns the life of the priest was delivered at the funeral of a friend, the Right Revd Dr Henry Weedall, the President of Oscott, 'whom there is no one I more revere or love in the whole Catholic body'.[32] This sermon, evocatively entitled 'The Tree Besides the Waters', paints an image of this priest's spirituality as like unto a tree which 'grows up gradually, silently, without observation; and in proportion as it rises aloft, so do its roots, with still less observation, strike deep into the earth.'[33] Weedall was one, recalls Newman, who was careful to observe the 'routine duties',[34] that formed the 'work *in* his day ... not the work of any other day, but of his own day', a work that he would not see complete but 'necessary in order to the work of that next day which is *not* his, as a stepping-stone on which we, who come next, are to raise our own work'.[35]

Whilst Newman understood the place of the priest in the priesthood of Christ that all the baptized shared, he also recognized the place of the priest as one of the Faithful, a man, like any of his brothers and sisters, who relied upon the mercy

---

[30] See Appendix 4.
[31] *Mix.* 20.
[32] *LD* xviii. 340. To Henry Weedall, 29 April 1858.
[33] *OS* 245.
[34] *OS* 246.
[35] *OS* 262.

of God. Rhetorically, Newman asks what type of being is a priest?

men they could not be, if they were to be preachers of the everlasting Gospel, and dispensers of its divine mysteries. If they were to sacrifice, as He had sacrificed; to continue, repeat, apply, the very Sacrifice which He had offered; to take into their hands that very Victim which was He Himself; to bind and to loose, to bless and to ban, to receive the confessions of His people, and to give them absolution for their sins; to teach them the way of truth, and to guide them along the way of peace; who was sufficient for these things but an inhabitant of those blessed realms of which the Lord is the never-failing Light?

And yet, my brethren, so it is, He has sent forth for the ministry of reconciliation, not Angels, but men; He has sent forth your brethren to you, not beings of some unknown nature and some strange blood, but of your own bone and your own flesh, to preach to you. "Ye men of Galilee, why stand ye gazing up into heaven?" Here is the royal style and tone in which Angels speak to men, even though these men be Apostles; it is the tone of those who, having never sinned, speak from their lofty eminence to those who have. But such is not the tone of those whom Christ has sent; for it is your brethren whom He has appointed, and none else, – sons of Adam, sons of your nature, the same by nature, differing only in grace, – men, like you, exposed to temptations, to the same temptations, to the same warfare within and without; with the same three deadly enemies – the world, the flesh, and the devil; with the same human, the same wayward heart: differing only as the power of God has changed and rules it. So it is; we are not Angels from Heaven that speak to you, but men, whom grace, and grace alone, has made to differ from you.[36]

A further example of Newman approaching the theme of priesthood is the sermon that he preached at the opening of St Bernard's Seminary, situated at Olton, near Birmingham, on 2 October 1873, a sermon starkly entitled 'The Infidelity of the Future'. To the prospective priests he warned 'that the trials which lie before us are such as would appal and make dizzy even such courageous hearts as St Athanasius, St Gregory I, or

St Gregory VII. And they would confess that, dark as the prospect of their own day was to them severally, ours has a darkness different in kind from any that has been before it.'[37] Catholics would one day be seen as 'the enemies' of 'civil liberty and of national progress'.[38] According to a member of the congregation on this occasion Newman did not even use notes whilst delivering this sermon, 'but held a small Bible in his hand, where he sought out in a curiously eager fashion the texts which he was about to recite. His voice sounded low and clear, with exquisite modulations, as if he were thinking aloud.'[39] Before setting his face towards the tenebrous future, Newman spoke of the institution of seminaries as a necessary means for the 'handing down of the truth from generation to generation'. The priests of the future 'are educated in one school, that is, in one seminary; under the rule, by the voice and example of him who is the One Pastor of all those collections or circles of Christians, of whom they all in time to come are to be the teachers.'[40]

Despite the difficulties that lay ahead for the students of St Bernard's, Newman also laid before them the tools needed for the contest that each was called to engage. He enjoined the students to learn and propose 'a sound, accurate, complete knowledge of Catholic theology'. But most of all he taught that

A seminary is the only true guarantee for the creation of the ecclesiastical spirit. And this is the primary and true weapon for meeting the age, not controversy. Of course every Catholic should have an intelligent appreciation of his religion, as St. Peter says, but still controversy is not the instrument by which the world is to be resisted and overcome. And this we shall see if we study that epistle, which comes with an authority of its own, as being put by the Holy Spirit into the mouth of him who was the chief of the Apostles. What he addresses to all Christians, is especially suitable for priests. Indeed he wrote it at a time when the duties of one and the other, as against the heathen world, were the same. In the first place he

---

[37] *CS* 116–17.
[38] *CS* 120.
[39] *LD* xxvi. 373 n. 1.
[40] *CS* 115.

reminds them of what they really were as Christians, and surely we should take these words as belonging especially to us ecclesiastics. "You are a chosen generation, a kingly priesthood, a holy nation, a purchased people ..." (1 Pet. ii. 9).

In this ecclesiastical spirit, I will but mention a spirit of seriousness or recollection. We must gain the habit of feeling that we are in God's presence, that He sees what we are doing; and a liking that He does so, a love of knowing it, a delight in the reflection, "Thou, God, seest me." A priest who feels this deeply will never misbehave himself in mixed society. It will keep him from over-familiarity with any of his people; it will keep him from too many words, from imprudent or unwise speaking; it will teach him to rule his thoughts. It will be a principle of detachment between him and even his own people; for he who is accustomed to lean on the Unseen God, will never be able really to attach himself to any of His creatures. And thus an elevation of mind will be created, which is the true weapon which he must use against the infidelity of the world. (Hence, what St. Peter says: 1, ii, 12, 15; iii, 16.)[41]

Now this I consider to be the true weapon by which the infidelity of the world is to be met.[42]

Thus Newman, as he always had done, puts his trust in the Lord, as he had preached at the ordination back in 1831,

In thoughts such as these we may take refuge, when pressed by difficulties – suspending our inquiries till we have strength to renew them, – God hath been mindful of us – Surely He *will* bless us still – He will bless the house of Israel, He will bless the house of Aaron < Ps 115[:9–10] > – and should it be His good pleasure ever again, to bring out into clearer view the form of His Church and to make His ordained ministry a rallying point as well a sacred bond of union, then (blessed be His name) we should enjoy the benefit of our calling, not only in the slow way of reasoning, but as a present energetic power kindling our hearts and strengthening us by the

---

[41] The three texts cited are, 'Having your conversation good among the Gentiles: that whereas they speak against you as evildoers, they may, by the good works, which they shall behold in you, glorify God in the day of visitation'; 'Be ye subject to every human creature for God's sake: whether it be to the king as excelling'; and 'But with modesty and fear, having a good conscience: that whereas they speak evil of you, they may be ashamed who falsely accuse your good conversation in Christ.'

[42] *CS* 126–8.

sympathy of each other – but great blessings are appointed against great trials, and we cannot expect to enjoy this rare privilege, till we especially need it – The Apostles laid the foundation of the Church in blood – shall we have unity again without grievous suffering first? We know not – but let us do our part towards it – and leave the rest to our Lord and Master to do according to His will in His good time.[43]

---

[43] B.O.A., A. 50. 2. 19+1 – from final preaching.

13

Letters

*I feel I am obliged to confess the truth of your remark that
Priests are generally too much employed to give much time to
correspondence, even on subjects to which they are drawn.* [1]

However difficult it might have been for Newman to write
letters, either due to other demands made on him or, in
advanced age, the painful action of literally putting pen to
paper, he has become celebrated for his gifts as a letter writer,
thirty-two volumes of correspondence having been published to
date. But it is, of course, the quality of these letters that are so
important because in private he could state the position of his
mind at any given time without the caution that any published
words might have had after necessarily having been carefully
honed. Newman's correspondence is the subject of many
articles. Here just a few are chosen to illustrate his great
epistolary apostolate with regard to ecclesiastical matters.
Frequently Newman gave informal spiritual direction by means
of his letters – he was clear that he was not trying to take on
the role of a spiritual director, 'Direction is a science, and I am
not up to it. Any use I can be to you short of this religious use,
I will most gladly,'[2] he wrote to one correspondent. That being
said, he gave much spiritual direction: writing to one friend he
encourages her not to be dispirited by her temptations:

---

[1] *LD* xiii. 74. To Catherine Ward, 5 March 1849. It has to be noted that
access to the letters of Newman by the public at large is thanks to the
outstanding work of Fr Charles Stephen Dessain of the Birmingham
Oratory who published the first volume of Newman's *Letters and Diaries*
in 1961, going on to publish a further twenty volumes of correspondence
before his death in 1976.

[2] *LD* xvi. 533. To Miss Holmes, 26 August 1855.

But you must recollect all places have their temptations, nay even the cloister. Our very work here is to overcome ourselves – and to be sensible of our hourly infirmities, to feel them keenly, is but the necessary step towards overcoming them. Never expect to be without such, while life lasts – if these were overcome, you would discover others, and that because your eyes would see your real state of imperfection more clearly than now, and also because they are in great measure a temptation of the Enemy, and he has temptations for all states, all occasions. He can turn whatever we do, whatever we do not do, into a temptation, as a skilled rhetorician turns every thing into an argument. It is plain, I am not saying this to make you *acquiesce* in the evils you speak of – if such be the *condition* of this life, to resist them is also its *duty*, and to resist them with success.[3]

Kind yet clear correction was also a work of his letters. After hearing of a speech made in Parliament by a former student, Newman determined to write to him:

Once on a time a young man made his Senior a present in token of his esteem for him. It was a Madonna, and that Senior put her over his bed-head, and whenever any one spoke of it, he used to say 'John Walter gave me that picture,' and he never said so without thinking kindly of him.

And so years passed, and changes came with them, and at length there was a day when the young man made a speech before a whole country; and after speaking by name of that elderly man of whom he once had felt esteem, he said that he wished that all who were such as that elderly man was, were kicked out of the kingdom.

What then could that elderly man do, before he was kicked out, but send back to that young man, who once had an innocent conscience and a gentle heart, that same sweet Madonna, to plead with the dear Child whom she holds in her arms for him, and with her gentle look and calm eyes to soften him towards that elderly man to whom he once gave it and who had kept it so safely.[4]

The recipient of this letter, John Walter, was indeed softened, professing his esteem for Newman in a letter hoping 'that the utterance of this Protestant remark may be forgiven him, and

[3]   *LD* ix. 184. To Miss Holmes, 27 December 1842.
[4]   *LD* xiv. 159. To John Walter, 6 December 1850.

not treated as an act of personal unkindness by one whom he believes to be as willing to pardon an unintentional offence as he has been gentle in rebuking it.'[5]

Discernment was a subject that Newman was not infrequently asked to assist in. To one of his correspondents Newman points out the path of discernment, in this case with regard to her possible conversion to Catholicism:

Some holy man, I think St Bonaventure, speaking about inward suggestions to a Monastic Life, observes to this effect: – 'Never trust a first suggestion – You cannot tell whether the voice is from above or from below – Your rule is, not to attend to it but to go on as usual – At first shrink from it. If it is from God, it will in due time return'.[6] And hence to all great changes, a season of thought and preparation is a necessary introduction, if we would know what God's will is.[7]

To a lady who was unsure about which Order she should join, Newman wrote,

We cannot have every thing in this world – but we can have the greatest of all, God's Presence, God's guidance. May you have it abundantly, wherever you are, and you will, but you must leave yourself in His hands, who loves you.[8]

While stating that 'God's inscrutable grace draws the young as well as the matured', Newman carefully counselled a friend, who was a mother, to be aware in case an apparent vocation was rather 'very much like a boy's whim.'[9] In the case in question, Newman was more than doubtful of the aspirant's

---

[5] *LD* xiv. 160. From John Walter, 10 December 1850.

[6] Gerard Tracey, the editor of Volume viii of *The Letters and Diaries of John Henry Newman*, notes that 'The ascription seems unlikely. Newman refers to a similar rule in an 1844 Memorandum: "I did not dare to trust my impression – and I resisted it. I trust I did so on principle; certainly I have long thought it a duty to resist such impressions – If true they will return", and gives the source as St Teresa, which seems more feasible.' *LD* viii. 239, note 1.

[7] *LD* viii. 239. To Miss Holmes, 8 August 1841.

[8] *LD* xv. 352-3. To Catherine Anne Bathurst, 16 April 1853.

[9] *LD* xv. 411. To Mrs J. W. Bowden, 24 August 1853.

professed calling, which had seemed to have been to the Dominicans. Newman felt that the young man was more motivated by individuals whom he had met than by the true spirit of the Order itself: 'I cannot understand how so high a vocation can be a mere attachment to persons,' he wrote. 'The Oratory, a local institution and not a religious order, may admit of it, but not surely the Friar Preachers.'[10]

In a similar case, when his advice was solicited, Newman confessed,

What I shrink from with dread ... is not the Church losing priests whom she ought to have had, but gaining priests whom she never should have been burdened with. The thought is awful, that boys should have had no trial of their hearts, till at the end of some 14 years, they go out into the world with the most solemn vows upon them, and then perhaps for the first time learn that the world is not a seminary; when they exchange the atmosphere of the Church, the lecture room, and the study, the horarium of devotion, work, meals and recreation, for this most bright, various, and seductive world.

Moreover, I dread too early a separation from the world for another reason – for the spirit of formalism, affectation, and preciseness, which it is very apt to occasion.[11]

Once again Newman is clear that he does not doubt 'that there are real vocations in the case of children' and he cites the calling of Samuel and the vocation of St Thomas as examples of this; St Ignatius and St Anselm as examples of vocations 'after life'; and Sts Charles Borromeo, Aloysius Gonzaga, Philip Neri and Alphonse De Liguori as examples of those who had their vocation from childhood but who 'nevertheless

---

[10] Ibid.

[11] *LD* xx. 21–2. To Edward Bellasis, 5 August 1861. Bellasis had written to Newman seeking advice as to the future education of his second son, Edward, who had showed signs of a vocation to the priesthood. In the first prospectus of the Oratory School, Newman had stated that the School was for those 'not intended for the ecclesiastical state.' A month after he had sent his initial letter, but before Newman's response, Bellasis had decided to send Edward to the Oratory School 'however much he may be inclined to the ecclesiastical state', seemingly a good decision as Edward Bellasis eventually became a lawyer. Cf. *LD* xxi. 161–3. To Robert Edmund Froude, 24 July 1864.

cherished it and matured it in the course of a secular training.'[12] With all this in mind Newman concludes,

Under then the two opposite difficulties, of depriving our Lord of His priests, and of giving to Him unworthy ones, I myself, if left to myself, should be disposed to act with far greater sensitiveness of the latter. I think a true vocation in a boy is not lost by secular education – at most it is but merged for a time, and comes up again – whereas a false vocation may be fatally and irreversibly fostered in a seminary.[13]

Newman rebuked himself when he felt that he had failed as Superior of the Birmingham Oratory in the exercise of prudence with regard to vocations. Of a novice, Philip Molloy, who had proceeded as far as ordination to the diaconate, he chastises himself in a letter to the Oratory's Novice Master, 'I dare say I have had a good deal to do with it. If he had taken to me he would *perhaps* have taken to St Philip; – but I never took to him.'[14] Molloy had first attempted to join the Redemptorists before succeeding in entering the Oratory, coming, Newman clearly knew, as a second-best scheme to make up for the failure of the first:

and when he came, he thought his immediate admission certain – at least so it seemed. Well, this I resisted, and it is a satisfaction to me that I did, though I was importuned to do otherwise. There is one other thing I was strongly against, but, being still more strongly importuned again and again, have to my sorrow weakly given way – and that is his ordination. . . . I have been weak enough to let him be ordained first Subdeacon then Deacon. It is very hard, I find, to act firmly when I have so little confidence, as I have, in my own opinion. If I prayed more, and lived more in the next world, I should not give way half as much, for I should have more trust in myself, which every Superior should have.[15]

Among those considering becoming Catholics and applying

---

[12] *LD* xx. 22. To Edward Bellasis, 5 August 1861.
[13] Ibid. Cf. *LD* xxi. 181. To Robert Edmund Froude, 3 August 1864.
[14] *LD* xvi. 130. To J. D. Dalgairns, 15 May 1854.
[15] Ibid. 130–1.

to Newman for guidance there were sometimes Anglican clergymen. Newman could fully identify with their predicament and recognized the pain of setting out into the Church without the assurance that priestly ordination would follow. 'Such pain as you are suffering,' he wrote to an Anglican curate,

is your price for that inestimable benefit which I doubt not God reserves for you, admission to Catholic communion.

I cannot doubt that it is your duty to make up your mind on the subject without reference to worldly matters – though of course such uncertainty, as you describe, is part of your trial. You do not speak distinctly on the point, but I take you to imply, that, were it not for this difficulty, there is nothing strong enough to keep you back.

It is easy to give good advice. I can only say, that, when I joined the Catholic Church, I had not so much as the sum you name as having yourself – nor would it be considered a small sum by most of my friends, *supposing* you have a vocation to the Priesthood. But no one can tell at present whether you will or will not have one – and I don't think it would be safe to take it for granted. And then, as to time of preparation, it varies with the individual. I was myself ordained within two years – but Dr Manning, I think, in only a week or two. So, I *believe*, was Mr Sibthorp. Others have been kept some years before they even had sacred orders. Some were found in the event to have no vocation.[16]

The curate's particular difficulty was an understandable concern for his future livelihood should he not be accepted for ordination. Replying to Newman's letter he confessed, 'if I had no Vocation to the Priesthood, or from illness could not study sufficiently, I might be left nearly destitute ... Were I *sure* it was God's will, I should not hesitate a moment.'[17]

Lighter themes were also given time in Newman's letters. He would express his appreciation and care with regard to churches and the liturgy. From Milan he wrote of the 'most sumptuous' churches,[18] his first impressions of Italian Catholicism there in its full liturgical splendour were

---

[16] *LD* xxii. 21. To Henry Bedford, 4 August 1865.
[17] *LD* xxii. 21. From Henry Bedford, 7 August 1865.
[18] *LD* xi. 254. To Mrs J. W. Bowden, 4 October 1846.

overwhelming. To Henry Wilberforce he wrote of 'that overpowering place, the Duomo.'

It has moved me more than St Peter's did – but then, I studiously abstained from all services etc. – when I was at Rome, and now of course I have gone when they were going on and have entered into them. And, as I have said for months past that I never knew what worship was, as an objective fact, till I entered the Catholic Church, and was partaker in its offices of devotion, so now I say the same on the view of its cathedral assemblages ... a Catholic Cathedral is a sort of world, every one going about his own business, but that business a religious one; groups of worshippers, and solitary ones – kneeling, standing – some at shrines, some at altars – hearing Mass and communicating – currents of worshippers intercepting and passing by each other – altar after altar lit up for worship, like stars in the firmament – or the bell giving notice of what is going on in parts you do not see – and all the while the canons in the choir going through [[their hours]] matins and lauds [[or Vespers]], and at the end of it the incense rolling up from the high altar, and all this in one of the most wonderful buildings in the world and every day – lastly, all of this without any show or effort, but what every one is used to – every one at his own work, and leaving every one else to his.[19]

Letters written whilst he was building St Clement's in Oxford, the Birmingham Oratory or the church for the Catholic University of Ireland clearly attest to his care for the beautiful expression of holiness in the liturgy, yet more letters portray his anxiety that all the rubrics should properly be observed.[20]

Nineteenth-century England was a time and a place for many prodigious writers of letters but, as the first editor of Newman's correspondence, Father Charles Stephen Dessain, observed, 'He [Newman] lived so long, he had so many friends, he was engaged upon such various enterprises, for so much of his life he carried on an intense apostolate by means of letters, that his output became enormous.'[21] And that output, ranging from pure business notes to lengthy expositions

---

[19] *LD* xi. 253. To Henry Wilberforce, 24 September 1846.
[20] E.g. *LD* xv. 228. To Austin Mills, 24 December 1852. Cf. *Diff.* i. 215–16.
[21] *LD* xi. xvii.

of Catholic doctrine, has, thanks to the indefatigable work of the late Fr Dessain, become a published source of knowledge about Newman and a reminder, in a world of such easy yet impersonal communication, of the power and warmth of the written word, even if just a short prayer inscribed to a correspondent:

> May the Blessed Mary
> be your Protection and Comfort
> this day and all days
> till she welcomes you
> to the eternal Home
> above.[22]

---

[22] *LD* xxxi. 176. To an Unknown Correspondent, 7 December 1886.

14

Giacinto Achilli and the Rambler

*Truth can fight its own battle. It has reality in it, which
shivers to pieces swords of earth. As far as we are
not on the side of truth, we shall shiver to bits,
and I am willing it should be so.*[1]

Whilst Vicar of St Mary the Virgin, Newman preached with
striking strength on the lot of those who would truly follow
Christ:

A work of blood is our salvation; and we, as we would be saved,
must draw near and gaze upon it in faith, and accept it as the way to
heaven. We must take Him, who thus suffered, as our guide; we
must embrace His sacred feet, and follow Him. No wonder, then,
should we receive on ourselves some drops of the sacred agony
which bedewed His garments; no wonder, should we be sprinkled
with the sorrows which He bore in expiation of our sins!

And so it has ever been in very deed; to approach Him has been,
from the first, to be partaker, more or less, in His sufferings; I do
not say in the case of every individual who believes in Him, but as
regards the more conspicuous, the more favoured, His choice
instruments, and His most active servants; that is, it has been the lot
of the Church, on the whole, and of those, on the whole, who had
been most like Him, as Rulers, Intercessors, and Teachers of the
Church ... As if He said, "Ye cannot have the sacraments of grace
without the painful figures of them. The Cross, when imprinted on
your foreheads, will draw blood. You shall receive, indeed, the
baptism of the Spirit, and the cup of My communion, but it shall be
with the attendant pledges of My cup of agony, and My baptism of
blood."[2]

---

[1] *LD* viii. 23. To Robert Belaney, 25 January 1841.
[2] *PS* iii. 140–1.

Newman must have thought that the trials to which he was subjected at the time leading up to his conversion could not ever be any harder to bear. And yet in the years that followed, new and terrible trials were visited upon him. In the midst of the first of these he wrote by way of a background note for his lawyers,

In the course of the foregoing year, Dr Achilli came down to Birmingham, and made a speech in the Town Hall against the Roman Inquisition. This speech had its weight as coming from one who had been a Priest and Friar in the Catholic Church, and professed to be witnessing what he had known. It had raised a great deal of odium against Catholics, and in particular attacked individuals who could not defend themselves. Moreover, it had actually perplexed some of our own Catholic congregation, who did not know how to disbelieve stories which came from what seemed so good an authority.[3]

Because of the enthusiastic support that Giacinto Achilli had received from the Evangelical Alliance, who had brought the ex-priest and friar Achilli to England from Italy in 1850, Newman believed that he had to defend the Church against the slanders that the Italian was peddling. Achilli had been suspended from the clerical state due to his sexual immorality. In June 1850, Wiseman had published a pamphlet that clearly set out Achilli's true background and the legal judgements that had been handed down to him due to his violence and immorality. Newman took legal advice as to whether or not he could expose the lack of veracity of Achilli's character. He was advised that it was possible that he might be indicted on charges of libel but that this was unlikely as no action had proceeded against Wiseman. Both Wiseman and Newman were in no doubt whatsoever as to the truth of what they told as the real life of Achilli. Newman later wrote that he presented his case against Achilli in his *Lectures on the Present Position of Catholics in England* not 'without a good deal of thought and anxious prayer' but he believed 'the risk so small as not to be regarded',[4] and to Richard Stanton, a Father of the London

---

[3]   *LD* xiv. 504. Extract from Newman's Memorandum for his lawyers.
[4]   *LD* xiv. 417. To Bishop Ullathorne, 5 November 1851.

Oratory he wrote, 'I went before the Blessed Sacrament and begged to be kept from doing it, if wrong.'[5]

Achilli, however denied under oath the charges against him and was thus enabled to pursue criminal proceedings against Newman which could have resulted in Newman's imprisonment. As Wiseman had mislaid his documentary evidence relating to Achilli's recent life, two members of the Birmingham Oratory were sent to Italy to attempt to bring together the necessary papers. If clear proof of only one of the cases had been produced at this stage, the case would have been stopped. Despite the publicity that was building, Wiseman managed to be less than conscientious in assisting the Oratorian Fathers in their increasingly desperate mission.

On 20 November the court refused to allow Newman any more time for the documentary evidence to be brought before them and Newman was committed to stand trial on a criminal charge. From the judge down there had been abundantly apparent a strong anti-Catholic bias in the courtroom and at first Newman's lawyers advised him not to fight the case in order to avoid jail and the legal expenses. More was at stake, in Newman's view, than his personal comfort and he chose to fight on. Yet it was a grisly nightmare for Newman: 'If the devil raised a physical whirlwind, rolled me up in sand, whirled me round, and then transported me some thousands of miles, it would not be more strange, though it be more imposing a visitation.'[6]

Wiseman eventually found his documents, which he then had dispatched to London. Meanwhile, a committee had been established to raise funds to cover the legal expenses and Maria Giberne, a close friend of Newman, was deputed to accompany the key women witnesses on their journey from Italy to England. At this time Newman had the further challenges of the establishment of the Oratory at Edgbaston and the invitation to Ireland to assist in the setting up of the Catholic University in Dublin.

Newman stood trial from 21 to 24 June 1852. He knew that

---

[5] *LD* xiv. 451. To Richard Stanton, 4 December 1851.
[6] *LD* xiv. 442. To J. M. Capes, 27 November 1851.

he could not win legally – he would have had to have been able to prove all his charges against Achilli in order to prevail legally and that was impossible – but he could win morally. Achilli's word on oath had brought Newman to trial and now it was apparent to all that Achilli's stand on oath during the trial was in clearest opposition to all the witnesses and testimonies Newman had brought to the attention of the jury. Newman's initial aim had at last been achieved – Achilli was discredited. The *Times* denounced the judge's conduct of the trial in a leading article, commenting that Roman Catholics could no longer be confident in British justice. Just weeks later Newman delivered his most famous Catholic sermon, 'The Second Spring' at the first Synod of Westminster at Oscott.

On 22 November 1852, Newman attended court to hear judgement but to the astonishment of judge and jury his lawyers called for a new trial. On 31 January 1853 a new trial was refused on technical grounds and Newman received a token fine of £100. Throughout the whole debacle Newman wrote letters similar to one he dispatched to his brother Oratorian, Richard Stanton: 'I am most thankful to say ... I have not had any interruption to the simple feeling, that I am in God's hands, who knows what He is about, and that every thing will be well, and that I shall be borne thro' every thing.'[7] He spent 'day and night almost, before the Tabernacle, and his serenity and calmness in the midst of the excitement without were remarkable.'[8] Newman had withstood the opprobrium of the Establishment during the turbulent years of the reestablishment of the Catholic Hierarchy, perhaps worse for him was to seemingly receive the same from some members of his very own Congregation of the Oratory and then from the Church.

The establishment of the London Oratory in 1849 had been a fraught affair and in 1855 serious differences arose over the interpretation of a canonical matter with regard to the compass of the Oratory's mission that caused Newman once again to travel to Rome to seek guidance. Newman believed that the

---

[7]   *LD* xiv. 451. To Richard Stanton, 4 December 1851.
[8]   *Positio* i. 232, quoting a note of events kept at the London Oratory.

London house had attempted to unilaterally alter the Rule of the Congregation. Writing at length to his community in Birmingham before setting off to Rome, Newman asks St Philip's intercession for a very particular grace:

For me, my dear Fathers, I do not think it unkind, if I say, that if there be one gift I would ask of St Philip for my Congregation, now and in time to come, [it] is that (while serving God zealously of course,) it should be unthought of and despised. I do not ask for *persecution*, I do not ask for *evil fame*; for I do not see that St Philip has suggested these trials to me; but I ask for our being overlooked, passed by, and not known to be true children of our Father, till men come close to us. I ask this, not only from love of St Philip, but from the experience which God has given me; for I know well, that, as to myself, all through life, when I have been despised most, I have succeeded most; and I feel confident that to ask for scorn, contempt, slight, and the like treatment for my Congregation, is to ask for a *great* success, for *real* work, for fruits, which are not unveiled here, in order that they may be reserved in all their freshness and bloom and perfection for manifestation at the marriage feast above.[9]

The quarrel was finally resolved in the summer of 1856 and less than three years later Newman's prayer was answered.

Truly, damno auctus sum; and I am in this position, because, as in so many cases in my life, I have done (what I never can repent) what seemed to me at the moment my duty, without looking at consequences. I cannot help saying this, for it is my only consolation.[10]

In 1859 Cardinal Wiseman had determined that Newman was the only person who could effect a solution to the conundrum of the moment. In the January edition of the *Rambler,* a Catholic monthly run by laymen, an article had appeared criticizing the English bishops for their handling of the question as to whether or not there should be state support for Catholic schools. The bishops were greatly aggrieved by the stance of the journal and were threatening to publicly censure it if the editor, Richard Simpson, did not resign. The only person who both the bishops

---

[9] *LD* xvii. 49. To Ambrose St John, 9 November 1855.
[10] *LD* xix. 75. To W. G. Ward, 10 March 1859.

and the supporters of the monthly felt they could trust was Newman, who reluctantly agreed to become the new editor. He wrote to his good friend Henry Wilberforce, 'I have the extreme mortification of being Editor of the Rambler. I have never had in my life (in its time) so great a one. It is like a bad dream, and oppresses me at times inconceivably.'[11]

Newman was thrust into the middle of not merely a diplomatic squall but, more decisively, into the heart of a debate that resulted in his essay *On Consulting the Faithful in Matters of Doctrine*. If, Newman proposed, the laity were consulted regarding the dogma of the Immaculate Conception, how much more should they be engaged alongside the hierarchy in the question of education. Episcopal reaction was instantaneous and Newman was prevailed upon to step down as editor of the *Rambler*. He did so, publishing his article 'On Consulting the Faithful' in the second, and last, edition of the journal that he was to edit, in July 1859. Newman had only accepted the post after much prayer, had spent a miserable few months trying to serve the bishops and the laity, was delated to Rome by Bishop Browne of Newport and ultimately suffered years of suspicion from the Roman authorities as a result of doing what he saw as his duty.

One thing I will add here for the sake of myself and others. I hope we shall all be on our guard against the indignation or anger which in various ways may at this moment or that be in danger of besetting us. Pride and passion are bad counsellors. In saying this I do not at all forget that reason would lead one to be quiet and composed, but it is very difficult at all times to go by reason. For myself, I think it is a portion of the fate of my life – and, if I anticipated it beforehand, I really cannot with any reason be annoyed with the instruments of it, when it takes place, for nothing can happen without instruments. All through life things happen to me which do not happen to others – I am the scapegoat. It was the Cardinal who got off in the Achilli matter while I suffered, as now Döllinger gets off not I.[12] It was on occasion of that Achilli matter that I anticipated what is taking place

---

[11] *LD* xix. 96. To Henry Wilberforce, 31 March 1859.

[12] The theologian Döllinger had also been threatened with delation to Rome for his article in the *Rambler* (Dec. 1858) 'The Paternity of Jansenism', but the threat was not carried through.

now. On looking back to my life, I found myself as one of those Roman Candles[?], or as Sisyphus, rolling my load up the hill for ten years and never cresting it, but falling back. Thus I failed in the schools in 1820; then I slowly mended things and built myself into some body with a prospect of something till 1830, and then on the 5th May I had to retire from College Office and was nobody again. Then again I set to work and by 1840 had become somebody once more, when on Febry 27, 1841, Number 90 was attacked, and down I fell again. Then slowly I went on and by 1850 I had as a Catholic so recovered my ground that the Pope made me a DD, when on July 28, 1851 I delivered the lecture in the Corn Exchange, which delivered me over into the hands of Achilli. On that occasion I said to several persons, to Ward, to Wilberforce, and I think to Ambrose, 'In 1820 I was cast out from among my equals – in 1830 from the Oxford carriera, in 1841 from the Tractarian party, in 1851 I am fully under the law – and in another ten years, I shall be had up before Rome.' Ward said, 'God forbid' – I answered, 'Don't misunderstand me – Even saints have fallen under displeasure at Rome – I am supposing nothing which I need be afraid to anticipate.' I add in speaking to one or other, 'And so I suppose, in 1870 I shall die, for nothing more is left for me.' Sometimes I think it may be that I shall have to give up my place in this Oratory – or that this Oratory may come to nought.

I have said all this to show why I ought not to be angry at what is the manifest disposition of Providence. Others, when they do wrong or act from infirmity, escape – I have always been smitten. I have steadily looked, forward to something or other like this though I could little conceive how it was to brought about.

It has been brought about by the Rambler.[13]

---

[13] Newman's reflection on the whole episode. *LD* xix. 282–83.

15

The Long Ladder

These are trials, which God puts upon us;
and we cannot at our will put them aside.[1]

Even in Newman's lifetime the notion had gathered force that his was an ethereal existence of ideas and musings, prayers and dreams. The most cursory viewing of his correspondence demolishes such thoughts at a stroke. Such an initiator of plans and schemes was hardly to escape the dirt and dust and debts that have to be faced in order to drive through such plans as are necessary. As one witness of his life in Dublin at the time of the founding of the Catholic University of Ireland later noted, 'I was pained by the very humble labours to which Newman seemed so willingly to subject himself . . . Such work should have fallen on subordinates.'[2] The more active years of his life produced hundreds of letters that deal with the minutiae of planning and funding, be it the Birmingham Oratory or the Oratory's school, the Catholic University of Dublin or the expense of his defence in the Achilli trial. Newman was a very practical priest who bore the lesser trials of life like many others. In a Chapter Address of 1852, Newman was clear,

It is the very rule then, my dear children, under which we live, if we are God's own, to sow in tears that we may reap in joy. When I was first a priest, and kissed the Cross on my maniple, and said, Merear, Domine, portare manipulam [sic] fletus et doloris,[3] I used to say to

---

[1] *LD* xxii. 194. To Lady Chatterton, Holy Thursday 1866.
[2] *Recollections of Aubrey de Vere,* New York and London, 1897, 266.
[3] The whole vesting prayer for the maniple being, 'Grant, O Lord, that I may so bear the maniple of weeping and sorrow, that I may receive the reward for my labours with rejoicing.'

myself, "Where is the sorrow? where the tears?" – and then I added, "I suppose it will come." It is our very portion here. If we had no punishment, then, as St Paul says, we should be but spurious sons, not true heirs of the promise. But if we have trial and bear it well, then we have two proofs of God's love upon us: one in the trial itself, and another in the grace which has enabled us to sustain it.[4]

Over twenty years earlier Newman expressed similar sentiments in a poem entitled 'A Thanksgiving' and subtitled with the words, 'Thou in faithfulness hast afflicted me.'

> Lord, in this dust Thy sovereign voice
> First quicken'd love divine;
> I am all Thine, – Thy care and choice,
> My very praise is Thine.
>
> I praise Thee, while Thy providence
> In childhood frail I trace,
> For blessings given, ere dawning sense
> Could seek or scan Thy grace;
>
> Blessings in boyhood's marvelling hour,
> Bright dreams, and fancyings strange;
> Blessings, when reason's awful power
> Gave thought a bolder range.
>
> Blessings of friends, which to my door
> Unask'd, unhoped, have come;
> And choicer still, a countless store
> Of eager smiles at home.
>
> Yet, Lord, in memory's fondest place
> I shrine those seasons sad,
> When, looking up, I saw Thy face
> In kind austereness clad.
>
> I would not miss one sigh or tear,
> Heart-pang, or throbbing brow;
> Sweet was the chastisement severe,
> And sweet its memory now.

[4] B.O.A., D. 4. 9. Quoted in *NO* 238.

Yes! let the fragrant scars abide,
    Love-tokens in Thy stead,
Faint shadows of the spear-pierced side
    And thorn-encompass'd head

And such Thy tender force be still,
    When self would swerve or stray,
Shaping to truth the froward will
    Along Thy narrow way.

Deny me wealth; far, far remove
    The lure of power or name;
Hope thrives in straits, in weakness love,
    And faith in this world's shame.[5]

Through the lesser trials, what might be the scuffing of the spirit by the incidents of the day is transformed into the burnishing of the soul and a preparation for perfection. With the clarity and simplicity that a Saint and Doctor of the Church, Thérèse of Lisieux, was soon to become renowned for, Newman encouraged the priests and brothers of his community to be holy in all that they did. Whilst some of the details of Newman's address, often called 'A Short Rule to Perfection', are specific to his particular community, the principle of what he has to say, and most of the specific points too, will resonate for many secular priests.

It is the saying of holy men that, if we wish to be perfect, we have nothing more to do than to perform the ordinary duties of the day well . . .
    We must bear in mind what is meant by perfection – it does not mean any extraordinary service, anything out of the way, or especially heroic in our obedience < not all have the opportunity of heroic acts, sufferings > but it means what the word perfection ordinarily means. By perfect we mean that which has no flaw in it, that which is complete, that which is consistent, that which is sound. We mean the opposite to imperfect. As we know well what imperfection in religious service means, we know by contrast what is meant by perfection.

[5]   *VV* 45-7.

He then is perfect who does the work of the day perfectly – and we need not go beyond this to seek for perfection. < You need not go out of the *round* of the day[.] > We are perfect, if we do perfectly our duty as members of the Oratory.

I insist on this, because I think it will simplify our views, fix our exertions on a definite aim. If you ask me what you are to do in order to be perfect, I say – first – Do not lie in bed beyond the due time of rising – give your first thoughts to God – make a good meditation – say or hear Mass and communicate with devotion – make a good thanksgiving – say carefully all the prayers which you are bound to say – say Office attentively, do the work of the day, whatever it is, diligently and for God – make a good visit to the Blessed Sacrament. Say the Angelus devoutly – eat and drink to God's glory – say the Rosary well, be recollected – keep out bad thoughts. Make your evening meditation well – examine yourself duly. Go to bed in good time, and you are already perfect.[6]

Evidently the temptation of burning the candle at both ends is perennial, as is the striving for holiness while, overworked, it is felt that we are getting no where. Hence Newman's most practical advice that, for most people, perfection will be worked out by God by not 'going out of the round of the day'.[7] Our sense of 'the round' of a typical day for Newman is somewhat sketchy. Written recollections of a contemporary father at the Oratory from Newman's time records that 'The early morning was devoted to meditation, prayers and ecclesiastical duties; the succeeding hours to study and work.'[8] He went for a walk in the afternoon and dined at 6 o'clock in the refectory, 'and when it fell to his turn Newman would serve his guests and brethren as though he had been the least among them.'[9]

---

6 Chapter Address, 27 September 1856, in *NO* 359–60. Newman had given a similar rule of life to George Ryder on 2 December 1850: 'I would not have you go to any mortifications. I will tell you what is the greatest – viz to do well the ordinary duties of the day. Determine to rise at a certain hour – to go through certain devotions – to give certain hours to your boys – Don't oppress yourself with them, but *keep to* your rules – and you will find it a sufficient trial.' *LD* xiv. 153.
7 Cf. *PS* i. 270 & *PS* viii. 165.
8 *Ward* ii. 352.
9 Ibid.

For Newman, each day would bring each person all the opportunities necessary for sanctification, usually not least of all when they are painfully aware of the imperfection of what they do and of the constraints of time to do it:

I was much pleased and encouraged by your letter, being in the midst of worry and fidget, if such uncomfortable words bear to be written down. It really is a great encouragement to know there are any persons who at all value what one tries to do in the cause of the Gospel. A person like myself hears of nothing but his failures or what others consider such – men do not flatter each other – and one's best friends act as one's best friends ought, tell one of all one's mistakes and absurdities. I know it is a good thing thus to be dealt with – nor do I wish it otherwise – All things one tries to do, *must* be mixed with great imperfection – and it is part of one's trial to be obliged to attempt things which involve incidental error, and give cause for blame. This is all very humbling, particularly when a person has foretold to himself his own difficulties and scrapes, and then is treated as if he was quite unconscious of them and thought himself a very fine fellow. But it is good discipline and I will gladly accept it. Nevertheless it is very pleasant to have accidentally such letters as yours to encourage one, though I know well that it goes far beyond the occasion, owing to you great kindness.[10]

Building works and moving house are two simple examples of common place nuisances – lesser trials – which Newman had to face like many others. Was the situation different then compared to today?

You will be interested to hear that we are in the act of moving into our new house at Edgbaston, but it is a slow act of months. As we creep in head foremost, I have gone up first, these three weeks, and am battling with the workmen, who, like aboriginal inhabitants, do not brook being dispossessed.[11]

---

[10] *LD* iv. 147. To Miss M. R. Giberne, 22 December 1833.
[11] *LD* xv. 48. To Cardinal Wiseman, 4 March 1852.

Another period of domestic turmoil was characterized as a
veritably Biblical torment:

> Painters, plasterers, carpenters, and brick layers are four out of the
> [ten] plagues of Egypt, the frogs, the lice, the flies, and the locusts.
> Their first throw off was to be found in our private rooms, e.g. in
> mine, – they said, 'out of curiosity.' They come and go almost at
> their pleasure. One sends for drink from the Ivy Bush in the
> forenoon, tumbles off a ladder, and breaks his eyebrow. They stop
> up the drains, white wash the closet-seats – and they never will go.[12]

For one who had in his early days imagined that he was called
to missionary work, moving house was to be a surprising
trauma. Leaving Littlemore and his former parishioners, in
particular, was 'very, very painful' and he felt that 'Perhaps I
shall never have such quiet again . . . I shall have a great many
anxieties of various kinds in time to come.'[13] To another friend
he wrote, 'You may think how lonely I am. "Obliviscere
populum tuum et domum patris tui,"[14] has been in my ears for
the last twelve hours. I realize more that we are leaving
Littlemore, and it is like going on the open sea.'[15] And on
leaving Maryvale to travel to Rome, Newman laments, 'It is
melancholy work, this leaving. Every one sad and out of spirits
– myself included – yet hardly daring to seem otherwise
myself'.[16] Moving to Alcester Street in Birmingham he
complains,

> It is an awful thing, beginning so new a life in the end of my days.
> How I wish I had in me the energy which I had when I began the
> Tracts for the Times! Now I am scarce more, to my own feelings,
> than an inutile lignum; so stiff so wooden. May you never have, dear
> Henry, the bitter reflection that you have left yourself but the dregs
> of life for God's service![17]

---

[12] *LD* xxii. 32–3: To Ambrose St John, 14 August 1865.
[13] *LD* xi. 126. To J. D. Dalgairns, 26 February 1846.
[14] 'Forget thy people and thy father's house.' Ps. 45:10.
[15] *LD* xxxii. 31. To a Friend, 20 January 1846.
[16] *LD* xi. 233. To Mrs J. W. Bowden, 27 August 1846.
[17] *LD* xiii. 16. To Henry Wilberforce, 24 January 1849.

The new life at Alcester Street brought into focus a different kind of difficulty for those called to live together in religious houses:

My Dearest Br Philip,

It is strange to write to you a note about nothing; but such is my fate just now and for some time, that, since I have nothing to say to you, I must either be silent or unseasonable.

Many is the time I have stood over the fire at breakfast or looked at you at Recreation, hunting for something to talk about. The song says that 'Love cannot live on flowers;' not so; yet it requires material, if not for sustenance, at least for display. And I have fancied too that younger and lighter minds perhaps could not, if they would, care much for one who has had so much to wear him down.

All blessing come on you, My dear Brother Philip, in proportion to my waning[18]

If they could not speak to each other, at least they could write, and Newman received a warm note from Br Philip the very next day. But what to talk about? It would seem that some subjects were less welcome than others:

I used to say at Oxford that lawyers and doctors ever talked of the shop – but parsons never – now I find priests do – I suppose that, where there is *science*, there is the tendency to be wrapped up in the profession. An English clergyman is primarily a gentleman – a doctor, a lawyer, and so a priest is primarily a professional man. In like manner the military calling has been abroad a profession, accordingly they never go in mufti; but always in full military fig, talking as it were, *always* of the shop. Now I have a great dislike of this shopping personally. Richmond told someone that, when he took my portrait, I was the only person he could not draw out.[19]

Agonizingly absurd trials were also a possibility, on one occasion, having arrived in Dublin at new lodgings Newman was presented with an ordeal seemingly perfect in its innocent power to utterly mortify him:

---

[18] *LD* xiii. 32. To William Philip Gordon, 7 February 1849.
[19] *LD* xxvi. 218–19. To R. W. Church, 22 December 1872.

When I got here, I found that the house-keeper, who would not let any other of the servants do it, had arranged, not only my clothes, but all my papers for me. I had put my letters in various compartments according to my relations towards them – and my Discourse papers, according as I had done with them or not. She had mixed every thing, laying them most neatly according to their *size*. To this moment I have not had courage to attempt to set them right – and one bit, which was to have come in, I have from despair not even looked for. And so of my linen; I had put the linen in wear separate from the linen in reserve. All was revolutionized. I could find nothing of any kind. Pencils, pen, pen knife, tooth brush, boots, 'twas a new world – the only thing left, I suppose from a certain awe, was, (woe's me,) my discipline.[20]

Whilst Newman certainly believed that each day brought with it the means to 'achieve' perfection, this did not mean that men and women striving for holiness of life should not voluntarily take up other forms of mortification, as his reference to his discipline demonstrates. On his success in the Achilli affair he attributed 'a *great deal* to the good prayers, the many Masses, and the various penitential works which have been offered up for my cause';[21] and writing to Robert Edmund Froude, who had been actively considering whether he was being called to the priesthood and/or the religious life, Newman proposed that he 'certainly' thought that he '*should* have some definite mortification. ... The anxiety is to fix on one which is fitting – which may neither be a burden on your conscience nor interfere with your duties to others, and yet answers its purpose.'[22] Feeling that he did not know Robert well enough, Newman wrote down on a separate piece of paper, that has not been preserved, 'two or three penances, which you might choose from, or use as suggestions for others which I do not happen to mention.'[23]

In St Philip Neri's time it was an established custom for religious to take the discipline, even in public. Newman

[20] *LD* xv. 95. To Austin Mills, 3 June 1852.
[21] *LD* xv. 329. To Alexander Grant, 9 March 1853.
[22] *LD* xxi. 179–80. To Robert Edmund Froude, 3 August 1864.
[23] Ibid.

assigned this mortification to the optional parts of his Rule for the English Oratory, he clearly choosing to follow it. Some years after having drawn up the Rule he discovered that the custom had been dropped in a large part of the north of Italy but he did not change his practise once he knew this. As recommended by Newman, the discipline was to be taken three times each week after the spiritual exercises of the Oratory.

From the beginning of February 1838, Newman began to note in his diary his regular fasting, a practice that he increased in its severity by trying to imitate the fasting until the evening of the Desert Fathers of the Church whose writings were such an inspiration to him.[24] In the context of a sermon entitled 'Love, the One Thing needful', Newman wrote,

If I must, before concluding, remark upon the mode of overcoming the evil, I must say plainly this, that, fanciful though it may appear at first sight to say so, the comforts of life are the main cause of it; and, much as we may lament and struggle against it, till we learn to dispense with them in good measure, we shall not overcome it. Till we, in a certain sense, detach ourselves from our bodies, our minds will not be in a state to receive divine impressions, and to exert heavenly aspirations. A smooth and easy life, an uninterrupted enjoyment of the goods of Providence, full meals, soft raiment, well-furnished homes, the pleasures of sense, the feeling of security, the consciousness of wealth, – these, and the like, if we are not careful, choke up all the avenues of the soul, through which the light and breath of heaven might come to us. A hard life is, alas! no certain method of becoming spiritually minded, but it is one out of the means by which Almighty God makes us so. We must, at least at seasons, defraud ourselves of nature, if we would not be defrauded of grace.[25]

Upon becoming a Catholic he relaxed this discipline considerably, although he was scrupulous in his observation of the various fasts that the Church then imposed. In 1847, before returning to England, he had outlined in some detail what he considered to be the life of an English Oratory stating that

---

[24] cf. *LD* vi. xix.
[25] *PS* v. 337–8.

'There were to be no fastings over and above what the Church prescribed, nor other austerities (except the discipline).'[26] He backs up this rule of life with references to the history of the Oratory and, of course, to St Philip himself of whom it was authoritatively said that 'He wished especially to offer to the men of his Congregation the daily hearing of the Word of God as something to be preferred to fasting, vigils, silence and psalmody, for the devout hearing of the Word of God is as good as all exercises.' Newman noted that, 'It is remarkable how strongly this is insisted on at various times in the history of the Oratory.'[27]

To Newman, for whom 'my life all along has to be in quiet and solitude, and no one but I can *understand* how things tire me which would not tire another',[28] community life itself was the great self-imposed mortification:

For, though to live in a family has great advantages, and human affection is a great stay of supernatural charity, yet, after all, this kind of community life, sustained and persevered in without vows, involves a great mortification, according to the saying ... "Vita communis, morticatio maxima"; and has, when encountered and undergone well, a special effect upon the character and perfection of our obedience; for it is conformity to the spirit of a body, and it is a voluntary act continually repeated.[29]

Voluntary mortification was to be an essential part of the Oratorian's life but this was to be an internal practice:

As *mortification of selfwill* is the vital principle of the Oratory, so *obedience* is the essential and necessary means by which it is exercised. We are to mortify ourselves *by* obedience, that is, by submitting our own will to that of another ... St Philip's demand upon his own penitents and sons in this respect was most absolute and unmeasured.[30]

---

[26] B.O.A., B. 9. 3. Quoted in *NO* 398.
[27] B.O.A., B. 9. 3. The authoritative source is the Annals of F. Marini, Ann, t. I. 27 quoted in *NO* 399.
[28] *LD* xv. 140. To Manuel Johnson, 3 August 1852.
[29] B.O.A., B. 9. 2. Quoted in *NO* 345-6. Cf *PS* ii.58.
[30] B.O.A., B. 9. 3. Quoted in *NO* 404.

Considering the trials of temptations, Newman pondered, 'It is a great mystery, but (I think) a truth, that good is wrought out through evil.'[31] Job's 'temptations and impatience', St Paul's 'thorn in the flesh' and David 'who fell into mortal sin' are corralled as witnesses for Newman to make his point that

Some saints have been in gloom, or in dryness of spirit for years – nay in a constant warfare with temptations which incurred a heavy amount of *sin* against them – nay and in consequence brought on them in some shape *punishment* – yet this warfare, and those punishments for incidental defeat during it, were the ordained means leading them to glory. It is as if to become great saints one must incur great penances – and, like David, defile one's hands in the battle.[32]

For Newman the 'battle' was long and although he felt keenly 'the girths of time'[33] he frequently accused himself of having wasted his time, writing in 1860, 'It is a cause of great sadness to me, when I look back at my life, to consider how my time has been frittered away, and how much I might have done, had I pursued one subject.'[34]

Twelve years later Newman had not changed his estimation of the worth of his toils, writing,

now that the end of life is come, I seem to have done nothing and to have frittered away all my time and labour upon dreams – to have made a great commotion, and to have done little more. The words of Scripture seem best to suit my case, 'I said, I have laboured in vain, I have spent my strength without cause and in vain' etc.[35] I suppose all men feel this in a way – but it is a very oppressive thought.[36]

Newman frequently had this 'very oppressive thought', considering, almost five years later, that, 'In a word, I have done my work, a bad work, as you think, but my best. I must

---

[31] *LD* vii. 475. To F. W. Faber, Sunday [1840].
[32] Ibid.
[33] *LD* iii. 88. To R. F. Wilson, 4 September 1832.
[34] *LD* xix. 284. To William Froude, 18 January 1860.
[35] Isaiah 49:4.
[36] *LD* xxvi. 7. To Lady Simeon, 5 January 1872.

put it into the hands of Him, whom I have tried, well or ill, to serve.'[37] It had ever been a worry to him, writing on his twenty-fifth birthday, 'The age I am getting quite frightens me. Life seems passing away, and what is done? Teach me, Lord, the value of time, and let me not have lived in vain.'[38]

At times the weight of what he believed to have been his failure in the various missions that he had been given, really took its toll on him. In 1861, having received medical advice, Newman had retreated, exhausted, to the Bristol Hotel in Brighton. From there he wrote to Edward Bellasis, briefly about himself and at length in regard to Bellasis's son's future education. Of himself he said,

I have had a very able opinion in London, and am assured in the strongest terms that there is nothing at all seriously the matter with me – but that the sorrows (for though not great ones, they have been various and continual) of thirty years have at last told upon my nerves – and that I want rest. In truth, though I have lived in the midst of blessings and comforts of all kinds, I have had, all through my life, nothing but disappointments, and gutta cavat lapidem.[39]

Bellasis wrote back the next day remarking that he had found Newman's letter 'quite affecting' and recognizing that 'it does indeed seem true that certain of the objects you had proposed to yourself have not been accomplished, at least, not in the manner and to the extent you hoped'; and yet

at the same time is there not a fable ... in which a son is induced to dig vigorously over the paternal estate in search of a specific treasure, which, he never finds, the real treasure showing itself in a general fertility, the result of his labours? How many are there who, like myself, owe every thing to your spade?[40]

[37] *LD* xxviii. 146. To Archdeacon Allen, 17 December 1876.

[38] *AW* 207.

[39] *LD* xx. 21. To Edward Bellasis, 5 August 1861, quoting Ovid, *Epistulae ex Ponto*, IV, x, 5. The gist of this ancient proverb is 'a drop of water hollows a stone, not by force, but by continuously dripping.'

[40] *LD* xx. 33. From Edward Bellasis, 6 August 1861.

Newman gratefully responded,

Your letter did me a great deal of good. The fable of the Diggings is very apposite. If I have been digging a field with my own ideas and my own hopes, and though they have failed, have been preparing ground for the sowing, the showers and the harvest, of divine grace, I have done a work, so far, though not the various definite works which I have proposed to myself; and I ought to be most thankful to be so employed. I was not so unmindful of God's mercy to myself and others, in making us Catholics, when I wrote, but I looked on this, as *His* work, as it was, not mine – however, a digging, though it is but turmoil, confusion, and unsettlement, *is* a co-operation.[41]

Still 'digging' in 1876, doubtless assured that the close of his life was quickly advancing, Newman reflected that

What is always to me a humbling thought (and doubt less intended by a good Providence to be humbling) is the little able and good men do, compared with what they might do, but there is no opening for them to do. F. Gratry wrote various important works which doubtless will live – but still after all, why was he not a luminary set up on one of the highest candle sticks? why was he so poorly recognized for what he was by those in the high places of the Church?

But, as our S. Philip says, 'God has no need of men'[42] and he uses them little when He might use them much, to show that he does *but* use them, and that the real Opifex of all that goes on is He Himself.[43]

As he knew at the start of his ecclesiastical life, perseverance was an indispensable virtue in living any vocation. 'Only may He complete His work and give us perseverance to the end.'[44] Preaching at Christ Church Cathedral on the occasion of an ordination, Newman was careful to remind the Anglican ordinands that no small importance of the joyful solemnity of the ceremony lay in its

---

[41] *LD* xx. 33–4. To Edward Bellasis, 20 August 1861.
[42] G. Bacci, *The Life of St Philip Neri,* Book i, Chapter xix.
[43] *LD* xxviii. 122. To John Baptist Hogan, 10 October 1876.
[44] *LD* xxviii. 276. To Sister Mary Gabriel du Boulay, 7 December 1877.

being imprinted on their minds against days of little joy and less clear hope:

If *all* our life were like the present hour, the object of life would cease to be what it now is – a *trial* of us. It is not difficult, and it is scarce a praise, to love God within the walls of His house. A man must indeed be destitute of the very elements of religious faith, who cannot worship from the heart, when his mind and feelings are excited. But such opportunities will not, cannot last. It is but for a moment, now and then in our lives, that the Kingdom of God thus comes upon us with observation. The *course* of our life is far otherwise. We are to labour in *the world* – it is there we are to shine as lights – there we are to earn our reward; – with our hearts in their ordinary unexcited state – or render our minds harassed perhaps, and our spirits depressed – not by high emotion, by stedfast [sic] faith, faith, disregarding what is actually seen without and felt within, and deliberately pressing forward on the narrow way while the world and the flesh move impetuously and unremittingly against it.

And thus it is, in our daily discourse with mankind, that days, such as the present, have their real and designed influence. – Their use does not lie in the actual enjoyment of them, but in the recollection – Faith is thus helped by sight – We now see for a short while, as in a picture, the Church of the first born which are written in heaven; – and that picture, imprinted on our hearts 'within us' as the text says, is our appropriate defence against the system of the visible and present world, whose blandishments, threats and sophistries have their chief power in that it *is* present and visible.[45]

In this context one of Newman's famous prayers seems most pertinent:

... let us beg of our Divine Lord to take to Him His great power, and manifest Himself more and more, and reign both in our hearts and in the world. Let us beg of Him to stand by us in trouble, and guide us on our dangerous way. May He, as of old, choose "the foolish things of the world to confound the wise, and the weak things

---

[45] B.O.A., A. 50. 2. 19+1 – Sermon No. 323, 'The Ministerial Order, as an existing divine institution'. This sermon was first preached on Sunday 18 December 1831, Newman taking as his text, 'The Kingdom of God cometh not with observation – neither shall they say, Lo here, or Lo there – for behold, the Kingdom of God is within you.' (Lk xvii, 20, 21)

of the world to confound the things which are mightly"! May He support us all the day long, till the shades lengthen, and the evening comes, and the busy world is hushed, and the fever of life is over, and our work is done! Then in His mercy may He give us safe lodging, and a holy rest, and peace at the last![46]

On a different occasion, writing of the challenges in pursuing a religious calling, Newman counsels that 'Another trial lies in the *distant future*. Masters in the spiritual life will tell you that the great difficulty in a high vocation is *perseverance*. This trial may not come for 20 years. I say this, not to deter you – but that you may in your prayers *now* pray for perseverance *then*.'[47] These lines come from real personal experience, as a letter of Newman's written two days after a significant birthday proves: 'A long life is like a long ladder, which sways and jumps dangerously under the feet of the man who mounts it, the higher he goes, and, if there is any one needs prayers for perseverance, it is a man of 80.'[48] But he prayed for this gift also at the age of twenty-five:

> O! may we follow undismay'd
>   Where'er our God shall call!
> And may His Spirit's present aid
>   Uphold us lest we fall!
> Till in the end of days we stand,
> As victors in a deathless land.[49]

Despite trials and failures, he did persevere. The letters to his friends may be like so many conversations, not necessarily depicting a settled view but rather a transitory phase, even if such a phase is obviously a recurring one. At the level of recorded prayer, at least, Newman was sure of his mission as earnestly seeking to obey the will of God as could best be discerned, accepting the fact that only in the life to come will

[46] *SD* 307.
[47] *LD* xxviii. 331. To Justin Sheil, 20 March 1878.
[48] *LD* xxix. 340. To Bishop Ilsley, 23 February 1881.
[49] *VV* 15.

the map of that mission become truly apparent. He knew in his heart the reality of his prayer's closing words:

God has created me to do Him some definite service; He has committed some work to me which He has not committed to another. I have my mission – I never may know it in this life, but I shall be told it in the next. Somehow I am necessary for His purposes, as necessary in my place as an Archangel in his – if, indeed, I fail, He can raise another, as He could make the stones children of Abraham. Yet I have a part in this great work; I am a link in a chain, a bond of connexion between persons. He has not created me for naught. I shall do good, I shall do His work; I shall be an angel of peace, a preacher of truth in my own place, while not intending it, if I do but keep His commandments and serve Him in my calling.

Therefore I will trust Him. Whatever, wherever I am, I can never be thrown away. If I am in sickness, my sickness may serve Him; in perplexity, my perplexity may serve Him; if I am in sorrow, my sorrow may serve Him. My sickness, or perplexity, or sorrow may be necessary causes of some great end, which is quite beyond us. He does nothing in vain; He may prolong my life, He may shorten it; He knows what He is about. He may take away my friends, He may throw me among strangers, He may make me feel desolate, make my spirits sink, hide the future from me – still He knows what He is about.[50]

---

[50] *MD* 301–2.

16

The Catholic Clergy

And he becomes a father true,
Spending and spent, when troubles fall,
A pattern and a servant too,
All things to all.[1]

Newman's early impressions of the continental Catholic priesthood were not good. On his first visit to the south of Italy he wrote, 'every thing seems to confirm the notion received among ourselves of the infidelity and profligacy of the priesthood'[2] and having experienced Rome:

The Roman Clergy are said to be a decorous orderly body – and certainly most things are very different from Naples ... the appearance of the priests is superior. But there is (seemingly) timidity, indolence, and that secular spirit which creeps on established religion every where. It is said that they got Mr Spencer quickly out of Rome, because his fastings shamed them – and that no one thinks of fasting here (a curious contrast with the Greeks.)[3]

With regard to the reaction to Mr Spencer's fasting, Newman jotted on the copy of the letter, at a later date, 'This is

[1] *VV* 275.
[2] *LD* iii. 224–25. To Jemima Newman, 15 January 1833. In another letter, to Henry Wilberforce, 9 March 1833, Newman declares, 'Here <at Rome> the clergy are far more moral and decent than at Naples.': *LD* iii. 246. To R. F. Wilson, 18 March 1833, 'the clergy, though sleepy, are said to be a decorous set of men ... (except for the Canons at service, who laugh and talk)': *LD* iii. 258. See also *AW* 42–3, quotations that Newman gives of a poem that he and a friend had written on the Massacre of St Bartholomew, Newman owning up to having written the theological parts of this poem, although he deleted the passage that concerned priests from his Autobiographical Memoir.
[3] *LD* iii. 232. To H. N., 5 March 1833.

nonsense.' One senses that Newman is utterly wide-eyed at the different culture he was discovering to Oxford clerical life. Despite the examples of 'profligacy' that he witnessed he also felt that

the clergy all through Italy and Sicily (as far as we have been) appear to be in a wretched state of destitution (*i.e.* more or less). In Sicily a great portion of their revenues is appropriated for the payment of Government pensions – in Naples, etc., their property seems to have been almost entirely confiscated, the French have completed and confirmed the spoliation. They subsist by their Masses in the most cowardly contemptible way possible, not having had spirit enough to resist, but keeping good friends with their robbers. They seem to have lost all hold on their people, and we learn (as at Malta and elsewhere) that there has been a considerable growth of avowed infidelity in the last fifteen years. It strikes me the superb religious edifices with which Italy abounds are a great snare to the clergy – they are a property of theirs which the State holds as a bond for their servility. 'We will take your rich churches' is a virtual threat which persuades them to submit to any insult or injury. At least, I think most men would be exposed to the temptation had they such wonderful structures.[4]

Indeed Newman's belief that the clergy could 'not bear to lose as a body such beautiful and rich structures' led him to reflect that, 'I am willing to believe this, as I think it will sufficiently account for their conduct, without imputing worse motives – and when I see outward decency, I am unwilling to attribute worse than I need.'[5]

Back in England Newman was suspicious and critical of what he perceived of the Catholic clergy with whom he came into contact, yet in all probability only a very particular kind

---

[4]   *LD* iii. 234–5. To Frederic Rogers, 5 March 1833. In part Newman was seeing this aspect of Italy in the light of having read, whilst at Naples, newspaper reports of the Irish Church Reform Bill of which he writes in the same letter to Rogers, 'It has surprised us to see how far Ministers have gone in their Irish Church Reform Bill – abolishing sees, taxing benefices immediately, etc.; not that we doubted their sacrilegious will ... If it is any consolation to have partners in misfortune, we have abundance here [i.e. in Italy]'.

[5]   *LD* iii. 246. To Henry Wilberforce, 9 March 1833.

of priest made his acquaintance with the Vicar of St Mary's –
a priest who was seeking Newman's conversion and was very
possibly sent by Bishop Wiseman. 'Rome must change first of
all in her spirit,' cried Newman. 'I must see more sanctity in
her than I do at present. Alas! I see no marks of sanctity – or
if any, they are chiefly confined to converts from us.'

'By their fruits ye shall know them', is the main canon our Lord
gives us, to know true pastors from false. I do verily think that, with
all our sins, there is more sanctity in the Church of England and
Ireland, than in the Roman Catholic bodies in the same countries.

I say not all this in reproach, but in great sorrow. ... What
Hildebrand did by faith and holiness, they do by political intrigue.
Their great object is to pull down the English Church. They join with
those who are *further* from them in creed to oppose those who are
nearer to them. ... Never can I think such ways the footsteps of
Christ. If they want to convert England, let them go barefooted into
our manufacturing towns, let them preach to the people, like St
Francis Xavier, let them be pelted and trampled on – and I will own
that they can do what we cannot; I will confess that they are our
betters far. ... What a day it will be, if God ever again raises up holy
men, Bernards or Bor[r]omeos, in their communion![6]

Perhaps not only Catholic priests fell below these standards,
certainly both Anglican and Catholic ministers were, in
increasing numbers and with greater effect, to penetrate the
nation's manufacturing towns, as indeed Newman himself was
to do. It seems that part of Newman's distrust of Rome and his
opinion that Rome lacked 'the Note of Sanctity', 'I am not
saying whether or not we exaggerate, but this would be our
common impression', was in no small part founded upon a lack

---

6 *LD* viii. 42, quoting Matthew 7:20. To J. R. Bloxam, 23 February 1841.
   Ambrose Lisle Philipps, a convert and a friend of Pugin, had been the
   occasion of Bloxam's letter to Newman. Having seen Newman's response he
   wrote to Bloxam that he agreed, 'that what we want is really apostolick Men
   ... To raise up such as these must be God's work ... let me add, Oxford
   contains many such Men, when once a reunion shall have put them in
   possession of the *inconceivable grace* of Catholick Communion. Yes, all
   Christendom needs regeneration. I firmly believe that God has raised you
   and your friends at Oxford for this very purpose; reunite yourselves to us and
   you shall reform not only us but the whole Universe.': *LD* viii. 42, note 2.

of written evidence. 'Let them put into our hands the hymns, or the meditations, or the prayers, or the essays, or the sermons which argue the man of God. We cannot but judge of them by what comes before us.'[7]

On a better day Newman could be more even-handed with regard to the Church of England and the Catholic Church, concluding a letter to Bishop Nicholas Wiseman by saying, 'I feel as much as any one the lamentable state of Christendom, and heartily wish that the Communions of Rome and England could be one – but the best way of tending to this great end seems to me to be, in charity and meekness, to state our convictions, not to stifle them.'[8]

By the time Newman had written to Wiseman, he had received at least one letter that might have signified better than any hymn, or meditation, or prayer, any essay or sermon, a true man of God. It was from Mr Thomas Doyle, 'a Catholic priest and an admirer of several writings' of Newman. He wrote simply of his life as a priest:

My every day work is to comfort the confessing and compunctive penitents that apply to *me* ah! how very unworthy a guide – my walks to the sick and dying is [sic] also my daily occupation – and in it I feel very much consoled that it is the work of love and for what are we sent but this. Mr Newman you do not know us – nor do the writers in the Critic know the heart and soul of a true Priest of the Catholic Church or they would never speak of us as they do. I am ready to be an Anathema for the love of Jesus – and yet no fanaticism is in me – no self-sufficiency – no independence, but all by and with authority. Let us know each other better and may God perfect in your soul all that He sees wanting.[9]

Such letters must have left their mark on Newman who, despite the strength of all his misgivings about Catholics, 'was scarcely ever for an half an hour in the same room with a Roman Catholic in my life. I have no correspondence with any

---

[7] *LD* viii. 49. To J. R. Bloxam, 2 March 1841.
[8] *LD* viii. 161. To Nicholas Wiseman, 6 April 1841.
[9] *LD* viii. 128, note 2. Newman's diary records that he received the letter on Saturday 27 March 1841.

one. I know absolutely nothing of them except that external aspect that is so uninviting.'[10] And this was written with less than a year to pass before Newman's conversion.

Blessed Dominic Barberi, who received Newman into the Catholic Church after hearing his confession, left an indelible impression on Newman's mind:

> Certainly Fr Dominic of the Mother of God was a most striking missioner and preacher and he had a great part in my own conversion and in that of others. His very look had a holy aspect which when his figure came in sight in my circle most singularly affected me, and his remarkable *bonhomie* in the midst of his sanctity was in itself a real and holy preaching. No wonder, then, I became his convert and penitent. He was a great lover of England.[11]

Once he was a Catholic and had become more closely acquainted with the lives and work of Catholic priests, Newman became generous in his praise, saying of priests that 'on the whole, they had been, as a body, the salt of the earth and the light of the world, through the power of divine grace, and that thus, in spite of frailty of human nature, they had fulfilled the blessed purposes of their institution'.[12] Having come to know the Irish clergy through his mission to set up the Catholic University of Ireland in Dublin, he wrote,

> the Irish Priesthood is a nobly devoted body of men. You must not judge of them by the newspapers. I admire them exceedingly. Many of them are persons of cultivated minds generally. Those whom I have met about the country are zealous, hardworking men. ... They are commonly taken out of the families of small farmers, they have strong constitutions, they know the habits of the people, and are fully trusted by them.[13]

The most extensive appreciation of Newman with regard to

---

[10] *LD* x. 416. To Edward Coleridge, 16 November 1844. Cf. *LD* x. 476. To John Keble, 29 December 1844: 'No one can have a more unfavourable view than I of the present state of the Roman Catholics'.
[11] *LD* xxxi. 277. To Cardinal Parocchi, 2 October 1889.
[12] *Prepos.* 339.
[13] *LD* xvi. 110. To Miss Holmes, 12 April 1854.

the priesthood comes towards the end of his autobiography, *Apologia pro Vita Sua.* His words come in a section entitled 'Position of my Mind Since 1845' and are worth quoting in full as they not only give fulsome praise of the men with whom he laboured as a priest but also directly deal with a scandalous accusation published in the January 1864 edition of *Macmillan's Magazine.* It was precisely these lines, from a review of the seventh and eighth volumes of Froude's *History of England,* and their author's persistence in maintaining his position that motivated Newman to set out clearly a history of his religious opinions in 1864. The reviewer, Charles Kingsley, had claimed,

Truth, for its own sake, had never been a virtue with the Roman clergy. Father Newman informs us that it need not, and on the whole ought not to be; that cunning is the weapon which Heaven has given to the saints wherewith to withstand the brute male force of the wicked world which marries and is given in marriage. Whether his notion be doctrinally correct or not, it is at least historically so.[14]

Newman pointed out that he had never held, let alone published, such an opinion and that it was 'a great affront to myself, and a worse insult to the Catholic priesthood',[15] one that he felt personally and one that touched upon the reputation of priests amongst the citizens of Britain. Newman's appreciation of his brother priests on the English mission was happily reciprocated, particularly at the time of the publication of his correspondence with regard to the calumnies of Charles Kingsley. The priests of Westminster expressed their admiration and gratitude for Newman's riposte:

We, the undersigned Priests of the Diocese of Westminster, tender to you our respectful thanks for the services you have done to religion, as well as to the interests of literary morality, by your Reply to the calumnies of [a popular writer of the day].
    We cannot but regard it as a matter of congratulation that your

14 *Apo.* 2.
15 *LD* xxi. 25. To Messrs Macmillan and Co., 22 January 1864.

assailant should have associated the cause of the Catholic Priesthood with the name of one so well fitted to represent its dignity, and to defend its honour, as yourself.

We recognize in this latest effort of your literary power one further claim, besides the many you have already established, to the gratitude and veneration of Catholics, and trust that the reception with which it has met on all sides may be the omen of new successes which you are destined to achieve in the vindication of the teaching and principles of the Church.[16]

The priests of Westminster were not to be disappointed in their hope for 'new successes', for, perhaps encouraged by such support, within a month Newman began composing and swiftly publishing *Apologia pro Vita Sua*. In response to the Address made by the priests of Westminster Newman wrote: 'I am well aware that it was the insult, which he [Kingsley] offered to the Catholic Priesthood, which alone gave value and meaning to my animadversions upon him; and it is my consolation to reflect that I was indirectly subserving the interests of religion, while I was engaged in protesting against a merely personal wrong.'[17]

The *Apologia* was written in the white heat of inspiration, each chapter being published in pamphlet form every week from Thursday 21 April 1864 until Thursday 2 June, with an appendix published on June 16. In this work Newman pays tribute to the priests he had encountered, whilst laying to rest the slur on their collective veracity.

There is only one other subject, which I think it necessary to introduce here, as bearing upon the vague suspicions which are

---

[16] *Apo.* 320. The Address that was sent to Newman was accompanied with a personal letter from Canons John Maguire and Frederick Oakeley that declared, 'Valuable as we are persuaded you will consider such a testimony in itself, its worth would be indefinitely enhanced, if, together with these names, we could also convey to you the expressions of deep and devoted sympathy and respect by which not a few of them have been accompanied.

You would thus perceive how eagerly your late brilliant exploit on the field of literature has been seized upon as an occasion of testifying the sentiments which our brethren habitually entertain towards you, and which have long sought some such opportunity of utterance.': *LD* xxi. 82. From John Maguire and Frederick Oakeley, 15 March 1864.

[17] *LD* xxi. 85. To George Rolfe, 18 March 1864.

attached in this country to the Catholic Priesthood. It is one of which my accusers have before now said much, – the charge of reserve and economy. They found it in no slight degree on what I have said on the subject in my History of the Arians, and in a note upon one of my Sermons in which I refer to it. The principle of Reserve is also advocated by an admirable writer in two numbers of the *Tracts for the Times*, and of these I was the Editor.

Now, as to the Economy itself, it is founded upon the words of our Lord, "Cast not your pearls before swine"; and it was observed by the early Christians, more or less, in their intercourse with the heathen populations among whom they lived. In the midst of the abominable idolatries and impurities of that fearful time, the Rule of the Economy was an imperative duty. But that rule, at least as I have explained and recommended it, in anything that I have written, did not go beyond (1) the concealing the truth when we could do so without deceit, (2) stating it only partially, and (3) representing it under the nearest form possible to a learner or inquirer, when he could not possibly understand it exactly. I conceive that to draw Angels with wings is an instance of the third of these economical modes; and to avoid the question, "Do Christians believe in a Trinity?" by answering, "They believe in only one God," would be an instance of the second. As to the first, it is hardly an Economy, but comes under what is called the *Disciplina Arcani*. The second and third economical modes Clement calls *lying*; meaning that a partial truth is in some sense a lie, as is also a representative truth. And this, I think, is about the long and the short of the ground of the accusation which has been so violently urged against me, as being a patron of the Economy.

Of late years I have come to think, as I believe most writers do, that Clement meant more than I have said. I used to think he used the word "lie" as an hyperbole, but I now believe that he, as other early Fathers, thought that, under certain circumstances, it was lawful to tell a lie. This doctrine I never maintained, though I used to think, as I do now, that the theory of the subject is surrounded with considerable difficulty; and it is not strange that I should say so, considering that great English writers declare without hesitation that in certain extreme cases, as to save life, honour, or even property, a lie is allowable. And thus I am brought to the direct question of truth, and of the truthfulness of Catholic priests generally in their dealings with the world, as bearing on the general question of their honesty, and of their internal belief in their religious professions.

It would answer no purpose, and it would be departing from the line of writing which I have been observing all along, if I entered into any formal discussion on this question; what I shall do here, as I have done in the foregoing pages, is to give my own testimony on the matter in question, and there to leave it. Now first I will say, that, when I became a Catholic, nothing struck me more at once than the English out-spoken manner of the Priests. It was the same at Oscott, at Old Hall Green, at Ushaw; there was nothing of that smoothness, or mannerism, which is commonly imputed to them, and they were more natural and unaffected than many an Anglican clergyman. The many years, which have passed since, have only confirmed my first impression. I have ever found it in the priests of this Diocese; did I wish to point out a straightforward Englishman, I should instance the Bishop, who has, to our great benefit, for so many years presided over it.

And next, I was struck, when I had more opportunity of judging of the Priests, by the simple faith in the Catholic Creed and system, of which they always gave evidence, and which they never seemed to feel, in any sense at all, to be a burden. And now that I have been in the Church nineteen years, I cannot recollect hearing of a single instance in England of an infidel priest. Of course there are men from time to time, who leave the Catholic Church for another religion, but I am speaking of cases, when a man keeps a fair outside to the world and is a hollow hypocrite in his heart.

I wonder that the self-devotion of our priests does not strike a Protestant in this point of view. What do they gain by professing a Creed, in which, if their enemies are to be credited, they really do not believe? What is their reward for committing themselves to a life of self-restraint and toil, and perhaps to a premature and miserable death? The Irish fever cut off between Liverpool and Leeds thirty priests and more, young men in the flower of their days, old men who seemed entitled to some quiet time after their long toil. There was a bishop cut off in the North;[18] but what had a man of his ecclesiastical rank to do with the drudgery and danger of sick calls, except that Christian faith and charity constrained him? Priests volunteered for the dangerous service. It was the same with them on the first coming of the cholera, that mysterious awe-inspiring infliction. If they did not heartily believe in the Creed of the Church, then I will say that the remark of the Apostle had its fullest illustration: – "If in this life only we have hope in Christ, we are of

---

[18] The bishop referred to was Bishop William Riddell, Vicar Apostolic of the Northern District for less than three months in 1847.

all men most miserable." What could support a set of hypocrites in the presence of a deadly disorder, one of them following another in long order up the forlorn hope, and one after another perishing? And such, I may say, in its substance, is every Mission-Priest's life. He is ever ready to sacrifice himself for his people. Night and day, sick or well himself, in all weathers, off he is, on the news of a sick call. The fact of a parishioner dying without the Sacraments through his fault is terrible to him; why terrible, if he has not a deep absolute faith, which he acts upon with a free service? Protestants admire this, when they see it; but they do not seem to see as clearly, that it excludes the very notion of hypocrisy.

Sometimes, when they reflect upon it, it leads them to remark on the wonderful discipline of the Catholic priesthood; they say that no Church has so well ordered a clergy, and that in that respect it surpasses their own; they wish they could have such exact discipline among themselves. But is it an excellence which can be purchased? is it a phenomenon which depends on nothing else than itself, or is it an effect which has a cause? You cannot buy devotion at a price. "It hath never been heard of in the land of Chanaan, neither hath it been seen in Theman. The children of Agar, the merchants of Meran, none of these have known its way." What then is that wonderful charm, which makes a thousand men act all in one way, and infuses a prompt obedience to rule, as if they were under some stern military compulsion? How difficult to find an answer, unless you will allow the obvious one, that they believe intensely what they profess![19]

It would be easy to read Newman's words believing that he was exaggerating his estimation of the priests whom he had encountered. It would seem that this was not the case. Firstly, the whole context in which Newman sings the praises of priests is a response to the slur that Catholic priests were economical with the truth – he was not one who would say one thing whilst believing another. Secondly, some years later he wrote to Henry Wilberforce with regard to the case of one Fr Suffield, a priest who had continued to preach missions up and down the country despite having privately given up Christianity for what he called 'Christian Theism'.[20] Newman asks,

---

[19] *Apo.* 241–4.
[20] cf. *LD* xxv. 193. To Mrs William Froude, 22 August 1870.

Now then what business had he to be giving Sermons on the Mysteries of Christianity, on the Incarnation and Resurrection, on the Holy Eucharist, on a future judgement upon our risen bodies and souls re-united to them, etc etc – while *all the time* he disbelieved in all these miracles.

This [is] to me in itself a breach of good faith, and most immoral.

Next, if it comes out < (I don't see that it has *yet*) > , observe how it will destroy confidence in priests, preachers, and confessors; for every one will say 'how do I know what is in this man's mind, who looks so fair? perhaps he is a second Fr S.' For myself I blush to think how I said in my Apologia that I had never met with an unbelieving priest, when there was so great an instance before me < (tho' I knew it not) > .[21]

In his eighty-fourth year Newman was corresponding with St George Jackson Mivart upon the subject of the lack of scientific knowledge of the clergy. Mivart had written in an article entitled 'The Conversion of England': 'We are strongly impressed with the absolute necessity of our clergy being so far instructed in physical science as to be able to intelligently discuss the religious difficulties which are so often supposed to be therewith connected.'[22] 'I pity and sympathize with the poor priests whom you animadvert on,' replied Newman,

Three centuries ago they would hear about the earth going round the sun, an idea so simple, so beautiful, so antecedently probable, but so utterly opposed to tradition, to the word of Scripture, and to the apparent necessity of Christian doctrine. What a threatening difficulty to faith and to catechetical teaching!, but what evidence, what scientific proof had they that the new doctrine was true?

Far more difficult is the position of priests and confessors now.

---

[21] *LD* xxv. 184. To Henry Wilberforce, 14 August 1870. Cf. *LD* xxv. 216, note 1 and *LD* xxi. 161–3 & 171. Letters to the Froude family, July 1864. Undoubtedly Fr Suffield's apostasy was more keenly felt by Newman because he resigned as Vicar of St Mary's precisely because of his growing certainty that not being in communion with Rome the Church of England was not part of the Catholic Church and therefore he 'could not honestly be a teacher in it any longer.' *LD* ix. 585. To H. E. Manning, 25 October 1843.

[22] *LD* xxx. 358, note 3, quoting from "The Conversion of England" *Dublin Review* (July 1884), 65–86.

They are in the front of a battle with unbelief, not merely against a school here or there of scientific research, and they have no time to get up a knowledge of physics, of biology so broad, so deep, as to have a right to judge of the strength and cogency of the views which at first sight are so difficult to harmonize with Scripture. How can they give up what is received by Catholic tradition without some better grounds for surrendering it than they have?

What increases their difficulty, and what supports them in their scepticism, their dislike, of the whole scientific movement is the sudden disappearance perhaps of supposed facts, which have been confidently urged against Scripture, and which at length are found by scientific men not to hold water, after some Catholic has elaborated an answer to them; – and they are naturally led to think that, as in other cases, error will eat up error, if they are but patient, without their trouble.

For myself, I confess I share these views to a great extent, and the more so because I am impressed especially by a fact which I have not yet noticed. What is the good of argument, unless opponents can join issue on some certain general principle? how can a priest combat a man of science, when the latter virtually denies the possibility of miracles, and the former holds that the most stupendous have actually occurred? The man of Science ought to know that he has not proved that miracles are impossible; yet he uses that assumption as confidently against the Catholic, as if it was the most necessary of truths. Why am I to deny that our Lord rose again the third day because Professor A or B says it is impossible? He brings no facts.

Before I can fairly be called upon to enter upon difficult questions which involve great study and research for the answering I have a right to make two conditions before I have that responsibility; first, does the inquirer allow the possibility of a miraculous revelation, and next, what are the *facts*, and what the *proof* of the alledged facts, which are supposed to interfere with the belief that such a revelation is to be found in Scripture.[23]

---

[23] *LD* xxx. 358-9. To St George Jackson Mivart, 8 May 1884. This letter was not sent. Cf *LD* xxx. 360. To St George Jackson Mivart, 8 May 1884: 'The primary point is does the writer believe that the Resurrection is a fact? and the second, is therefore the Deluge possible? He may have many good reasons for thinking so strange an event improbable, or not to be taken literally – but if he begins with the avowal that it is too great a matter to accept on faith, I don't see how good can come from arguing.' This letter also was not sent.

Great Catholic priests of nineteenth-century Europe also interested Newman. During his last days, he requested that a Life of the Curé d'Ars was read to him and he took great interest in hearing it. After this book had been completed Newman had selected Jaques Melchior Villefranche's *Life of Don Bosco, founder of the Salesian Society*, which had been sent to him by its translator, Lady Martin, but according to Fr Neville, 'it had not the same interest for him. It lacked life and variety. He was always in good luck. Let him have a rebuff, it ever brought a tenfold harvest of good. There was a monotony in this to him, and the reading was broken off.'[24]

17

The Allocutions of Dr Moriarty

... one of the most instructive and edifying volumes I have read,[1]

The volume in question was *Allocutions and Pastorals of the late Right Rev. Dr. Moriarty*, a volume containing addresses to the clergy on the occasion of Diocesan Synods and the bishop's pastoral letters. As an Anglican, Newman was involved in the re-publication of books that he considered to be of continuing benefit, one such being the *Imitation of Christ* by the fifteenth-century mystic Thomas à Kempis, referring to it as 'a most deeply valuable work.'[2] Newman sometimes recommended books to others in his letters: a number of times he suggested that a correspondent read Bishop Challoner's *Garden of the Soul*, 'For preparation for Confession, you cannot have anything better',[3]

---

[1] *LD* xxx. 364. To Arthur Sandes Griffin, 21 May 1884.
[2] *LD* vii. 341. Looking forward to publishing the *Imitation of Christ*, Newman commented that of all the translations then available, 'very different from each other', the older ones were best, though none very good. Thus 'A new translation is wanted.' Cf. *LD* vi. 125. To Henry Wilberforce, 10 September 1837. Newman's friend, Henry Wilberforce, had been enthusiastically supporting this idea for over a year, an idea that Newman thought was 'excellent'. The edition most accessible at this time was a translation by George Stanhope published in London as *The Christian's Pattern* in 1698, a translation that Newman described as being 'notoriously languid.' In 1841 a new edition of an earlier translation was published in Oxford.
[3] *LD* xx. 540. To William Robert Brownlow, 16 October 1863. See also *LD* xxi. 387. To Lavinia Wilson, 14 January 1865 & *LD* xxii. 28. To Henry Bedford, 10 August 1865. The full title of Bishop Challoner's book clearly describes its purpose: *The Garden of the Soul: A Manual of Spiritual Exercises and Instructions for Christians Who, Living in the World, Aspire to Devotion; Whereto Are Added the Public and Private Devotions Now in Most Frequent Use*, London, 1775.

he wrote. Only in the case of Dr Moriarty's *Allocutions* is he recorded as having not only commended a book for priests but also to have actively promoted it.

Newman had known Dr Moriarty, the Bishop of Kerry, for many years having first become acquainted with him whilst the Irishman stayed at Alcester Street on 24 May 1849, not long after Newman's community had moved there. From his dealings with Moriarty during his time in Dublin establishing the Catholic University of Ireland, so great was Newman's esteem that he hoped that Dr Moriarty would succeed him as Rector of the University. Newman knew that the chances for this to occur were slim as, in February 1854, David Moriarty had been appointed coadjutor Bishop of Kerry.[4]

Bishop Moriarty succeeded as Bishop of Kerry on 22 July 1856 and energetically laid new foundations for his successors to build upon. Having previously been President of All Hallows College, Dublin, he knew well the importance of a good seminary, so he founded one for his diocese. He constantly travelled the length and breadth of his diocese visiting parishes, conferring the Sacraments and encouraging the parishes to hold missions. A major church building programme was carried out whilst on the national scene he supported the role of a nationally organized system of schooling that included careful catechizing of the children. Newman remained on friendly terms with the bishop, dedicating the first volume of his *Historical Studies* to him, until the latter's death on 1 October 1877. Seven years later, on the publication of Bishop Moriarty's writings, Newman was sent a copy. Inside the volume was printed a warm dedication to Cardinal Newman:

We deem it a high honour to have the privilege of dedicating this volume to a Prince of the Church, so distinguished for learning, piety, and love for Ireland.

We are well aware of the great affection the late illustrious Bishop of Kerry entertained during life for your Eminence, and hence we determined to seek your permission to connect his most important utterances with your name.

[4] *LD* xviii. 72–3. To Joseph Dixon, Archbishop of Armagh, 2 July 1857.

Very many of the Clergy to whom the Allocutions were addressed by our late lamented Bishop, have passed away. A new generation of Priests has taken their place, and we feel confident you will say, when you read these utterances – so full of learning, wisdom, and piety – that they will afford a wide field for meditation, not only to those Priests in Kerry who never heard them, but even to all English-speaking Priests.[5]

The confidence of the editors was well placed – Newman ordered a dozen copies which he swiftly distributed to friends having written to the editors thanking them for the dedication and reflecting, 'I have ever felt the truest love and gratitude towards him [Dr Moriarty]. He was indeed a rare friend, one in ten thousand. He is in Heaven doubtless, but I mention him always in Mass, from the good which I am sure I can get from him.'[6]

Of the allocutions to the clergy, the titles alone point to clear, pastoral guidelines and direction for the priests of his Diocese – for example 'Sacrament of Penance – Zeal'; 'Pastoral Vigilance'; 'Care of the Sick and Dying'; 'Care of the Dead'; 'Devotions to be Introduced and Encouraged'; 'The Holy Sacrifice'. Each examines the strengths and weaknesses of the exercise of these ministries in his Diocese. 'It is a book which must be welcome to every priest', Newman wrote.[7]

One of the allocutions, however, did not please a recipient of Newman's largesse:

a Catholic Priest, to whom I gave the Volume, in my admiration of it, disappointed me by criticizing the Allocution on Avarice. I don't agree with him at all . . . I am sure it would in many good Protestants raise their opinion of the Catholic Church and of its authorities; but we have fierce enemies.[8]

5   *Allocutions and Pastorals of the late Right Rev. Dr. Moriarty* (hereafter *Allocutions*), Dublin, 1884, iii.
6   Ibid. iv.
7   *LD* xxx. 376. To Arthur Sandes Griffin, 1 July 1884.
8   *LD* xxx. 377–8. To Arthur Sandes Griffin, 5 July 1884.

The editors concurred with Newman in thinking that the allocution on Avarice was necessarily forthright. Canon Griffin replied to Newman's letter,

Is it not better to make known to all that Bishops warn their Clergy against possible vices and denounce them when they exist? This very sin of Avarice dragged Judas down to hell, and his crime is published to the entire world in the Sacred Volume and stands as a warning to all priests.

An old avaricious parish priest died lately in this diocese and left all his money, some thousands of pounds to his relatives, and a ruin of a Church to his people and successor. Our revered Bishop would not attend his burial – his fellow priests remained away in disgust, and the few who did go to the place, not having heard of the facts, would not chant the office or join the Curate of the Parish in reading the short service when they heard of his will. This emphatic condemnation of his sin, edified the people of the entire diocese.[9]

The whole volume comprises seventeen allocutions to the clergy and eight pastoral letters, these in total running to 397 pages. The shared friendship of Newman and Moriarty clearly extended to their vision of priesthood. The addresses given by the bishop are naturally authoritative in tone, very practical and range through the life of the priest in his preaching the Sacred Scriptures, administering the Sacraments and his care for souls. He does not stint in his use of classical illustrations from Greek antiquity or the Fathers of the Church, all given in Latin.

With regard to avarice, Moriarty notes at the beginning of his address that the Lord took 'most special care to warn them [his disciples] against everything that might savour of avarice, or that might cause them to be even remotely suspected of this vice.'[10] He notes that the Lord did not give his disciples particular warnings against intemperance, the life of chastity, the 'duties of prayer or religious worship' or anything else but 'we can say, without any exaggeration, that there is no other point of missionary training, on which He more earnestly dwelt, than that of disinterestedness.' The Lord says to his

---

[9] *LD* xxx. 378, n. 1. From Arthur Sandes Griffin, 8 July 1884.
[10] *Allocutions*, 54.

disciples 'Bestow these gifts of heaven on man as freely, as generously, as gratuitously as I have bestowed them on you. Ask no payment; seek no reward or payment for your work: for what you give has cost you nothing.'[11]

The disciples were bidden to take with them no possessions, 'they must go forth as poor men, depending on Providence', 'they are not to be paid for their labours', 'They are to receive their daily bread from those to whom they preach'

Hence that grand discipline of the Church – one of the brightest glories of her history – which deprived the clergy of the dominion of ecclesiastical property; allowing them to take from it merely what was necessary for their support, and requiring them to refund what was superfluous, that it might be applied to the support of the poor, or to the maintenance of the temple of God.[12]

This lesson is given to the seventy-two at their sending out as it is given with great force to the young man who desired to be perfect.[13] But after Peter 'with that manly and straightforward courage of his [said] "Well, we have left all things and have followed You!"'[14] Jesus replies, 'Truly, I say to you, there is no one who has left house or brothers or sisters or mother or father or children or lands, for my sake and for the gospel, who will not receive a hundredfold now in this time, houses and brothers and sisters and mothers and children and lands, with persecutions, and in the age to come eternal life.'[15]

The life of the apostles, taught Moriarty, exemplified this ideal starting from St Peter's first miracle when he exclaims, 'Silver and gold I have not.'[16] After further scriptural illustrations the bishop asks, 'We might have supposed, dear and Reverend Brethren, that there are vices more dangerous than avarice; we might have supposed that there are virtues more important than disinterestedness.' 'The reasons which, with the light of Faith, we can discover, shall be motives for

[11] Ibid. 55.
[12] Ibid. 56.
[13] Mark 10:17–31.
[14] *Allocutions* 57.
[15] Mark 10:29–30.
[16] Acts 3:9.

us, to remove from our hearts, every taint of avarice, and to
show forth, in our character and in our whole bearing the true
nobility of Ministers of the Gospel.' In short, Moriarty states
that, 'The ministry of an avaricious man ... must be barren
and ineffectual.'[17]

The allocution to the clergy for the Diocesan Synod of 1875
took as its theme fraternal charity amongst the clergy
themselves and took as its text one verse from John's Gospel,
'This is my commandment, that you love one another.'[18] This
commandment is addressed to all the followers of Christ but is
especially important and beneficial to the Church when it is
lived out amongst the clergy. 'Fraternal charity should be
eminently conspicuous in the body of Christ's ministers'.[19]

How is such fraternity to be nurtured? Firstly, 'the example
of your priestly life, your habits, your conversation, the honest
sincerity of your friendship, will have more effect than all the
vigilance of a Bishop, than all the canons of the Church.'
Sometimes the priest may need to give advice as a form of
fraternal correction to another priest, 'The rank of your
brother clergyman does not therefore exempt you from the
duty of giving him fraternal advice or warning, if perchance he
is going wrong.' There is a real challenge in Bishop Moriarty's
words – 'You know that a neighbouring priest is spoken of for
his bad temper or for his violence of language, for his
exactions, sordid manner of living, or for his neglect of duty.
Do not speak *of* him, but speak *to* him.' As a bishop, Moriarty
fully comprehended the difficulty of fraternal correction but he
saw that it was more often than not the honest and most helpful
way for a priest to be steered back on to the right path than if
he, as bishop, became involved.

There is another exercise of brotherly love of which we need to be
reminded – the mutual help we should give to each other in the work
of the ministry. In this respect, the spirit of the Diocese seems
somewhat opposed to united action. Some parishes, like certain game
covers, might have the words "strictly preserved" inscribed on their

[17] *Allocutions*, 58-9.
[18] John 15:12.
[19] *Allocutions*, 274.

frontiers ... Working together, we manifest our union, we edify the people,[20]

The particular point at issue for such collaboration was the administration of the Sacrament of Confession, some very restrictive rules having been applied by a previous bishop in Moriarty's diocese. But the gist of the argument bears larger application, 'the spirit of union should make us seek opportunities of working together, that all may see that we are one.'[21] The 'spirit of union' is manifest in other ways too:

If I go back in memory some thirty or forty years, I would say, that as far as I then knew the clergy, they were more social – that a friendly hospitality was more frequent. Some grave and holy priests may not regret the change, thinking that such social meetings were not edifying – that they might have led to over-indulgence. Let us not confound the use and the abuse ...

Priests are not often called upon to practise charity, by helping each other in a pecuniary way, though I have heard with pleasure of some very generous acts of that kind; but in our corporate capacity we can do so. In other professions we observe more of what is called *l'espirit de corps,* than in our own, we see more zeal in collecting funds to support the sick, and to provide for the widows and families of deceased members. Are we not rather remarkable for a spirit of individuality – every man for himself? We contribute what is required to our clergy fund; but I do not remember that we ever had a bequest or donation for that purpose. Yet, if we really loved our brethren in the ministry, if we loved the body of our priesthood, would not this be a way to show our love? What a wretched thing it is, to see a poor priest in sickness or old age, thrown aside on a pittance less than the wages of a tradesman, when he should end his days in decency and comfort? A competent clergy fund brings other advantages with it: it creates a sense of security, and removes the pretext for avaricious hoarding; but I allude to it here, as one of the ways by which we can show that we are one body, animated by one spirit; – and that, a spirit of generous, sacerdotal charity: *"Filioli mei,"* writes St. John, *"non diligamus verbo, neque lingua, sed opera et veritate."* (I *John* 3, 18)[22]

---

[20] Ibid. 282.
[21] Ibid. 283.
[22] Ibid. 283–4. The quotation from I John 3:18, being, 'Little children, let us not love in word or speech but in deed and truth.'

As he concludes his address, Moriarty counsels, 'Remember that while the poor priest is helping thousands to save their souls, no one is helping him, unless his brother priest does so.'

There are many standards by which I estimate the relative value of a priest; first of all his work in his mission; then his prudence and tact in the management of the people, and in his relations with the world; his knowledge, his love of study, his gentleness and unselfishness; the esteem and reverence in which he is held by the people. But there is one standard of comparison, the sweetest of all – the degree of confidence reposed in him by his brother-priests – the affectionate regard with which they surround him. We have known such men; they are centres of union, and strong props of support in a diocese.[23]

Such a man was John Henry Newman, a priest of the Birmingham Oratory, who so strongly recommended Bishop Moriarty's book.

---

[23] Ibid. 285.

18

In veritatem

Thou art calling me . . .[1]

In an article on Newman's preaching, the Oratorian Father, Paul Chavasse, records a note that Newman made on a collection headed: 'Packet of Sermons, St Clement's, 1824–1826'. Newman had written, 'May 17th 1881. None of these sermons are worth anything in themselves . . .'[2] Yet his last sermon, at least, as a curate at St Clement's, Oxford, preached on 23 April 1826, is of special value:

For this at least I can thank God that from the first I have looked upon myself solely as an instrument in His hand, and have looked up to Him for all the blessing and all the grace by which any good could be effected. For I have felt and feel now that it is only as He makes use of me that I can be useful – only as I put myself entirely into His hands that I can promote His glory, and that to attempt even the slightest work in my own strength is an absurdity too great for words to express. He has been pleased to bring me into His ministry and to lay the weight of an high office upon me – and wherever His good providence may lead me I trust I shall never forget that I am dedicated and made over entirely to Him as the minister of Christ, and that the grand and blessed object of my life must be to promote the interest of His cause, and to serve His church, and contribute to the strength of His Kingdom, and make use of all my powers of mind and body, external and acquired, to bring sinners to Him, and to help in purifying a corrupt world – In this good work I willingly would be spent; and I pray God to give me grace to keep me from falling, and ever true to that vow by which I have bound

---

[1] *VV* 323.
[2] B.O.A., A.17.1. quoted here from Lefebvre, P. & Mason, C. (eds), *John Henry Newman in His Time*, 118.

myself to Him that I may at length finish my course with joy and the ministry which I have received of the Lord Jesus to testify the gospel of the grace of God. . . .[3]

Newman was indeed 'to finish' his 'course with joy' as in 1879 Pope Leo XIII created John Henry Newman a Cardinal. Writing of his being raised to the Sacred College, Newman said 'it is a wonderful Providence, that even before my death that acquittal of me comes, which I knew would come some day or other, though not in my life time.'[4] This 'acquittal' came in a prodigious manner, as Lord Blanchford wrote to Newman, 'It is really an extraordinary historical event – that a Prince of the Church should go about receiving indiscriminate homage at London and Oxford with the applause of all men.'[5] Another correspondent mused to Newman:

I wonder if you know how much you are loved by England. I wonder if any man, at least of our time, was ever so loved by England – by all religiously minded England. And even the enemies of faith are softened by their feeling for you. And I wonder whether this extraordinary and unparalleled love might not be – was not meant to be – utilized, as one means to draw together into one fold all Englishmen who believe. I can conceive no more powerful nor truer *eirenicon*.[6]

Writing down his memories of the Cardinal's last years, Fr Neville prefixed some of Newman's own words to his manuscript, words spoken by Newman at the funeral of his friend the Rev. Walter Mayer, but 'applying', according to Neville, 'exactly to the Cardinal himself':

His was a life of prayer. The works and ways of God, the mercies of Christ, the real purpose and uses of this life, the unseen things of the spiritual world, were always uppermost in his mind. His speech and conversation showed it . . . It pleased God to show to all around him the state of his heart and spirit, not only by the graces of a meek and

---

[3]   B.O.A., A.17.1. Sermon no. 150.
[4]   *LD* xxix. 63. To Mother Mary Imelda Poole, 6 March 1879.
[5]   *LD* xxix. 275, n. 2. From Lord Blanchford, 26 May 1880.
[6]   *LD* xxix. 195, n. 1. From Octavius Ogle, 6 November 1879.

peaceable and blameless conversation ... but also by the direct religiousness of his conversation. Not that he ever spoke for the sake of display – he was quite unaffected, and showed his deep religion quite naturally.[7]

Newman would certainly not have wished any achievement of his to be ascribed to himself but rather to the grace of Christ granted through the inspiration and the intercession of the Oratory's founder, St Philip Neri. Preaching at the Birmingham Oratory on the Feast of St Philip Neri, 26 May 1956, the legendary preacher Mgr Ronald Knox asked, 'What was it, under Providence, that made, that makes the institute of St Philip so congenial to our English way of life?' Various possibilities are put forward but Knox felt that there was a simple answer to his rhetorical question: 'I think the fact was that St Philip had, in an unusual degree, and passed on to his children, an individual love of souls.'

A love of souls; he didn't just love people, with a fond love that made him blind to their shortcomings; he loved their souls; loved, with a fierce, supernatural jealousy, the image of Christ in them. And at the same time it was an individual love of souls; there was nothing in him of the ecclesiastical recruiting sergeant who tries to send people to heaven by numbers. And that is the meaning of the Oratorian vocation; to be a son of St Philip is not to be burdened with a whole régime of obligations and prohibitions, but to be the prisoner of love; chained to your house, to your church, and above all to your confessional by a permanent readiness to woo souls for Christ.[8]

Above all, Newman would have admired St Philip Neri's 'permanent readiness to woo souls for Christ'. Consistency in striving to live well the Christian life, Newman held, was the *sine qua non* of sanctity. Consistency in accepting that

All God's providences, all God's dealings with us, all His judgments, mercies, warnings, deliverances, tend to peace and repose as their ultimate issue. All our troubles and pleasures here, all our anxieties,

---

[7] *Ward* ii. 512.
[8] P. Caraman, S.J., (ed.) *The Occasional Sermons of Ronald Knox*, 78.

fears, doubts, difficulties, hopes, encouragements, afflictions, losses, attainments, tend this one way ... after our Soul's anxious travail; after the birth of the Spirit; after trial and temptation; after sorrow and pain; after daily dyings to the world; after daily risings unto holiness; at length comes that "rest which remaineth unto the people of God." After the fever of life; after wearinesses and sicknesses; fightings and despondings; languor and fretfulness; struggling and failing, struggling and succeeding; after all the changes and chances of this troubled unhealthy state, at length comes death, at length the White Throne of God, at length the Beatific Vision.[9]

Death came to Newman after a great length of life, yet when it did it came quite quickly. He was taken ill during the early hours of the morning of Sunday 10 August 1890, dying of pneumonia the evening of the following day. After his Requiem Mass was offered on 19 August, Newman's mortal remains were borne out of the City of Birmingham to Rednal, the country retreat and burial ground of the Oratorian Fathers. The pall that covered his coffin was inscribed with his cardinalatial motto, 'cor ad cor loquitor', 'heart speaks to heart', and, in fulfilment of his wishes, his memorial tablet bears the words 'Ex umbris et imaginibus in veritatem' – from shadows and images into truth – words that echo Newman's assessment of his conversion 'I have come from clouds and darkness into light'.[10]

---

[9] *PS* vi. 369–70.
[10] *LD* xi. 257. To Miss Parker, 9 October 1846.

Part III

I

The Ventures of Faith*

"They say unto Him, We are able." Matt. xx. 22

These words of the holy Apostles James and John were in
reply to a very solemn question addressed to them by their
Divine Master. They coveted, with a noble ambition, though as
yet unpractised in the highest wisdom, untaught in the holiest
truth,—they coveted to sit beside Him on His Throne of Glory.
They would be content with nothing short of that special gift
which He had come to grant to His elect, which He shortly
after died to purchase for them, and which He offers to us.
They ask the gift of eternal life; and He in answer told them,
not that they should have it (though for them it was really
reserved), but He reminded them what *they must venture for it*;
"Are ye able to drink of the cup that I shall drink of and to be
baptized with the baptism that I am baptized with? They say
unto Him, We are able."* Here then a great lesson is impressed
upon us, that our duty as Christians lies in this, in making
ventures for eternal life without the absolute certainty of
success.

Success and reward everlasting they will have, who
persevere unto the end. Doubt we cannot, that the ventures of
all Christ's servants must be returned to them at the Last Day
with abundant increase. This is a true saying, – He returns far

* This is one of Newman's most famous Anglican sermons, delivered at St
  Mary the Virgin, Oxford, and published on 30 November 1838 as Sermon
  No. 20 in the fourth volume of *Parochial and Plain Sermons*. Although it is a
  sermon not centred upon the subject of the ministry, it includes a short
  section directly addressing this theme. The whole sermon is given here as the
  force of Newman's argument is greatly weakened if taken out of the context
  of the calling of every Christian, this being the subject of this sermon.

more than we lend to Him, and without fail. But I am speaking of individuals, of ourselves one by one. No one among us knows for certain that he himself will persevere; yet every one among us, to give himself even a chance of success at all, must make a venture. As regards individuals, then, it is quite true, that all of us must for certain make ventures for heaven, yet without the certainty of success through them. This, indeed, is the very meaning of the word "venture"; for that is a strange venture which has nothing in it of fear, risk, danger, anxiety, uncertainty. Yes; so it certainly is; and in this consists the excellence and nobleness of *faith*; this is the very reason why *faith* is singled out from other graces, and honoured as the especial means of our justification, because its presence implies that we have the heart to make a venture.

St. Paul sufficiently sets this before us in the eleventh chapter of his Epistle to the Hebrews, which opens with a definition of faith, and after that, gives us examples of it, as if to guard against any possibility of mistake. After quoting the text, "the just shall live by faith," and thereby showing clearly that he is speaking of what he treats in his Epistle to the Romans as *justifying* faith, he continues, "Now faith is the substance," that is, the realizing, "of things hoped for, the evidence," that is, the ground of proof, "of things not seen." It is in its very essence the making present what is unseen; the acting upon the mere prospect of it, as if it really were possessed; the venturing upon it, the staking present ease, happiness, or other good, upon the chance of the future. And hence in another epistle he says pointedly, "If in this life only we have hope in Christ, we are of all men most miserable." [1 Cor. xv. 19] If the dead are not raised, we have indeed made a most signal miscalculation in the choice of life, and are altogether at fault. And what is true of the main doctrine itself, is true also of our individual interest in it. This he shows us in his Epistle to the Hebrews, by the instance of the Ancient Saints, who thus risked their present happiness on the chance of future. Abraham "went out, not knowing whither he went." He and the rest died "not having received the promises, but having seen them afar off, and were persuaded of them, and embraced them, and confessed that they were strangers

and pilgrims on the earth." Such was the faith of the
Patriarchs: and in the text the youthful Apostles, with an
untaught but generous simplicity, lay claim to the same. Little
as they knew what they said in its fulness, yet their words were
any how expressive of their hidden hearts, prophetic of their
future conduct. They say unto Him, "We are able." They
pledge themselves as if unawares, and are caught by One
mightier than they, and, as it were, craftily made captive. But,
in truth, their unsuspicious pledge was, after all, heartily
made, though they knew not what they promised; and so was
accepted. "Are ye able to drink of My cup, and be baptized
with My baptism? They say unto Him, We are able." He in
answer, without promising them heaven, graciously said, "Ye
shall drink indeed of My cup, and be baptized with the baptism
that I am baptized with."

Our Lord appears to act after the same manner towards St.
Peter: He accepted his office of service, yet warned him how
little he himself understood it. The zealous Apostle wished to
follow his Lord at once: but He answered, "Whither I go thou
canst not follow Me now, but thou shalt follow me
afterwards." [John xiii. 36] At another time, He claimed the
promise already made to Him; He said, "Follow thou Me";
and at the same time explained it, "Verily, verily, I say unto
thee, when thou wast young, thou girdedst thyself, and
walkedst whither thou wouldest: but when thou shalt be old,
thou shalt stretch forth thy hands, and another shall gird thee,
and carry thee whither thou wouldest not." [John xxi. 18–22]

Such were the ventures made in faith, and in uncertainty, by
Apostles. Our Saviour, in a passage of St. Luke's Gospel,
binds upon us all the necessity of deliberately doing the like, –
"Which of you, intending to build a tower, sitteth not down
first and counteth the cost, whether he have sufficient to finish
it? Lest haply, after he hath laid the foundation, and is not able
to finish it, all that behold it, begin to mock him, saying, This
man began to build, and is not able to finish." And then He
presently adds, "So likewise, whosoever he be of you that
forsaketh not all that he hath, he cannot be My disciple":
[Luke xiv. 28–33] thus warning us of the full sacrifice we must
make. We give up our all to Him; and He is to claim this or

that, or grant us somewhat of it for a season, according to His good pleasure. On the other hand, the case of the rich young man, who went away sorrowful, when our Lord bade him give up his all and follow Him, is an instance of one who had *not* faith to make the venture of this world for the next, upon His word.

If then faith be the essence of a Christian life, and if it be what I have now described, it follows that our duty lies in risking upon Christ's word what we have, for what we have not; and doing so in a noble, generous way, not indeed rashly or lightly, still without knowing accurately what we are doing, not knowing either what we give up, nor again what we shall gain; uncertain about our reward, uncertain about our extent of sacrifice, in all respects leaning, waiting upon Him, trusting in Him to fulfil His promise, trusting in Him to enable us to fulfil our own vows, and so in all respects proceeding without carefulness or anxiety about the future.

Now I dare say that what I have said as yet seems plain and unexceptionable to most of those who hear me; yet surely, when I proceed to draw the practical inference which immediately follows, there are those who in their secret hearts, if not in open avowal, will draw back. Men allow us Ministers of Christ to proceed in our preaching, while we confine ourselves to general truths, until they see that they themselves are implicated in them, and have to act upon them; and then they suddenly come to a stand; they collect themselves and draw back, and say, "They do not see *this* – or do not admit *that*" – and though they are quite unable to say *why* that should not follow from what they already allow, which we show *must* follow, still they persist in saying, that they do not see that it does follow; and they look about for excuses, and they say we carry things too far, and that we are extravagant, and that we ought to limit and modify what we say, that we do not take into account times, and seasons, and the like. This is what they pretend; and well has it been said, "where there is a will there is a way"; for there is no truth, however overpoweringly clear, but men may escape from it by shutting their eyes; there is no duty, however urgent, but they may find ten thousand good reasons against it, in their own case. And they are sure to say we carry things too far, when we carry them home to themselves.

This sad infirmity of men, called Christians, is exemplified in the subject immediately before us. Who does not at once admit that faith consists in venturing on Christ's word without seeing? Yet in spite of this, may it not be seriously questioned, whether men in general, even those of the better sort, venture any thing upon His truth at all?

Consider for an instant. Let every one who hears me ask himself the question, what stake has *he* in the truth of Christ's promise? How would he be a whit the worse off, supposing (which is impossible), but, supposing it to fail? We know what it is to have a stake in any venture of this world. We venture our property in plans which promise a return; in plans which we trust, which we have faith in. What have we ventured for Christ? What have we given to Him on a belief of His promise? The Apostle said, that he and his brethren would be of all men most miserable, if the dead were not raised. Can we in any degree apply this to ourselves? We think, perhaps, at present, we have some hope of heaven; well, *this* we should lose of course; but after all, how should we be worse off as to our *present* condition? A trader, who has embarked some property in a speculation which fails, not only loses his prospect of gain, but somewhat of his own, which he ventured with the *hope* of the gain. This is the question, What have *we* ventured? I really fear, when we come to examine, it will be found that there is nothing we resolve, nothing we do, nothing we do not do, nothing we avoid, nothing we choose, nothing we give up, nothing we pursue, which we should not resolve, and do, and not do, and avoid, and choose, and give up, and pursue, if Christ had not died, and heaven were not promised us. I really fear that most men called Christians, whatever they may profess, whatever they may think they feel, whatever warmth and illumination and love they may claim as their own, yet would go on almost as they do, neither much better nor much worse, if they believed Christianity to be a fable. When young, they indulge their lusts, or at least pursue the world's vanities; as time goes on, they get into a fair way of business, or other mode of making money; then they marry and settle;

and their interest coinciding with their duty, they seem to be, and think themselves, respectable and religious men; they grow attached to things as they are; they begin to have a zeal against vice and error; and they follow after peace with all men. Such conduct indeed, as far as it goes, is right and praiseworthy. Only I say, it has not necessarily any thing to do with religion at all; there is nothing in it which is any proof of the presence of religious principle in those who adopt it; there is nothing they would not do still, though they had nothing to gain from it, except what they gain from it now: they do gain something now, they do gratify their present wishes, they are quiet and orderly, because it is their interest and taste to be so; but they *venture* nothing, they risk, they sacrifice, they abandon nothing on the faith of Christ's word.

For instance: St. Barnabas had a property in Cyprus; he gave it up for the poor of Christ. Here is an intelligible sacrifice. He did something he would not have done, unless the Gospel were true. It is plain, if the Gospel turned out a fable (which God forbid), but if so, he would have taken his line most unskilfully; he would be in a great mistake, and would have suffered a loss. He would be like a merchant whose vessels were wrecked, or whose correspondents had failed. Man has confidence in man, he trusts to the credit of his neighbour; but Christians do not risk largely upon their Saviour's word; and this is the one thing they have to do. Christ tells us Himself, "Make to yourselves friends of the mammon of unrighteousness; that, when ye fail, they may receive you into everlasting habitations"; [Luke xvi. 9] *i.e.* buy an interest in the next world with that wealth which this world uses unrighteously; feed the hungry, clothe the naked, relieve the sick, and it shall turn to "bags that wax not old, a treasure in the heavens that faileth not." [Luke xii. 33] Thus almsdeeds, I say, are an intelligible *venture* and an evidence of faith.

So again the man who, when his prospects in the world are good, gives up the promise of wealth or of eminence, in order to be nearer Christ, to have a place in His temple, to have more opportunity for prayer and praise, he makes a sacrifice. Or he who, from a noble striving after perfection, puts off the desire of worldly comforts, and is, like Daniel or St. Paul, in much labour and business, yet with a solitary heart, he too ventures something upon the certainty of the world to come.

Or he who, after falling into sin, repents in deed as well as in word; puts some yoke upon his shoulder; subjects himself to punishment; is severe upon his flesh; denies himself innocent pleasures; or puts himself to public shame, – he too shows that his faith is the realizing of things hoped for, the warrant of things not seen.

Or again: he who only gets himself to pray against those things which the many seek after, and to embrace what the heart naturally shrinks from; he who, when God's will seems to tend towards worldly ill, while he deprecates it, yet prevails on himself to say heartily, "Thy will be done"; he, even, is not without his sacrifice. Or he who, being in prospect of wealth, honestly prays God that he may never be rich; or he who is in prospect of station, and earnestly prays that he may never have it; or he who has friends or kindred, and acquiesces with an entire heart in their removal while it is yet doubtful, who can say, "Take them away, if it be Thy will, to Thee I give them up, to Thee I commit them," who is willing to be taken at his word; he too risks somewhat, and is accepted.

Such a one is taken at his word, while he understands not, perhaps, what he says; but he is accepted, as meaning somewhat, and risking much. Generous hearts, like James and John, or Peter, often speak largely and confidently beforehand of what they will do for Christ, not insincerely, yet ignorantly; and for their sincerity's sake they are taken at their word as a reward, though they have yet to learn how serious that word is. "They say unto Him, We are able"; – and the vow is recorded in heaven. This is the case of all of us at many seasons. First, at Confirmation, when we promise what was promised for us at Baptism, yet without being able to understand how much we promise, but rather trusting to God gradually to reveal it, and to give us strength according to our day. So again they who enter Holy Orders promise they know not what, engage themselves they know not how deeply, debar themselves of the world's ways they know not how intimately, find perchance they must cut off from them the right hand, sacrifice the desire of their eyes and the stirring of their hearts at the foot of the Cross, while they thought, in their simplicity, they were but choosing the quiet easy life of "plain men dwelling in tents." And so again, in various ways, the circumstances of the times cause men at certain seasons to take this path or that, for religion's sake. They know not whither they are being carried; they see not the end of their course; they know no more than this, that it is right to do what they are now doing; and they hear a whisper within them, which assures them, as it did the two holy brothers, that whatever their present conduct involves in time to come, they shall, through God's grace, be equal to it. Those blessed Apostles said, "We are able"; and in truth they were enabled to do and suffer as they had said. St. James was given strength to be steadfast unto death, the death of martyrdom; being slain with the sword in Jerusalem. St. John, his brother, had still more to bear, dying last of the Apostles, as St. James first. He had to bear bereavement, first, of his brother, then of the other Apostles. He had to bear a length of years in loneliness, exile, and weakness. He had to experience the dreariness of being solitary, when those whom he loved had been summoned away. He had to live in his own thoughts, without familiar friend, with those only about him who belonged to a younger generation. Of him were demanded by his gracious Lord, as pledges of his faith, all his eye loved and his heart held converse with. He was as a man moving his goods into a far country, who at intervals and by portions sends them before him, till his present abode is well-nigh unfurnished. He sent forward his friends on their journey, while he stayed himself behind, that there might be those in heaven to have thoughts of him, to look out for him, and receive him when his Lord should call. He sent before him, also, other still more voluntary pledges and ventures of his faith, – a self-denying walk, a zealous maintenance of the truth, fasting and prayers, labours of love, a virgin life, buffetings from the heathen, persecution, and banishment. Well might so great a Saint say, at the end of his days "Come, Lord Jesus!" as those who are weary of the night, and wait for the morning. All his thoughts, all his contemplations, desires, and hopes, were stored in the invisible world; and death, when it came, brought back to him the sight of what he had worshipped, what he had loved, what he had held intercourse with, in years long past away. Then, when again brought into the presence of what he had lost, how would remembrance revive, and familiar thoughts long buried come to life! Who shall dare to describe the blessedness of those who find all their pledges safe returned to them, all their ventures abundantly and beyond measure satisfied?

Alas! that we, my brethren, have not more of this high and unearthly spirit! How is it that we are so contented with things as they are, – that we are so willing to be let alone, and to enjoy this life, – that we make such excuses, if any one presses on us the necessity of something higher, the duty of bearing the Cross, if we would earn the Crown, of the Lord Jesus Christ?

I repeat it; what are our ventures and risks upon the truth of His word? for He says expressly, "Every one that hath forsaken houses, or brethren, or sisters, or father, or mother, or wife, or children, or lands, for My Name's sake, shall receive an hundred-fold, and shall inherit everlasting life. But many that are first shall be last; and the last shall be first." [Matt. xix. 29, 30]

II

Men, not Angels,
the Priests of the Gospel*

When Christ, the great Prophet, the great Preacher, the great
Missionary, came into the world, He came in a way the most
holy, the most august, the most glorious. Though He came in
humiliation, though He came to suffer, though He was born in
a stable, though He was laid in a manger, yet He issued from
the womb of an Immaculate Mother, and His infant form shone
with heavenly light. Sanctity marked every lineament of His
character and every circumstance of His mission. Gabriel
announced His incarnation; a Virgin conceived, a Virgin bore,
a Virgin suckled Him; His foster-father was the pure and
saintly Joseph; Angels proclaimed His birth; a luminous star
spread the news among the heathen; the austere Baptist went
before His face; and a crowd of shriven penitents, clad in
white garments and radiant with grace, followed Him wherever
He went. As the sun in heaven shines through the clouds, and
is reflected in the landscape, so the eternal Sun of justice,
when He rose upon the earth, turned night into day, and in His
brightness made all things bright.

He came and He went; and, seeing that He came to
introduce a new and final Dispensation into the world, He left
behind Him preachers, teachers, and missionaries, in His
stead. Well then, my brethren, you will say, since on His
coming all about Him was so glorious, such as He was, such
must His servants be, such His representatives, His ministers,
in His absence; as He was without sin, they too must be

* This sermon was originally published in 1849 as Discourse 3 in
Discourses Addressed to Mixed Congregations, the first work that
Newman published under his own name as a Catholic priest.

without sin; as He was the Son of God, they must surely be Angels. Angels, you will say, must be appointed to this high office, Angels alone are fit to preach the birth, the sufferings, the death of God. They might indeed have to hide their brightness, as He before them, their Lord and Master, had put on a disguise; they might come, as they came under the Old Covenant, in the garb of men; but still men they could not be, if they were to be preachers of the everlasting Gospel, and dispensers of its divine mysteries. If they were to sacrifice, as He had sacrificed; to continue, repeat, apply, the very Sacrifice which He had offered; to take into their hands that very Victim which was He Himself; to bind and to loose, to bless and to ban, to receive the confessions of His people, and to give them absolution for their sins; to teach them the way of truth, and to guide them along the way of peace; who was sufficient for these things but an inhabitant of those blessed realms of which the Lord is the never-failing Light?

And yet, my brethren, so it is, He has sent forth for the ministry of reconciliation, not Angels, but men; He has sent forth your brethren to you, not beings of some unknown nature and some strange blood, but of your own bone and your own flesh, to preach to you. "Ye men of Galilee, why stand ye gazing up into heaven?" Here is the royal style and tone in which Angels speak to men, even though these men be Apostles; it is the tone of those who, having never sinned, speak from their lofty eminence to those who have. But such is not the tone of those whom Christ has sent; for it is your brethren whom He has appointed, and none else, – sons of Adam, sons of your nature, the same by nature, differing only in grace, – men, like you, exposed to temptations, to the same temptations, to the same warfare within and without; with the same three deadly enemies – the world, the flesh, and the devil; with the same human, the same wayward heart: differing only as the power of God has changed and rules it. So it is; we are not Angels from Heaven that speak to you, but men, whom grace, and grace alone, has made to differ from you. Listen to the Apostle: – When the barbarous Lycaonians, seeing his miracle, would have sacrificed to him and St. Barnabas, as to gods, he rushed in among them, crying out, "O men, why do ye this? we also are mortals, men like unto you"; or, as the words run more forcibly in the original Greek, "We are of like passions with you". And again to the Corinthians he writes, "We preach not ourselves, but Jesus Christ our Lord; and ourselves your servants through Jesus. God, who commanded the light to shine out of darkness, He hath shined in our hearts, to give the light of the knowledge of the glory of God in the face of Christ Jesus: *but* we hold this treasure *in earthen vessels.*" And further, he says of himself most wonderfully, that, "lest he should be exalted by the greatness of the revelations," there was given him "an angel of Satan" in his flesh "to buffet him". Such are your Ministers, your Preachers, your Priests, O my brethren; not Angels, not Saints, not sinless, but those who would have lived and died in sin except for God's grace, and who, though through God's mercy they be in training for the fellowship of Saints hereafter, yet at present are in the midst of infirmity and temptation, and have no hope, except from the unmerited grace of God, of persevering unto the end.

What a strange, what a striking anomaly is this! All is perfect, all is heavenly, all is glorious, in the Dispensation which Christ has vouchsafed us, except the persons of His Ministers. He dwells on our altars Himself, the Most Holy, the Most High, in light inaccessible, and Angels fall down before Him there; and out of visible substances and forms He chooses what is choicest to represent and to hold Him. The finest wheat-flour, and the purest wine, are taken as His outward symbols; the most sacred and majestic words minister to the sacrificial rite; altar and sanctuary are adorned decently or splendidly, as our means allow; and the Priests perform their office in befitting vestments, lifting up chaste hearts and holy hands; yet those very Priests, so set apart, so consecrated, they, with their girdle of celibacy and their maniple of sorrow, are sons of Adam, sons of sinners, of a fallen nature, which they have not put off, though it be renewed through grace, so that it is almost the definition of a Priest that he has sins of his own to offer for. "Every high Priest," says the Apostle, "taken from among men, is appointed for men, in the things that appertain unto God, that he may offer gifts and sacrifices for sins; who can condole with those who are in ignorance and error, because he also himself is compassed with infirmity. And therefore he ought, as for the people, so also for himself, to offer for sins." And hence in the Mass, when he offers up the Host before consecration, he says, *Suscipe, Sancte Pater, Omnipotens, æterne Deus*, "Accept, Holy Father, Almighty, Everlasting God, this immaculate Host, which I, Thine unworthy servant, offer to Thee, my Living and True God, for *mine* innumerable sins, offences, and negligences, *and* for all who stand around, and for all faithful Christians, living and dead."

Most strange is this in itself, my brethren, but not strange, when you consider it is the appointment of an all-merciful God; not strange in Him, because the Apostle gives the reason of it in the passage I have quoted. The priests of the New Law are men, in order that they may "condole with those who are in ignorance and error, because they too are compassed with infirmity". Had Angels been your Priests, my brethren, they could not have condoled with you, sympathised with you, have had compassion on you, felt tenderly for you, and made allowances for you, as we can; they could not have been your patterns and guides, and have led you on from your old selves into a new life, as they can who come from the midst of you, who have been led on themselves as you are to be led, who know well your difficulties, who have had experience, at least of your temptations, who know the strength of the flesh and the wiles of the devil, even though they have baffled them, who are already disposed to take your part, and be indulgent towards you, and can advise you most practically, and warn you most seasonably and prudently. Therefore did He send you men to be the ministers of reconciliation and intercession; as He Himself, though He could not sin, yet even He, by becoming man, took on Him, as far as was possible to God, man's burden of infirmity and trial in His own person. He could not be a sinner, but He could be a man, and He took to Himself a man's heart that we might entrust our hearts to Him, and "was tempted in all things, like as we are, yet without sin".

Ponder this truth well, my brethren, and let it be your

comfort. Among the Preachers, among the Priests of the Gospel, there have been Apostles, there have been Martyrs, there have been Doctors; – Saints in plenty among them; yet out of them all, high as has been their sanctity, varied their graces, awful their gifts, there has not been one who did not begin with the old Adam; not one of them who was not hewn out of the same rock as the most obdurate of reprobates; not one of them who was not fashioned unto honour out of the same clay which has been the material of the most polluted and vile of sinners; not one who was not by nature brother of those poor souls who have now commenced an eternal fellowship with the devil, and are lost in hell. Grace has vanquished nature; that is the whole history of the Saints. Salutary thought for those who are tempted to pride themselves in what they do, and what they are; wonderful news for those who sorrowfully recognise in their hearts the vast difference that exists between them and the Saints; and joyful news, when men hate sin, and wish to escape from its miserable yoke, yet are tempted to think it impossible!

Come, my brethren, let us look at this truth more narrowly, and lay it to heart. First consider, that, since Adam fell, none of his seed but has been conceived in sin; none, save one. One exception there has been, – who is that one? not our Lord Jesus, for He was not conceived of man, but of the Holy Ghost; not our Lord, but I mean His Virgin Mother, who, though conceived and born of human parents, as others, yet was rescued by anticipation from the common condition of mankind, and never was partaker in fact of Adam's transgression. She was conceived in the way of nature, she was conceived as others are; but grace interfered and was beforehand with sin; grace filled her soul from the first moment of her existence, so that the evil one breathed not on her, nor stained the work of God. *Tota pulchra es, Maria; et macula originalis non est in te.* "Thou art all fair, O Mary, and the stain original is not in thee." But putting aside the Most Blessed Mother of God, every one else, the most glorious Saint, and the most black and odious of sinners, I mean, the soul which, in the event, became the most glorious, and the soul which became the most devilish, were both born in one and the same original sin, both were children of wrath, both were unable to attain heaven by their natural powers, both had the prospect of meriting for themselves hell.

They were both born in sin; they both lay in sin; and the soul, which afterwards became a Saint, would have continued in sin, would have sinned wilfully, and would have been lost, but for the visitings of an unmerited supernatural influence upon it, which did for it what it could not do for itself. The poor infant, destined to be an heir of glory, lay feeble, sickly, fretful, wayward, and miserable; the child of sorrow; without hope, and without heavenly aid. So it lay for many a long and weary day ere it was born; and when at length it opened its eyes and saw the light, it shrank back, and wept aloud that it had seen it. But God heard its cry from heaven in this valley of tears, and He began that course of mercies towards it which led it from earth to heaven. He sent His Priest to administer to it the first sacrament, and to baptise it with His grace. Then a great change took place in it, for, instead of its being any more the thrall of Satan it forthwith became a child of God; and had it died that minute, and before it came to the age of reason, it would have been carried to heaven without delay by Angels, and been admitted into the presence of God.

But it did not die; it came to the age of reason, and, oh, shall we dare to say, though in some blessed cases it may be said, shall we dare to say, that it did not misuse the great talent which had been given to it, profane the grace which dwelt in it, and fall into mortal sin? In some instances, praised be God! we dare affirm it; such seems to have been the case with my own dear father, St. Philip, who surely kept his baptismal robe unsullied from the day he was clad in it, never lost his state of grace, from the day he was put into it, and proceeded from strength to strength, and from merit to merit, and from glory to glory, through the whole course of his long life, till at the age of eighty he was summoned to his account, and went joyfully to meet it, and was carried across purgatory, without any scorching of its flames, straight to heaven.

Such certainly have sometimes been the dealings of God's grace with the souls of His elect; but more commonly, as if more intimately to associate them with their brethren, and to make the fulness of His favours to them a ground of hope and an encouragement to the penitent sinner, those who have ended in being miracles of sanctity, and heroes in the Church, have passed a time in wilful disobedience, have thrown themselves out of the light of God's countenance, have been led captive by this or that sin, by this or that religious error, till at length they were in various ways recovered, slowly or suddenly, and regained the state of grace, or rather a much higher state, than that which they had forfeited. Such was the blessed Magdalen, who had lived a life of shame; so much so, that even to be touched by her was, according to the religious judgment of her day, a pollution. Happy in this world's goods, young and passionate, she had given her heart to the creature, before the grace of God prevailed with her. Then she cut off her long hair, and put aside her gay apparel, and became so utterly what she had not been, that, had you known her before and after, you had said it was two persons you had seen, not one; for there was no trace of the sinner in the penitent, except the affectionate heart, now set on heaven and Christ; no trace besides, no memory of that glittering and seductive apparition, in the modest form, the serene countenance, the composed gait, and the gentle voice of her who in the garden sought and found her Risen Saviour. Such, too, was he who from a publican became an Apostle and an Evangelist; one who for filthy lucre scrupled not to enter the service of the heathen Romans, and to oppress his own people. Nor were the rest of the Apostles made of better clay than the other sons of Adam; they were by nature animal, carnal, ignorant; left to themselves, they would, like the brutes, have grovelled on the earth, and gazed upon the earth, and fed on the earth, had not the grace of God taken possession of them, and set them on their feet, and raised their faces heavenward. And such was the learned Pharisee, who came to Jesus by night, well satisfied with his station, jealous of his reputation, confident in his reason; but the time at length came, when, even though disciples fled, he remained to anoint the abandoned corpse of Him, whom when living he had been ashamed to own. You see it was the grace of God that triumphed in Magdalen, in Matthew, and in Nicodemus; heavenly grace came down upon corrupt nature; it subdued impurity in the youthful woman, covetousness in the publican, fear of man in the Pharisee.

Let me speak of another celebrated conquest of God's grace in an after age, and you will see how it pleases Him to make a Confessor, a Saint and Doctor of His Church, out of sin and heresy both together. It was not enough that the Father of the Western Schools, the author of a thousand works, the triumphant controversialist, the especial champion of grace, should have been once a poor slave of the flesh, but he was the victim of a perverted intellect also. He, who of all others, was to extol the grace of God, was left more than others to experience the helplessness of nature. The great St. Augustine (I am not speaking of the holy missionary of the same name, who came to England and converted our pagan forefathers, and became the first Archbishop of Canterbury, but of the great African Bishop, two centuries before him) – Augustine, I say, not being in earnest about his soul, not asking himself the question, how was sin to be washed away, but rather being desirous, while youth and strength lasted, to enjoy the flesh and the world, ambitious and sensual, judged of truth and falsehood by his private judgment and his private fancy; despised the Catholic Church because it spoke so much of faith and subjection, thought to make his own reason the measure of all things, and accordingly joined a far-spread sect, which affected to be philosophical and enlightened, to take large views of things, and to correct the vulgar, that is the Catholic notions of God and Christ, of sin, and of the way to heaven. In this sect of his he remained for some years; yet what he was taught there did not satisfy him. It pleased him for a time, and then he found he had been eating as if food what had no nourishment in it; he became hungry and thirsty after something more substantial, he knew not what; he despised himself for being a slave to the flesh, and he found his religion did not help him to overcome it; thus he understood that he had not gained the truth, and he cried out, "O, who will tell me where to seek it, and who will bring me into it?"

Why did he not join the Catholic Church at once? I have told you why; he saw that truth was nowhere else; but he was not sure it was there. He thought there was something mean, narrow, irrational, in her system of doctrine; he lacked the gift of faith. Then a great conflict began within him, – the conflict of nature with grace; of nature and her children, the flesh and false reason, against conscience and the pleadings of the Divine Spirit, leading him to better things. Though he was still in a state of perdition, yet God was visiting him, and giving him the first fruits of those influences which were in the event to bring him out of it. Time went on; and looking at him, as his Guardian Angel might look at him, you would have said that, in spite of much perverseness, and many a successful struggle against his Almighty Adversary, in spite of his still being, as before, in a state of wrath, nevertheless grace was making way in his soul, – he was advancing towards the Church. He did not know it himself, he could not recognise it himself; but an eager interest in him, and then a joy, was springing up in heaven among the Angels of God. At last he came within the range of a great Saint in a foreign country; and, though he pretended not to acknowledge him, his attention was arrested by him, and he could not help coming to sacred places to look at him again and again. He began to watch him and speculate about him, and wondered with himself whether he was happy. He found himself frequently in Church, listening to the holy preacher, and he once asked his advice how to find what he was seeking. And now a final conflict came on him with the flesh: it was hard, very hard, to part with the indulgences of years, it was hard to part and never to meet again. O, sin was so sweet, how could he bid it farewell? how could he tear himself away from its embrace, and betake himself to that lonely and dreary way which led heavenwards? But God's grace was sweeter far, and it convinced him while it won him; it convinced his reason, and prevailed; – and he who without it would have lived and died a child of Satan, became, under its wonder-working power, an oracle of sanctity and truth.

And do you not think, my brethren, that he was better fitted than another to persuade his brethren as he had been persuaded, and to preach the holy doctrine which he had despised? Not that sin is better than obedience, or the sinner than the just; but that God in His mercy makes use of sin against itself, that He turns past sin into a present benefit, that, while He washes away its guilt and subdues its power, He leaves it in the penitent in such sense as enables him, from his knowledge of its devices, to assault it more vigorously, and strike at it more truly, when it meets him in other men; that, while our Lord, by His omnipotent grace, can make the soul as clean as if it had never been unclean, He leaves it in possession of a tenderness and compassion for other sinners, an experience how to deal with them, greater than if it had never sinned; and again that, in those rare and special instances, of one of which I have been speaking, He holds up to us, for our instruction and our comfort, what He can do, even for the most guilty, if they sincerely come to Him for a pardon and a cure. There is no limit to be put to the bounty and power of God's grace; and that we feel sorrow for our sins, and supplicate His mercy, is a sort of present pledge to us in our hearts, that He will grant us the good gifts we are seeking. He can do what He will with the soul of man. He is infinitely more powerful than the foul spirit to whom the sinner has sold himself, and can cast him out.

O my dear brethren, though your conscience witnesses against you, He can disburden it; whether you have sinned less or whether you have sinned more, He can make you as clean in His sight and as acceptable to Him as if you had never gone from Him. Gradually will He destroy your sinful habits, and at once will He restore you to His favour. Such is the power of the Sacrament of Penance, that, be your load of guilt heavier or be it lighter, it removes it, whatever it is. It is as easy to Him to wash out the many sins as the few. Do you recollect in the Old Testament the history of the cure of Naaman the Syrian, by the prophet Eliseus? He had that dreadful, incurable disease called the leprosy, which was a white crust upon the skin, making the whole person hideous, and typifying the hideousness of sin. The prophet bade him bathe in the river Jordan, and the disease disappeared; "his flesh," says the inspired writer, was "restored to him as the flesh of a little child". Here, then, we have a representation not only of what sin is, but of what God's grace is. It can undo the past, it can realise the hopeless. No sinner, ever so odious, but may become a Saint; no Saint, ever so exalted, but has been, or might have been, a sinner. Grace overcomes nature, and grace only overcomes it. Take that holy child, the blessed St. Agnes, who, at the age of thirteen, resolved to die rather than deny the faith, and stood enveloped in an atmosphere of purity, and diffused around her a heavenly influence, in the very home of evil spirits into which the heathen brought her; or consider the angelical Aloysius, of whom it hardly is left upon record that he committed even a venial sin; or St. Agatha, St. Juliana, St. Rose, St. Casimir, or St. Stanislas, to whom the very notion of any unbecoming imagination had been as death; well, there is not one of these seraphic souls but might have been a degraded, loathsome leper, except for God's grace, an outcast from his kind; not one but might, or rather would, have lived the life of a brute creature, and died the death of a reprobate, and lain down in hell eternally in the devil's arms, had not God put a new heart and a new spirit within him, and made him what he could not make himself.

All good men are not Saints, my brethren – all converted souls do not become Saints. I will not promise, that, if you turn to God, you will reach that height of sanctity which the Saints have reached: – true; still, I am showing you that even the Saints are by nature no better than you; and so (much more) that the Priests, who have the charge of the faithful, whatever be their sanctity, are by nature no better than those whom they have to convert, whom they have to reform. It is God's special mercy towards you that we by nature are no other than you; it is His consideration and compassion for you that He has made us, who are your brethren, His legates and ministers of reconciliation.

This is what the world cannot understand; not that it does not apprehend clearly enough that we are by nature of like passions with itself; but what it is so blind, so narrow-minded as not to comprehend, is, that, being so like itself by nature, we may be made so different by grace. Men of the world, my brethren, know the power of nature; they know not, experience not, believe not, the power of God's grace; and since they are not themselves acquainted with any power that can overcome nature, they think that none exists, and therefore, consistently, they believe that every one, Priest or not, remains to the end such as nature made him, and they will not believe it possible that any one can lead a supernatural life. Now, not Priest only, but every one who is in the grace of God, leads a supernatural life, more or less supernatural, according to his calling, and the measure of the gifts given him, and his faithfulness to them. This they know not, and admit not; and when they hear of the life which a Priest must lead by his profession from youth to age, they will not credit that he is what he professes to be. They know nothing of the presence of God, the merits of Christ, the intercession of the Blessed Virgin; the virtue of recurring prayers, of frequent confession, of daily Masses; they are strangers to the transforming power of the Most Holy Sacrament, the Bread of Angels; they do not contemplate the efficacy of salutary rules, of holy companions, of long-enduring habit, of ready spontaneous vigilance, of abhorrence of sin and indignation at the tempter, to secure the soul from evil. They only know that when the tempter once has actually penetrated into the heart, he is irresistible; they only know that when the soul has exposed and surrendered itself to his malice, there is (so to speak) a necessity of sinning. They only know that when God has abandoned it, and good Angels are withdrawn, and all safeguards, and protections, and preventives are neglected, that then (which is their own case), when the victory is all but gained already, it is sure to be gained altogether. They themselves have ever, in their best estate, been all but beaten by the Evil One before they began to fight; this is the only state they have experienced: they know this, and they know nothing else. They have never stood on vantage ground; they have never been within the walls of the strong city, about which the enemy prowls in vain, into which he cannot penetrate, and outside of which the faithful soul will be too wise to venture. They judge, I say, by their experience, and will not believe what they never knew.

If there be those here present, my dear brethren, who will not believe that grace is effectual within the Church, because it does little outside of it, to them I do not speak: I speak to those who do not narrow their belief to their experience; I speak to those who admit that grace can make human nature what it is not; and such persons, I think, will feel it, not a cause of jealousy and suspicion, but a great gain, a great mercy, that those are sent to preach to them, to receive their confessions, and to advise them, who can sympathise with their sins, even though they have not known them. Not a temptation, my brethren, can befall you, but what befalls all those who share your nature, though you may have yielded to it, and they may not have yielded. They can understand you, they can anticipate you, they can interpret you, though they have not kept pace with you in your course. They will be tender to you, they will "instruct you in the spirit of meekness," as the Apostle says, "considering themselves lest they also be tempted". Come then unto us, all ye that labour and are heavy laden, and ye shall find rest to your souls; come unto us, who now stand to you in Christ's stead, and who speak in Christ's name; for we too, like you, have been saved by Christ's all-saving blood. We too, like you, should be lost sinners, unless Christ had had mercy on us, unless His grace had cleansed us, unless His Church had received us, unless His saints had interceded for us. Be ye saved, as we have been saved; "come, listen, all ye that fear God, and we will tell you what He hath done for our souls". Listen to our testimony; behold our joy of heart, and increase it by partaking in it yourselves. Choose that good part which we have chosen; join ye yourselves to our company; it will never repent you, take our word for it, who have a right to speak, it will never repent you to have sought pardon and peace from the Catholic Church, which alone has grace, which alone has power, which alone has Saints; it will never repent you, though you go through trouble, though you have to give up much for her sake. It will never repent you, to have passed from the shadows of sense and time, and the deceptions of human feeling and false reason, to the glorious liberty of the sons of God.

And O, my brethren, when you have taken the great step, and stand in your blessed lot, as sinners reconciled to the Father you have offended (for I will anticipate, what I surely trust will be fulfilled as regards many of you), O then forget not those who have been the ministers of your reconciliation; and as they now pray you to make your peace with God, so do you, when reconciled, pray for them, that they may gain the great gift of perseverance, that they may continue to stand in the grace in which they trust they stand now, even till the hour of death, lest, perchance, after they have preached to others, they themselves become reprobate.

III

The Gainsaying of Korah[*]

"Woe unto them; for they have gone in the way of Cain, and
ran greedily after the error of Balaam for reward, and
perished in the gainsaying of Core." Jude 11

There are two special sins which trouble the Church, and are
denounced in Scripture, ambition and avarice, the sin of Korah
and the sin of Balaam; both of which are spoken of in the text.
The sin of Balaam is denounced again and again by St. Paul,
in his Epistles to Timothy and Titus; as where he says, "A
Bishop must be ... not greedy of filthy lucre ... not
covetous"; "the Deacons must be ... not greedy of filthy
lucre"; noticing the while that some supposed that "gain was
godliness," and "taught things which they ought not for filthy
lucre's sake." [1 Tim. iii. 8; vi. 5. Tit. i. 7, 11] And the sin
of Korah, or ambition, is condemned by our Lord, when He
commands, "Whosoever will be great among you, let him be
your minister"; by St. James, when he says, "Be not many
masters, knowing that we shall receive the greater
condemnation"; and by St. Paul, when he directs that a Bishop
should not be a "novice, lest being lifted up with pride he fall
into the condemnation of the devil." [Matt. xx. 26. James iii.
1. 1 Tim. iii. 6] And both sins together are spoken of by St.
Peter, in his exhortation to the Elders to "feed the flock of God
... not for filthy lucre, but of a ready mind; neither as being
lords over God's heritage, but being examples to the flock."
[1 Pet. v. 2, 3]

---

[*] A sermon from Newman's Anglican years and published as Sermon 18 in
Volume iv of *Parochial and Plain Sermons*. The notes appended to the end
of this and subsequent sermons in this section are Newman's own notes.

Accordingly, these are the two sins brought before us by our Church in the first lessons of the first Sunday after Easter, which is, as it were, the festival in commemoration of the Ministerial Commission. After celebrating the resurrection of Christ, when He became "a Priest for ever after the order of Melchizedek," we proceed to make mention of the means which He has instituted for exercising His Priesthood on earth continually, – for commemorating and applying in the Spirit, among His elect people, again and again, day after day, to the end of the world, that atoning death and glorious resurrection, which He wrought out once for all in His own person on Calvary. He Himself instituted that means on the very day that He rose from the dead, ordaining man, frail and fallible as he is, to be the vessel of His gifts, and to represent Him. When He was risen, He did not first show Himself to His enemies, nor manifest the Spirit, nor unfold His new law, nor destroy the Temple; but He consecrated His Ministers: "As My Father hath sent Me," He said to His Apostles, "even so send I you." And, as if after His pattern, we too, even at this day, follow up the celebration of His "taking to Himself His great power," with that of His delegating it to His Church, as the Gospel selected for the same Sunday shows.

Of such high importance then, in our Church's judgment, is the subject of the Christian Ministry; so intimately connected with the Divine scheme of mercy, so full of reverence and awe. This will be best seen by proceeding, as I shall now do, to consider the lesson derived from the rebellion of Korah, Dathan, and Abiram, which, though properly belonging to the Old Covenant, our Church certainly considers applicable to us Christians.

The history in question contains an account, not only of the ambition of Korah himself, who was a Levite or minister, but of the rebellion of Dathan and Abiram, who were not ministers, but, as we now speak, laymen.

In considering it, I shall confine myself to this point, viz. to determine the feelings and circumstances under which these wicked men rebelled against Moses and Aaron, and that, with a view of warning those who speak lightly of schism, separation, and dissent, in this day. For I think it will be seen that they are feelings and circumstances which prevail very widely now as well as then, and, if they do prevail, are as evil now as they were then; St. Jude, in the text plainly intimating that such gainsaying as Korah's is a sin in a Christian, as well as formerly in the Jews, and that those who commit it are in the way to perish. This, then, is a very serious thought; considering, as I have said, how men in these days make light of it.

The outline of the history of Korah, Dathan, and Abiram is this: they rebelled against Moses and Aaron, and in consequence Dathan and Abiram were swallowed up by an earthquake, and Korah's company was burnt with fire. Now, then let us proceed to the remarks proposed.

1. First, then, let the number and dignity of the offenders be observed. They seem to have been some of the most eminent and considerable persons in Israel. Dathan and Abiram's party are said more than once, with some emphasis, to have been "famous in the congregation, men of renown." [Numb. xvi. 2; xxvi. 9] Moreover there were among them as many as two hundred and fifty princes, or as we should now say, noblemen. A very great and formidable opposition to Moses and Aaron was it, when so great a number of eminent persons rebelled against, or (in modern language) became dissenters from the Church. Nor was this all, – a portion of God's appointed ministers joined them. The Levites, as we all know, were the especially holy tribe: a portion of them, viz. the family of Aaron, were priests; but all of them were ministers. Such was Korah; but, dissatisfied with being merely what God had made him, he aspired to be something more, to have the priesthood. And it appears that just as many of his brethren joined him in his rebellion as there were princes who joined Dathan and Abiram. Two hundred and fifty Levites, or ministers, were banded together in this opposition to Moses, forming, from their rank and number a body (to use once more modern language) of very high respectability, to say the least, that is, respectability in the eyes of men.

2. Next, let us observe how confident they were that they were right. They seemed to have entertained no kind of doubt or hesitation. When Moses denounced Dathan and Abiram, and bade all those who wished to escape their curse, to "depart" at once "from the tents of those wicked men," "Dathan and Abiram came out, and stood in the door of their tents, and their wives, and their sons, and their little children." You see they had no misgivings, no fears, no perplexity; they saw their way clear; they were sure they were in the right; and they came out, to stand any test, any sentence of wrath which Moses might attempt, as thinking that nothing could come of it. Nor was Korah's confidence less. Moses challenged him and the rest to appear before God, to perform the priest's office, and so to stand the test whether or not He would accept them; and they promptly accepted the proposal. They were to "take their censers, and put fire therein, and put incense in them before the Lord," "and it shall be, that the man whom the Lord doth choose, he shall be holy." Korah and his company accordingly "stood in the door of the tabernacle of the congregation with Moses and Aaron"; nay, in that sacred and awful place, where was the glory of the Lord visibly displayed, did Korah endure to "gather all the congregation" against Moses and Aaron. Sceptics, were there such standing by, might have made the remark, that both parties were equally sincere, equally confident; and therefore neither was more pleasing to God than the other.

Such was the confidence of Korah, Dathan, and Abiram, of the two hundred and fifty princes or nobles, and the two hundred and fifty ministers of God. And we, who believe that in spite of their confidence Almighty God was against them, are perhaps at first sight tempted to attribute it to some extraordinary infatuation, judicial blindness, special hard-heartedness, or the like, – something quite out of the way, peculiar perhaps to the Jews, – something which cannot happen now. We cannot comprehend how their confidence could possibly be based on reason – I do not say on correct reason, but on even apparent reason. We do not consider that perhaps they thought they had good reasons for what they did, as we often think in our own case, when we really have not.

Rather we attribute their conduct to something irrational, to pride, obstinacy, or hatred of the truth, as indeed it was in its origin; but I mean, to some such evil principle operating on the soul at once, and not operating on it through the pretence of reason, not so operating as to be hidden whether from themselves or others. And thus we lose the lesson which this solemn history is calculated to convey to us at this day; because, since the opposition made to God's Church in these days is professedly based upon reason, not upon mere prejudice, passion, or wilfulness, persons think that the confidence with which they oppose themselves to it, is a very different sort of confidence from that of Korah, Dathan, and Abiram, whereas it is really very much the same.

3. What, then, were the reasons or arguments which made Korah, Dathan, and Abiram so confident they were in the right, – so confident, that they even ventured to appeal to God, and to rise up against Moses and Aaron as if in the Name of the Lord? Their ground was this: they accused Moses and Aaron of what is now called priestcraft. Let us pay attention to this circumstance.

Now, let it be observed, that there were many rebellions of the people, founded on open and professed unbelief. This was not the character of the particular sin under review: it was not a disbelief in God, but in Moses. Distrust in Moses, indeed, was mixed up in all their rebellions; but generally their rebellion was more strictly directed against Almighty God. Thus, when the spies returned, and spread about an evil report of the good land, and the people believed them, this implied a disbelief in the Divine Arm altogether, as manifested in their deliverance and protection. Thus they complained of the manna; and thus they went out on the seventh day to gather it. But it is remarkable, that in the rebellion before us, there is no hint of the promoters of it disbelieving in the power or providence of God over the chosen people; only they accuse Moses of altering or (as we should say) corrupting the divine system. Dathan and Abiram were sons of Reuben, the first-born of the tribes: they might consider that Moses was interfering with their prerogative by birth to lead and govern the people. But, any how, they seem to have relied on their rank and eminence; they and their companions were "famous in the congregation, men of renown," and they could not bring themselves to submit to God's appointment, by which the nation was formed into a Church, and Levi was chosen, at God's inscrutable will, to be the priest instead of Reuben. Accordingly, far from denying that God was with the nation, they maintained it; they only said that He was not specially with Moses and Aaron; they only claimed an equality of honour and power with Moses and Aaron; they only denounced Moses and Aaron as usurpers, tyrants, and hypocrites. Far from showing any scoffing or lightness of mind, or profaneness, such as Esau's who rejected the blessing, they so esteemed it as to claim it as their own, in all its fulness; nay, they claimed it for the whole people. They were only opposed to what is now called exclusiveness; they were champions of the rights of the people against what they called the encroachments, the arrogant pretensions, the priestcraft of Moses their Lawgiver, and Aaron the Saint of the Lord. They said, "Ye take too much upon you, seeing all the congregation are holy, every one of them; and the Lord is among them; wherefore then lift ye up yourselves above the congregation of the Lord?" Their objection was, that Moses was interposing himself as a mediator between God and them, – limiting the mercies of God, restraining the freedom, obscuring the glory of His grace, and robbing them of their covenanted privileges; that he had instituted an order of priests, whereas they were all priests, every one, and needed no human assistance, no voice or advice, or direction, or performance, from fallible man, from men of like passions and imperfections with themselves, in order to approach God withal, and serve Him acceptably. "All the congregation are holy," say they, "every one of them; and the Lord is among them." "The Lord is not far off; He is not in the clouds only, He is not on Sinai, He is not on the mercy-seat, He is not with Aaron; but He is among us, in the congregation, as near one man as another, as near to all of us as He is to Moses." Their partisans affect the same tone even after God's judgment has fallen on the rebels. The people say to Moses and Aaron, "Ye have killed the people of the Lord." Yes; they call those separatists and schismatists "the Lord's people," and they accuse Moses and Aaron forsooth of having, by some device of juggling priests, some strange and diabolical stratagem, some secret of magic or science, compassed the death of their enemies, while they pretended to refer it to a miraculous judgment; and they seem as if to pride themselves on their discernment, on the clearness of intellectual vision by which they saw through the fraud, and brought it home to the impostors.

Awful guilt indeed in these self-wise men, if this representation be true! yet it is apparently true, as the words show with which the rebels themselves answer the summons of Moses to come to him. "Wilt thou," say they, "put out the eyes of these men? we will not come up." No, we have eyes; we are not mere dull, brutish, superstitious bigots, to crouch before a priest, and submit to his yoke of bondage; we can reason, we can argue, we are resolved to exercise our free unfettered private judgment, and to determine (candidly indeed and dispassionately), but still to determine for ourselves before we act. We will indeed give a fair hearing to what is told us; we will listen with a becoming deference and with all patience, nay with a sort of consideration and prepossession to what you, O Moses and Aaron, say to us; but still we will not have our eyes put out. No, seeing is believing; we will not go by instinctive feeling, by conscience, by mere probabilities; but everything shall be examined in a rational and enlightened way, everything searched, and sifted, and scrutinized, and rigidly tested, before it is admitted. The burden of proof lies with you; till you have proved to us your claims, we will not go up, we will not obey. To tell the truth, we are suspicious of you. We are "jealous with a godly jealousy" (alas! for men do so speak!) of any encroachments on our spiritual liberty, any assumption of superior holiness, superior acceptableness in one of us over another. We are all brethren, we are all equal, all independent. "Wilt thou make thyself altogether a prince over us?" "Moreover," they continue, "thou hast not brought us into a land that floweth with milk and honey, or given us inheritance of fields and vineyards"; or as men now speak, The present system does not work well; there are many abuses, abundant need of reform, much still undone which should be done, much idleness, much inefficiency, many defects in the Church. We see it quite plainly. Do not seek to defend yourselves. "Wilt thou put out the eyes of these men? we will not come up."

Something of the same kind of spirit had already shown itself in the sin of the golden calf, though that sin was open idolatry. Then also the people thought that they had found a better religion than Moses had taught them. They were far from denying God's miraculous providences; but they said that Moses had taken to himself what belonged to the nation; he had taught them in his own way, and they had a right to choose for themselves. "Up," they said, "make us gods, which shall go before us; for as for this Moses, the man that brought us up out of the land of Egypt, we wot not what is become of him." [Exod. xxxii. 1] And where was Moses? He was with God in prayer and vision. They did not know, or at least understand this. So they said, "What a time for a ruler to be absent! in what a crisis! how much is there that wants doing! – forty days are gone, and he is still away. Is he lost? has he left us here to ourselves? is he feigning any communication from heaven? any how, what binds us to him? We are bound indeed to the God who has brought us out of Egypt, but not to the rule of Moses or the line of Aaron." Moses was away; and where was Aaron? – where? the people could not ask, for they were partakers in his sin, rather, they had forced him into their sin, the sin of the golden calf. Aaron was receiving their gold ornaments, and was moulding them into an idol. Alas! the people could not accuse him, who had seduced him into the sin. But there were those who might, who did complain; and who they were, since I have been led to the subject, it will be found to our present purpose to inquire.

They were the Levites. While Aaron sinned, they, the inferior ministers, stood silent, but wondering and distressed. These had no part in the sin; and when Moses came down from the mount and said, "Who is on the Lord's side?" [Exod. xxii. 26] then they, and they only, answered the call. "All the sons of Levi gathered themselves together unto him"; and when he ordered them, they promptly "put every man his sword by his side, and went in and out from gate to gate throughout the camp, and slew every man his brother, and every man his companion, and every man his neighbour"; and "there fell of the people that day about three thousand men." This is considered in Scripture [Note 1] the act of consecration by which the Levites became the sacred tribe; so that their advancement to the ministerial office is historically coincident with Aaron's temporary defection from his more sacred duties in it. All this had happened, as some suppose shortly before, as others think as much as twenty years before, the occurrence which has been under our immediate review; but whether or not the one occurrence, as has been reasonably conjectured, led to the other, whether or not Korah's stouthearted rebellion was the result [Note 2] of ambitious views in the Levites, which their advancement to the sacred ministry had occasioned, still certain it is that at this time "it seemed but a small thing unto them" (in Moses' words) "that the God of Israel had separated them from the congregation of Israel, to bring them near to Himself to do the service of the tabernacle of the Lord, and to stand before the congregation to minister unto them"; and "they sought the priesthood also," Aaron's portion, on whom they were appointed to attend [Note 3]. And the circumstance that Aaron had failed on that trying occasion when they were rewarded, might dispose them to contemn him at this time, not recollecting that God's will made the difference between man and man, and that He who gave them His covenanted blessings through bulls and calves, might also vouchsafe them, did it please Him, through frail and erring men; and might dispense with inward perfection, and take up with mere earthen vessels, and be content with faith instead of consistent obedience, as He dispensed with eloquence, or wisdom, or strength. Such then were the circumstances under which the Levites rebelled, being elated by their existing privileges, as the Reubenites were stimulated by jealousy.

The parties then concerned in this formidable conspiracy were not besotted idolaters; they were not infidels; they were not obstinate, prejudiced, unreasoning zealots; they were not the victims of unscrupulous and desperate ambition; but though ambitious, proud, head-strong, obstinate, unbelieving, they veiled all these bad principles, even from their own conscience, under a show of reason, of clear, simple, straight-forward, enlightened reason, under a plain argument open to the meanest capacity: "All the congregation," they said, "were holy, every one." God had signified no exception or exclusion; all had been baptized in the Red Sea, all had been at Sinai. Moses, however, thus they might speak, had added to this simple and primitive religion a system of his own, a system of priestcraft. The especial favours which God had shown Moses were done twenty years before, and could be denied without much chance of contradiction; or if the rebellion took place (as others say) shortly after the Exodus, then it came close upon Aaron's sin in the matter of the golden calf. Any how, an excuse was easily found for explaining away the authority of Moses and Aaron, for denying the priesthood, and accusing it of being a corruption; and for professing to be the champions of a pure and enlightened, and uncorrupt worship, – a worship which would be quite clear of the idolatrous acts of Aaron, because in it Aaron's prerogative would be destroyed altogether.

Such is the history of the Church in the wilderness, in which we see as in a type the history of the Gospel. And how did it end? I stated in the commencement. The earth opened, and swallowed up Dathan, and covered the congregation of Abiram, their houses, their families, their possessions, and all that belonged to them. Fire went out from the Lord, and consumed the two hundred and fifty men who offered incense.

A very few words will suffice to suggest the lesson to be derived from this awful history; it is this: – If the Old Testament is still our rule of duty, except in such details as imply a local religion and a material sanctuary; if it is our rule of duty in its principles, its doctrines, its precepts; if the Gospel is but the fulfilment and development of the Law: if the parts in both are the same, only the circumstances without and the Spirit within new; if though Circumcision is abolished, yet there is Baptism instead of it; the Passover abolished, yet Holy Communion instead; the Sabbath abolished, yet instead of it the Lord's Day; if the two tables of stone which contained the

Law are destroyed, yet the Sermon on the Mount takes their place; if though Moses is gone, Christ is come; and if in like manner, though Aaron is gone and his priestly line, another order of priests is come instead; (and unless this is so, the Old Testament is in a great measure but a dead letter to Christians; and if there be but a chance that it is so, and if it has always been taken to be so, it is a most serious matter to act as if it were not so;) how great must be the sin of resisting the ministers of Christ, or of intruding into their office! How great the sin of presuming to administer the rites of the Church, to baptize, to celebrate the Holy Communion, or to ordain, or to bless, without a commission! Korah's sin was kept in remembrance for ever on the covering of the Altar, "to be a memorial," says the inspired writer, "that no stranger which is not of the seed of Aaron, come near to offer incense before the Lord, that he be not as Korah and his company"; in other words (as the warning is to be interpreted now), "that no one, who is not descended from the Apostles by laying on of hands, come near to perform the ministerial office before the Lord, that he be not such as Korah and his company." Many, you will say, intrude into it in this day in ignorance. True, it is so. Therefore, for them let us pray in our Lord's words, "Father, forgive them, for they know not what they do."

Notes
1. Exod. xxxii. 29.
2. Vid. Patrick on Numb. xvi. 2.
3. Numb. iii. 10.

IV

The Christian Ministry*

*"I say unto you, Among those that are born of women
there is not a greater prophet than John the Baptist; but
he that is least in the Kingdom of God is greater than he."*

Luke vii. 28

[Note 1] St. Peter's day suitably follows the day of St. John the
Baptist; for thus we have a striking memento, as the text
suggests, of the especial dignity of the Christian Ministry over
all previous Ministries which Almighty God has appointed. St.
John was "much more than a Prophet"; he was as great as any
messenger of God that had ever been born; yet the least in the
Kingdom of heaven, the least of Christ's Ministers, is greater
than he. And this, I observe, is a reflection especially fitted for
this Festival, because the Apostle Peter is taken in various
parts of the Gospel, as the appropriate type and representative
of the Christian ministry [Note 2].

Now, let us consider in what the peculiar dignity of the
Christian Minister consists. Evidently in this, that he is the
representative of Christ; for, as Christ is infinitely above all
other messengers from God, he who stands in His stead, must
be superior, beyond compare, to all Ministers of religion,
whether Prophets, Priests, Lawgivers, Judges, or Kings, whom
Almighty God ever commissioned. Moses, Aaron, Samuel,
and David, were shadows of the Saviour; but the Minister of
the Gospel is His present substitute. As a type or prophecy of
Grace is less than a pledge and means, as a Jewish sacrifice is
less than a Gospel sacrament, so are Moses and Elias less by

---

* Sermon 25 from Volume ii of *Parochial and Plain Sermons.*

office than the representatives of Christ. This I consider to be
evident, as soon as stated; the only question being, whether
there is reason for thinking, that Christ *has*, in matter of fact,
left representatives behind Him; and this, as I proceed to show,
Scripture enables us to determine in the affirmative.

Now, in the first place, as we all know, Christ chose twelve
out of His disciples, whom He called Apostles, to be His
representatives even during His own ministry. And He gave
them the power of doing the wonderful works which He did
Himself. Of course I do not say He gave them equal power
(God forbid!); but He gave them a certain sufficient portion of
His power. "He gave them power," says St. Luke, "and
authority over all devils, and to cure diseases; and He sent
them to preach the Kingdom of God, and to heal the sick."
[Luke ix. 1, 2] And He expressly made them His substitutes to
the world at large; so that to receive them was to receive
Himself. "He that receiveth you, receiveth Me." [Matt. x. 40]
Such was their principal power before His passion, similar to
that which He principally exercised, viz. the commission to
preach and to perform bodily cures. But when He had wrought
out the Atonement for human sin upon the Cross, and
purchased for man the gift of the Holy Ghost, then He gave
them a higher commission; and still, be it observed, parallel to
that which He Himself then assumed. "*As My Father hath sent
Me, even so send I you.* And when He had said this, He
breathed on them, and saith unto them, Receive ye the Holy
Ghost. Whose soever sins ye remit, they are remitted unto
them; and whose soever sins ye retain, they are retained."
[John xx. 21–23] Here, then, the Apostles became Christ's
representatives in the power of His Spirit, for the remission of
sins, as before they were His representatives as regards
miraculous cures, and preaching His Kingdom.

The following texts supply additional evidence that the
Apostles were commissioned in Christ's stead, and inform us
likewise in detail of some of the particular offices included in
their commission. "Let a man so account of us, as of the
Ministers of Christ, and *Stewards of the Mysteries* of God."
"Ye received me as an *Angel*" or heavenly Messenger "of
God, even *as Christ Jesus.*" "We *are Ambassadors* for Christ,

as though God did beseech you by us; we pray you *in Christ's stead*, be ye reconciled to God." [1 Cor. iv. 1. Gal. iv. 14. 2 Cor. v. 20]

The Apostles then, standing in Christ's place, were consequently exalted by office far above any divine Messengers before them. We come to the same conclusion from considering the sacred treasures committed to their custody, which (not to mention their miraculous powers, which is beside our present purpose) were those peculiar spiritual blessings which flow from Christ as a Saviour, as a Prophet, Priest, and King.

These blessings are commonly designated in Scripture as "the Spirit," or "the gift of the Holy Ghost." John the Baptist said of himself and Christ, "I indeed baptize you with water unto repentance; but He shall baptize you with the Holy Ghost, and with fire." [Matt. iii. 11] In this respect, Christ's ministrations were above all that had ever been before Him, in bringing with them the gift of the Holy Ghost, that one gift, one, yet multiform, sevenfold in its operation, in which all spiritual blessedness is included. Accordingly, our Lord was solemnly anointed with the Holy Ghost Himself, as an initiation into His Ministerial office. He was manifested as receiving, that He might be believed on as giving. He was thus commissioned, according to the Prophet, "to preach good tidings," "to heal the broken-hearted," "to give the oil of joy for mourning." Therefore, in like manner, the Apostles also were anointed with the same heavenly gift for the same Ministerial office. "He breathed on them, and saith unto them, Receive ye the Holy Ghost." Such as was the consecration of the Master, such was that of the Disciples; and such as His, were the offices to which they were thereby admitted.

Christ is a Prophet, as authoritatively revealing the will of God and the Gospel of Grace. So also were the Apostles; "He that heareth you, heareth Me; and he that despiseth you, despiseth Me; and he that despiseth Me, despiseth Him that sent Me"; "He that despiseth, despiseth not man, but God, who hath also given unto us His Holy Spirit." [Luke x. 16. 1 Thess. iv. 8]

Christ is a Priest, as forgiving sin, and imparting other

needful divine gifts. The Apostles, too, had this power; "Whose soever sins ye remit, they are remitted unto them; and whose soever sins ye retain, they are retained." "Let a man so account of us as ... Stewards of the Mysteries of God."

Christ is a King, as ruling the Church; and the Apostles rule it in His stead. "I appoint unto you a Kingdom, as My Father hath appointed unto Me; that ye may eat and drink at My table in My Kingdom, and sit on thrones judging the twelve tribes of Israel." [Luke xxi. 29, 30]

The gift, or office, cannot be named, which belongs to our Lord as the Christ, which He did not in its degree transfer to His Apostles by the communication of that Spirit, through which He Himself wrought; one of course excepted, the One great work, which none else in the whole world could sustain, of being the Atoning Sacrifice for all mankind. So far no one can take His place, and "His glory He does not give to another." His Death upon the Cross is the sole Meritorious Cause, the sole Source of spiritual blessing to our guilty race; but as to those offices and gifts which flow from this Atonement, preaching, teaching, reconciling, absolving, censuring, dispensing grace, ruling, ordaining, these all are included in the Apostolic Commission, which is instrumental and representative in His absence. "As My Father hath sent Me, so send I you." His gifts are not confined to Himself. "The whole house is filled with the odour of the ointment."

This being granted, however, as regards the Apostles themselves, some one may be disposed to inquire, whether their triple office has descended to Christian Ministers after them. I say their *triple* office, for few persons will deny that some portion of their commission still remains among us. The notion that there is no divine appointment of one man above another for Ministerial duties is not a common one, and we need not refute it. But it is very common for men to believe only as far as they can see and understand; and, because they are witnesses of the process and effects of instructing and ruling, and not of (what may be called) "the ministry of reconciliation," to accept Christ's Ministers as representatives of His Prophetic and Regal, not of His Priestly authority. Assuming then their claim to inherit two portions of His

Anointing, I shall confine myself to the question of their possessing the third likewise: not however with a view of proving it, but rather of removing such antecedent difficulties as are likely to prejudice the mind against it.

By a Priest, in a Christian sense, is meant an appointed channel by which the peculiar Gospel blessings are conveyed to mankind, one who has power to apply to individuals those gifts which Christ has promised us generally as the fruit of His mediation. This power was possessed by the Apostles; I am now to show that it is possessed by their successors likewise.

1. Now, first, that there is a strong line of distinction between the Apostles and other Christian Ministers, I readily grant; nay, rather I would maintain it to be so clearly marked that there is no possibility of confusing together those respects in which they resemble with those in which they differ from their brethren. The Apostles were not only Ministers of Christ, but first founders of His Church; and their gifts and offices, so far forth as they had reference to this part of their commission, doubtless were but occasional and extraordinary, and ended with themselves. They were organs of Revelation, inspired Teachers, in some respects infallible, gifted with divers tongues, workers of miracles; and none but they are such. The duration of any gift depends upon the need which it supplies; that which has answered its purpose ends, that which is still necessary is graciously continued. Such at least seems to be the rule of a Merciful Providence. Therefore it is, that the Christian Ministry still includes in it the office of teaching, for education is necessary for every soul born into the world; and the office of governing, for "decency and order" are still necessary for the quiet and union of the Christian brotherhood. And, for the same reason, it is natural at first sight to suppose that the office of applying the gifts of grace should be continued also, while there is guilt to be washed away, sinners to be reconciled, believers to be strengthened, matured, comforted. What warrant have we from the nature of the case, for making any distinction between the ministry of teaching and the ministry of reconciliation? if one is still committed to us, why not the other also?

And it will be observed, that the only real antecedent difficulty which attaches to the doctrine of the Christian Priesthood, is obviated by Scripture itself. It might be thought that the power of remitting and retaining sins was too great to be given to sinful man over his fellows; but in matter of fact it was committed to the Apostles without restriction, though they were not infallible in what they did. "*Whose soever* sins ye remit they are remitted unto them; and *whose soever* sins ye retain, they are retained.*"* The grant was in the very form of it unconditional, and left to their Christian discretion. What has once been given, may be continued. I consider this remark to be of weight in a case like the present, where the very nature of the professed gift is the only considerable reason against the fact of its bestowal.

2. But all this is on the bare antecedent view of the case. In fact, our Lord Himself has decided the question, by declaring that His presence, by means of His Apostles, *should* be with the Church to the end of the world. He promised this on the solemn occasion of His leaving them; He declared it when He bade them make converts, baptize, and teach. As well may we doubt whether it is our duty to preach and make proselytes, and prepare men for Heaven, as that His Apostolic Presence is with us, for those purposes. His words then at first sight even go to include *all* the gifts vouchsafed to His first Ministers; far from having a scanty grant of them, so large is the promise, that we are obliged to find out reasons to justify us in considering the Successors of the Apostles in any respects less favoured than themselves. Such reasons we know are to be found, and lead us to distinguish the extraordinary gifts from the ordinary, a distinction which the event justifies; but what is there either in Scripture or in Church History to make us place the commission of reconciliation among those which are extraordinary?

3. In the next place, it is deserving of notice that this distinction between ordinary and extraordinary gifts, is really made in Scripture itself, and that among the extraordinary there is no mention made of the sacerdotal power. No one can

doubt, that on the day of Pentecost the formal inauguration of the Apostles took place into their high and singular office of building the Church of Christ. They were "wise Master-builders, according to the grace given them"; and that grace was extraordinary. However, among those gifts, "tongues and visions, prophecies and wonders," their priestly power is not enumerated. On the contrary, that power had been previously conferred, according to the passage already cited, when Christ breathed on them, and gave them, through the Holy Ghost, the authority to remit and retain sins [Note 3]. And further, I would remind you, that this is certainly our Church's deliberate view of the subject: for she expressly puts into the Bishop's mouth at ordination the very words here used by our Saviour to His Apostles. "Receive the Holy Ghost"; "Whose soever sins ye remit, they are remitted to them; and whose soever sins ye retain, they are retained"; words, which it were inexpressibly profane for man to use to man, except by a plain divine commission to do so.

4. But again, has not the Gospel Sacraments? and have not Sacraments, as pledges and means of grace, a priestly nature? If so, the question of the existence of a Christian Priesthood is narrowed at once to the simple question whether it is or is not probable that so precious an ordinance as a channel of grace would be committed by Providence to the custody of certain guardians. The tendency of opinions at this day is to believe that nothing more is necessary for acceptance than faith in God's promise of mercy; whereas it is certain from Scripture, that the gift of reconciliation is not conveyed to individuals except through appointed ordinances. Christ has interposed something between Himself and the soul; and if it is not inconsistent with the liberty of the Gospel that a Sacrament should interfere, there is no antecedent inconsistency in a keeper of the Sacrament attending upon it. Moreover, the very circumstance that a standing Ministry has existed from the first, leads on to the inference that that Ministry was intended to take charge of the Sacraments; and thus the facts of the case suggest an interpretation of our Lord's memorable words, when He committed to St. Peter "the *keys* of the Kingdom of Heaven."

I would have this Scripture truth considered attentively; viz. that Sacraments are the channels of the peculiar Christian privileges, and not merely (as many men think, and as the rite of Confirmation really is) *seals* of the covenant. A man may object, indeed, that in St. Paul's Epistle to the Romans nothing is said about channels and instruments; that faith is represented as the sole medium of justification. But I will refer him, by way of reply, to the same Apostle's speech to Festus and Agrippa, where he describes Christ as saying to him on his miraculous conversion, "Rise and stand upon thy feet; for I have appeared unto thee for this purpose, to make thee a Minister and a Witness," sending him forth, as it might appear, to preach the Gospel, without instrumentality of Ordinance or Minister. Had we but this account of his conversion, who would not have supposed, that he who was "to open men's eyes, and turn them from darkness to light," had been pardoned and accepted at once upon his faith, without rite or form? Yet from other parts of the history, we learn what is here omitted, viz. that an especial revelation was made to Ananias, lest Saul should go without baptism; and that, so far from his being justified immediately on his faith, he was bid not to tarry, but "to arise and be baptized, and *to wash away his sins* calling on the name of the Lord." [Acts xxvi. 16–18; xxii. 16; ix. 17 (Note 4)] So dangerous is it to attempt to prove a negative from insulated passages of Scripture.

Here then we have a clear instance in St. Paul's own case, that there are priestly Services between the soul and God, even under the Gospel; that though Christ has purchased inestimable blessings for our race, yet that it is still necessary ever to apply them to individuals by visible means; and if so, I confess, that to me at least it seems more likely antecedently, that such services should have, than that they should lack, an appropriate minister. But here again we are not left to mere conjecture, as I proceed to show.

5. You well know that the benefits of the Atonement are frequently represented in Scripture under the figure of spiritual food, bread from heaven, the water that never faileth, and in more sacred language, as the communion of the Body and

Blood of the Divine Sacrifice. Now, this special Christian benefit is there connected, as on the one hand with an outward rite, so on the other with certain appointed Dispensers. So that the very context of Scripture leads us on from the notion of a priestly service to that of a priesthood.

"Who then is that faithful and wise *Steward*," says Christ, "whom his Lord shall make ruler over His household, to give them their *portion of food* in due season? Blessed is that servant, whom his Lord when He cometh shall find so doing." [Luke xii. 43] Now, I infer from this passage; first, that there are, under the Gospel, especial Dispensers of the Christian's spiritual food, in other words (if the word "food" [Note 5] may be interpreted from the parallel of the sixth chapter of St. John), Dispensers of invisible grace, or Priests; – next, that they are to continue to the Church in every age till the end, for it is said, "Blessed is he, whom his Lord, *when He cometh*, shall find so doing;" – further, that the Minister mentioned is also "Ruler over His household," as in the case of the Apostles, uniting the Regal with the Sacerdotal office; – lastly, the word "Steward," which incidentally occurs in the passage, a title applied by St. Paul to the Apostles, affords an additional reason for supposing that other like titles, such as "Ambassadors of Christ," given to the Apostles, do also belong in a true and sufficient sense to their Successors.

6. These considerations in favour of the existence of a Christian Priesthood, are strengthened by observing that the office of intercession, which though not a peculiarity, is ever characteristic of the Priestly Order, is spoken of in Scripture as a sort of prerogative of the Gospel Ministry. For instance, Isaiah, speaking of Christian times, says, "I have set watchmen upon thy walls, O Jerusalem, which shall never hold their peace day nor night. Ye that make mention of the Lord, keep not silence; and give Him no rest, till He establish, and till He make Jerusalem a praise in the earth." [Isa. lxii. 6, 7] In the Acts of the Apostles, we find Christ's ministers engaged in this sacred service, according to the prophecy. "There were in the Church that was at Antioch certain prophets and teachers, as Barnabas, and Simeon called Niger, and Lucius of Cyrene, and

Manaen, foster brother to Herod the Tetrarch, and Saul. As they *ministered* to the Lord, and fasted," [Acts xiii. 1, 2] the Holy Ghost separated two of them for His work. This "ministering" to the Lord with fasting was surely some solemn intercessory service. And this agrees with a passage in St. James's Epistle, which seems to invest the Elders of the Church with this same privilege of the priesthood. "Is any sick among you? Let him call for the Elders of the Church, *and let them pray over him* (not pray *with* him merely), anointing him with oil in the name of the Lord; and *the prayer of faith* (not the oil merely) shall save the sick, and the Lord shall raise him up." In like manner St. Paul speaks of Epaphras as "our dear fellow-servant, who is *for* you," that is, for the Colossians to whom he is writing, "a faithful minister of Christ." Presently he explains what was the service which Epaphras did for them: "always *labouring fervently for you in prayer*, that ye may stand perfect and complete in all the will of God." [James v. 14, 15. Col. i. 7; iv. 12]

7. We may end these remarks by recurring to the instances of St. Peter and St. John the Baptist; who, as types of God's ordained servants, before and after His Son's coming, may serve to explain the office of ordinary Christian Ministers. Even the lowest of them is "greater than John." Now what was it that he wanted? Was it the *knowledge of Gospel doctrine*? No, surely; no words can be clearer than his concerning the New covenant. "Behold the Lamb of God, which taketh away the sin of the world." "He that cometh from above, is above all ... He whom God hath sent speaketh the words of God, for God giveth not the Spirit by measure unto Him. The Father loveth the Son, and hath given all things into His hand. He that believeth on the Son hath everlasting life, and he that believeth not the Son shall not see life, but the wrath of God abideth on him." [John i. 29; iii. 31–36] Therefore, the Baptist lacked not the full Christian *doctrine*; what he did lack was (as he says himself) the Baptism of *the Spirit*, conveying a commission from Christ the Saviour, in all His manifold gifts, ordinary and extraordinary, Regal and Sacerdotal. John was not inferior to us Gospel Ministers in knowledge, but in power.

On the other hand, if, as I have made appear, St. Peter's ministerial office continues as regards ordinary purposes, in the persons of those who come after him, we are bound to understand our Lord's blessing, pronounced in the first instance upon him, as descending in due measure on the least of us His ministers who "keep the faith," Peter being but the representative and type of them all. "Blessed art thou, Simon Barjona; for flesh and blood hath not revealed it unto thee, but My Father, which is in heaven. And I say also unto thee, that thou art Peter, and upon this rock I will build My Church, and the gates of hell shall not prevail against it. And I will give unto thee the keys of the Kingdom of Heaven; and whatsoever thou shalt bind on earth shall be bound in heaven, and whatsoever thou shalt loose on earth shall be loosed in heaven." August and glorious promise! Can it be, that it is all expended on St. Peter, how great soever that noble Apostle? Is it inserted in the "everlasting Gospel," to witness merely of one long since departed? Is it the practice of the inspired word to exalt individuals? Does not the very exuberance of the blessing resist any such niggardly use of it? Does it not flow over in spite of us, till our unbelief is vanquished by the graciousness of Him who spoke it? Is it, in short, anything but the prejudices of education, which prevent so many of us from receiving it in that fulness of grace in which it was poured out?

I say our *prejudices*, – for these surely are the cause of our inconsistency in faith; adopting, as we do, a rule of Scripture interpretation, which carries us a certain way, and stops short of the whole counsel of God, and should teach us nothing, or a great deal more. If the promises to Christ's Apostles are not fulfilled in the Church for ever after, why should the blessing attaching to the Sacraments extend after the first age? Why should the Lord's Supper be now the Communion of the Lord's Body and Blood? Why should Baptism convey spiritual privileges? Why should any part of Scripture afford permanent instruction? Why should the way of life be any longer narrow? Why should the burden of the Cross be necessary for every disciple of Christ? Why should the Spirit of adoption any longer be promised us? Why should separation from the world be now a duty? Happy indeed it is for men that they *are* inconsistent; for then, though they lose some part of a Christian's faith, at least they keep a portion. This will happen in quiet times, and in the case of those who are of mature years, and whose minds have been long made up on the subject of religion. But should a time of controversy arise, then such inconsistencies become of fearful moment as regards the multitude called Christian, who have not any decided convictions to rest upon. Inconsistency of creed is sure to attract the notice of the intellect, unless habit has reconciled the heart to it. Therefore, in a speculative age, such as our own, a religious education which involves such inconsistency, is most dangerous to the unformed Christian, who will set straight his traditionary creed by unlearning the portion of truth it contains, rather than by adding that in which it is deficient. Hence, the lamentable spectacle, so commonly seen, of men who deny the Apostolic commission proceeding to degrade the Eucharist from a Sacrament to a bare commemorative rite; or to make Baptism such a mere outward form, and sign of profession, as it would be childish or fanciful to revere. And reasonably; for they who think it superstitious to believe that particular persons are channels of grace, are but consistent in denying virtue to particular ordinances. Nor do they stop even here; for denying the grace of baptism, they proceed to deny the doctrine of original sin, for which that grace is the remedy [Note 6]. Further, denying the doctrine of original sin, they necessarily impair the doctrine of the Atonement, and so prepare a way for the denial of our Lord's Divinity. Again, denying the power of the Sacraments on the ground of its *mysteriousness*, demanding from the very text of Scripture the fullest proof of it conceivable, and thinking little of the blessedness of "not seeing, and yet believing," they naturally proceed to object to the doctrine of the Trinity as obstructing and obscuring the simplicity (as they consider it) of the Gospel, and but indirectly deducible from the extant documents of inspiration. Lastly, after they have thus divested the divine remedies of sin, and the treatment necessary for the sinner, of their solemnity and awe, having made the whole scheme of salvation of as intelligible and ordinary a character as the repair of any accident in the works of man, having robbed

Faith of its mysteries, the Sacraments of their virtue, the Priesthood of its commission, no wonder that sin itself is soon considered a venial matter, moral evil as a mere imperfection, man as involved in no great peril or misery, his duties of no very arduous or anxious nature. In a word, religion, as such, is in the way to disappear from the mind altogether; and in its stead a mere cold worldly morality, a decent regard to the claims of society, a cultivation of the benevolent affections, and a gentleness and polish of external deportment, will be supposed to constitute the entire duties of that being, who is conceived in sin, and the child of wrath, is redeemed by the precious blood of the Son of God, is born again and sustained by the Spirit through the invisible strength of Sacraments, and called, through self-denial and sanctification of the inward man, to the Eternal Presence of the Father, Son, and Holy Ghost.

Such is the course and issue of unbelief, though beginning in what the world calls trifles. Beware then, O my Brethren, of entering a way which leads to death. Fear to question what Scripture says of the Ministers of Christ, lest the same perverse spirit lead you on to question its doctrine about Himself and His Father. "Little children, it is the last time; and as ye have heard that Antichrist shall come, even now are there many Antichrists ... They went out from us, but they were not of us." [1 John ii. 18, 19] "Ye shall know them by their fruits." [Matt. vii. 16] If any man come to you, bringing any scoff against the power of Christ's Ministers, ask him what he holds concerning the Sacraments, or concerning the Blessed Trinity; look narrowly after his belief as regards the Atonement, or Original Sin. Ascertain whether he holds with the Church's doctrine in these points; see to it whether at very best he does not try to evade the question, has recourse to explanations, or professes to have no opinion at all upon it. Look to these things, that you may see whither you are invited. Be not robbed of your faith blindfold. Do what you do with a clear understanding of the consequences. And if the arguments which he uses against you tend to show that your present set of opinions is in some measure inconsistent, and force you to see in Scripture more than you do at present, or else less, be not afraid to add to it, rather than to detract from it. Be quite sure that, go as far as you may, you will never, through God's grace, be led to see more in it than the early Christians saw; that, however you enlarge your creed, you will but carry yourselves on to Apostolic perfection, equally removed from the extremes of presumption and of unbelief, neither intruding into things not seen as yet, nor denying, on the other hand, what you cannot see.

Notes

1. The Feast of St. Peter the Apostle.
2. *Vide* Matt. xvi. 18, 19. Luke xxii. 29, 30. John xxi. 15–17.
3. The following passage supplies a corroboration of the above argument, and carries it on to the doctrine of the Apostolical Succession: – "The very first act of the Apostles after Christ was gone out of their sight, was the ordination of Matthias in the room of the traitor Judas. That ordination is related very minutely. Every particular of it is full of instruction; but at present I wish to draw attention to one circumstance more especially: namely, the *time* when it occurred. It was contrived (if one may say so) exactly to fall within *the very short interval* which elapsed between the departure of our Lord, and the arrival of the Comforter in His place: on that 'little while,' during which the Church was comparatively left alone in the world. Then it was that St. Peter rose and declared with authority, that the time was come for supplying the vacancy which Judas had made. 'One,' said he, 'must be ordained;' and without delay they proceeded to the ordination. Of course, St. Peter must have had from our Lord express authority for this step. Otherwise it would seem most natural to defer a transaction so important until the unerring Guide, the Holy Ghost, should have come among them, as they knew He would in a few days. On the other hand, since the Apostles were eminently Apostles of our Incarnate Lord, since their very being, *as* Apostles, depended entirely on their personal mission from Him (which is the reason why catalogues are given of them, with such scrupulous care, in many of the holy books): in that regard one should naturally have expected that He Himself before His departure would have supplied the vacancy by personal designation. But we see it was not His pleasure to do so. As the Apostles afterwards brought on the ordination sooner, so He had deferred it longer than might have been expected. Both ways it should seem as if there were a purpose of bringing the event within those ten days, *during which*, as I said, *the church was left to herself*; left to exercise her faith and hope, much as Christians are left now, without any *miraculous* aid or extraordinary illumination from above. Then, at that moment of the New Testament history in which the circumstances of believers corresponded most nearly to what they have been since miracles and inspiration ceased, – just at that time it pleased

our Lord that a fresh Apostle should be consecrated, with authority and commission as ample as the former enjoyed. In a word, it was His will that the eleven Disciples alone, not Himself personally, should name the successor of Judas; and that they chose the right person, He gave testimony very soon after, by sending His Holy Spirit on St. Matthias, as richly as on St. John, St. James, or St. Peter." – *Tracts for the Times*, vol. ii, No. 52.

4. *Vide* also Acts xiii. 2, 3.

5. [*sitometoion*]

6. *E.g.* A Dissenting Catechism has lately been published in the country for popular use, in which the doctrine of original sin is denied, by way of meeting the charge of cruelty towards children, as involved in the omission of infant baptism.

V

Excerpts from:
The Salvation of the Hearer
the Motive of the Preacher*

When a body of men come into a neighbourhood to them unknown, as we are doing, my brethren, strangers to strangers, and there set themselves down, and raise an altar, and open a school, and invite, or even exhort all men to attend them, it is natural that they who see them, and are drawn to think about them, should ask the question, What brings them hither? Who bids them come? What do they want? What do they preach? What is their warrant? What do they promise? – You have a right, my brethren, to ask the question.

Many, however, will not stop to ask it, as thinking they can answer it without difficulty for themselves. Many there are who would promptly and confidently answer it, according to their own habitual view of things, on their own principles, the principles of the world. The views, the principles, the aims of the world are very definite, are everywhere acknowledged, and are incessantly acted on. They supply an explanation of the conduct of individuals, whoever they be, ready at hand, and so sure to be true in the common run of cases, as to be probable and plausible in any case in particular. When we would account for effects which we see, we of course refer them to causes which we know of. To fancy causes of which we know nothing, is not to account for them at all. The world then naturally and necessarily judges of others by itself. Those who live the life of the world, and act from motives of the world,

---

* Preached at the opening of the Oratory at Alcester Street, Birmingham, on 2 February 1849 and published as Discourse 1 in *Discourses to Mixed Congregations*.

and live and act with those who do the like, as a matter of course ascribe the actions of others, however different they may be from their own, to one or other of the motives which weigh with themselves; for some motive or other they must assign, and they can imagine none but those of which they have experience . . .

My brethren, if these things be so, or rather (for this is the point here), if we, Catholics, firmly believe them to be so, so firmly believe them, that we feel it would be happy for us to die rather than doubt them, is it wonderful, does it require any abstruse explanation, that men minded as we are should come into the midst of a population such as this, and into a neighbourhood where religious error has sway, and where corruption of life prevails both as its cause and as its consequence – a population, not worse indeed than the rest of the world, but not better; not better, because it has not with it the gift of Catholic truth; not purer, because it has not within it that gift of grace which alone can destroy impurity; a population, sinful, I am certain, given to unlawful indulgences, laden with guilt and exposed to eternal ruin, because it is not blessed with that Presence of the Word Incarnate, which diffuses sweetness, and tranquillity, and chastity over the heart; – is it a thing to be marvelled at, that we begin to preach to such a population as this, for which Christ died, and try to convert it to Him and to His Church? Is it necessary to ask for reasons? is it necessary to assign motives of this world, for a proceeding which is so natural in those who believe in the announcements and requirements of the other? My dear brethren, if we are sure that the Most Holy Redeemer has shed His blood for all men, is it not a very plain and simple consequence that we, His servants, His brethren, His priests, should be unwilling to see that blood shed in vain, – wasted I may say, as regards you, and should wish to make you partakers of those benefits which have been vouchsafed to ourselves? Is it necessary for any bystander to call us vain-glorious, or ambitious, or restless, greedy of authority, fond of power, resentful, party-spirited, or the like, when here is so much more powerful, more present, more influential a motive to which our eagerness and zeal may be ascribed? What is so powerful an incentive to preaching as the sure belief that it is the preaching of the truth? What so constrains to the conversion of souls, as the consciousness that they are at present in guilt and in peril? What so great a persuasive to bring men into the Church, as the conviction that it is the special means by which God effects the salvation of those whom the world trains in sin and unbelief? Only admit us to believe what we profess, and surely that is not asking a great deal (for what have we done that we should be distrusted?) – only admit us to believe what we profess, and you will understand without difficulty what we are doing. We come among you, because we believe there is but one way of salvation, marked out from the beginning, and that you are not walking along it; we come among you as ministers of that extraordinary grace of God, which you need; we come among you because we have received a great gift from God ourselves, and wish you to be partakers of our joy; because it is written, "Freely ye have received, freely give"; because we dare not hide in a napkin those mercies, and that grace of God, which have been given us, not for our own sake only, but for the benefit of others.

Such a zeal, poor and feeble though it be in us, has been the very life of the Church, and the breath of her preachers and missionaries in all ages. It was a fire such as this which brought our Lord from heaven, and which He desired, which He travailed, to communicate to all around Him. "I am come to send fire on the earth," He says, "and what will I, but that it be kindled?" Such, too, was the feeling of the great Apostle to whom his Lord appeared in order to impart to him this fire. "I send thee to the Gentiles," He had said to him on his conversion, "to open their eyes, that they may be converted from darkness to light, and from the power of Satan unto God." And, accordingly, he at once began to preach to them, that they should do penance, and turn to God with worthy fruits of penance, "for," as he says, "the charity of Christ constrained him," and he was "made all things to all that he might save all," and he "bore all for the elect's sake, that they might obtain the salvation which is in Christ Jesus, with heavenly glory." Such, too, was the fire of zeal which burned within those preachers, to whom we English owe our Christianity. What brought them from Rome to this distant isle and to a barbarous people, amid many fears, and with much suffering, but the sovereign uncontrollable desire to save the perishing, and to knit the members and slaves of Satan into the body of Christ? This has been the secret of the propagation of the Church from the very first, and will be to the end; this is why the Church, under the grace of God, to the surprise of the world, converts the nations, and why no sect can do the like; this is why Catholic missionaries throw themselves so generously among the fiercest savages, and risk the most cruel torments, as knowing the worth of the soul, as realising the world to come, as loving their brethren dearly, though they never saw them, as shuddering at the thought of the eternal woe, and as desiring to increase the fruit of their Lord's passion, and the triumphs of His grace ...

We come to you in the name of God; we ask no more of you than that you would listen to us; we ask no more than that you would judge for yourselves whether or not we speak God's words; it shall rest with you whether we be God's priests and prophets or no. This is not much to ask, but it is more than most men will grant; they do not dare listen to us, they are impatient through prejudice, or they dread conviction. Yes! many a one there is, who has even good reason to listen to us, nay, on whom we have a claim to be heard, who ought to have a certain trust in us, who yet shuts his ears, and turns away, and chooses to hazard eternity without weighing what we have to say. How frightful is this! but you are not, you cannot be such; we ask not *your* confidence, my brethren, for you have never known us: we are not asking you to take for granted what we say, for we are strangers to you; we do but simply bid you first to consider that you have souls to be saved, and next to judge for yourselves, whether, if God has revealed a religion of His own whereby to save those souls, that religion can be any other than the faith which we preach.

VI

The Infidelity of the Future[*]

It is no common occasion of thankfulness to the Giver of all
good, the Divine Head of the Church, that has led our Rt. Revd.
Father, the Bishop of this Diocese, to call us this morning from
our several homes to this place. It is with no common gladness,
with no ordinary words of rejoicing and congratulations on their
lips, that so many of his priests and of his devout laity have met
him here today in consequence of his invitation. At length this
Seminary is completed and in occupation, which has been for so
long a course of years a vision before his mind, and the subject
of his prayers and exertions. Years and years ago I have heard
him say, that he never could be at rest, till he was enabled by
God's mercy to accomplish this great work, and God has heard
his persevering prayers and blessed his unwearied exertions. I
might say with truth, that even before some of you, my dear
Brethren, were born, or at least from the time that you were in
your cradles, he, as the chief Pastor of this diocese, when as yet
you knew him not, has been engaged in that great undertaking,
of which you, by God's inscrutable grace, enjoy the benefits
without your own labours.

It is indeed a great event in this diocese, a great event, I may
say, in the history of English Catholics, that at length the
injunctions of Ecumenical Councils, the tradition of the
Church, the desire of the Sovereign Pontiff, are fulfilled
among us, and the Bishop's Throne is erected not merely in a
dwelling of brick or stone, in the midst of those in whom
Christ is to be formed by his teaching, that they in turn may be
the edification and light and strength of the generation which is
to come after him.

---

[*] The occasion of the preaching of this sermon was the opening of St
Bernard's Seminary, Olton (near Birmingham), 2 October 1873.

This handing down of the truth from generation to generation is obviously the direct reason for the institution of seminaries for the education of the clergy. Christianity is one religious idea. Superhuman in its origin, it differs from all other religions. As man differs from quadruped, bird or reptile, so does Christianity differ from the superstitions, heresies, and philosophies which are around it. It has a theology and an ethical system of its own. This is its indestructible idea. How are we to secure and perpetuate in this world that gift from above? How are we to preserve to the Christian people this gift, so special, so divine, so easily hid or lost amid the imposing falsehoods with which the world abounds?

The divine provision is as follows. Each circle of Christians has its own priest, who is the representative of the divine idea to that circle in its theological and ethical aspects. He teaches his people, he catechizes their children, bringing them one and all into that form of doctrine, which is his own. But the Church is made up of many such circles. How are we to secure that they may all speak one and the same doctrine? and that the doctrine of the Apostles? Thus: by the rule that their respective priests should in their turn all be taught from one and the same centre, viz. their common Father, the Bishop of the diocese. They are educated in one school, that is, in one seminary; under the rule, by the voice and example of him who is the One Pastor of all those collections or circles of Christians, of whom they all in time to come are to be the teachers. Catholic doctrine, Catholic morals, Catholic worship and discipline, the Christian character, life, and conduct, all that is necessary for being a good priest, they learn one and all from this religious school, which is the appointed preparation for the ministerial offices. As youths are prepared for their secular calling by schools and teachers who teach what their calling requires, as there are classical schools, commercial schools, teachers for each profession, teachers of the several arts and sciences, so the sacred ministers of the Church are made true representatives of their Bishop when they are appointed to the charge of the Christian people, because they come from one centre of education and from the tutelage of one head.

Hence it is that St. Ignatius, the Martyr Bishop of Antioch, in the first century of the Church, speaking of the ecclesiastical hierarchy, comparing the union of the sacred orders with the Bishop, likens it to a harp which is in perfect tune. He says in his Epistle to the Ephesians, "It becomes you to concur in the mind of your Bishop, as indeed you do. For your estimable body of clergy, worthy of God, is in exact harmony with your Bishop, as the strings to the harp. Hence it is that in your unanimity and concordant charity Jesus Christ is sung. And one by one you take your parts in the choir, so as to sing with one voice through Jesus Christ to the Father that He may hear your petitions" (ad Eph. 4).

And if at all times this simple unity, this perfect understanding of the members with the Head, is necessary for the healthy action of the Church, especially is it necessary in these perilous times. I know that all times are perilous, and that in every time serious and anxious minds, alive to the honour of God and the needs of man, are apt to consider no times so perilous as their own. At all times the enemy of souls assaults with fury the Church which is their true Mother, and at least threatens and frightens when he fails in doing mischief. And all times have their special trials which others have not. And so far I will admit that there were certain specific dangers to Christians at certain other times, which do not exist in this time. Doubtless, but still admitting this, still I think that the trials which lie before us are such as would appal and make dizzy even such courageous hearts as St. Athanasius, St. Gregory I, or St. Gregory VII. And they would confess that dark as the prospect of their own day was to them severally, ours has a darkness different in kind from any that has been before it.

The special peril of the time before us is the spread of that plague of infidelity, that the Apostles and our Lord Himself have predicted as the worst calamity of the last times of the Church. And at least a shadow, a typical image of the last times is coming over the world. I do not mean to presume to say that this is the last time, but that it has had the evil prerogative of being like that more terrible season, when it is said that the elect themselves will be in danger of falling away.

This applies to all Christians in the world, but it concerns me at this moment, speaking to you, my dear Brethren, who are being educated for our own priesthood, to see how it is likely to be fulfilled in this country.

1. And first [Note 1] it is obvious that while the various religious bodies and sects which surround us according to God's permission have done untold harm to the cause of Catholic truth in their opposition to us, they have hitherto been of great service to us in shielding and sheltering us from the assaults of those who believed less than themselves or nothing at all. To take one instance, the approved miracles of the Saints are not more wonderful than the miracles of the Bible. Now the Church of England, the Wesleyans, the Dissenters, nay the Unitarians have defended the miracles of the Bible and thereby have given an indirect protection to the miracles of ecclesiastical history. Nay, some of their divines have maintained certain ecclesiastical miracles, as the appearance of the Cross to Constantine, the subterranean fire in Julian's attempt to build the Jewish Temple, etc. And so again the doctrines of the Holy Trinity, the Incarnation, Atonement, etc., though as strange to the reason as those Catholic doctrines which they reject, have been held by many of these bodies with more or less distinctness, and thereby we have been unassailed when we have taught them. But in these years before us it will be much if those outlying bodies are able to defend their own dogmatic professions. Most of them, nearly all of them, already give signs of the pestilence having appeared among them. And as time goes on, when there will be a crisis and a turning point, with each of them, then it will be found that, instead of their position being in any sense a defence for us, it will be found in possession of the enemy. A remnant indeed may be faithful to their light, as the great Novatian body stood by the Catholics and suffered with them during the Arian troubles, but we shall in vain look for that safeguard from what may be called the orthodoxy of these Protestant communions, which we have hitherto profited by.

2. Again another disadvantage to us will arise from our very growth in numbers and influence in this country. The Catholic Religion, when it has a free course, always must be a power in a country. This is the mere consequence of its divine origin. While Catholics were few and oppressed by disabilities, they were suffered and were at peace. But now that those disabilities are taken off and Catholics are increasing in number, it is impossible that they should not come in collision with the opinions, the prejudices, the objects of a Protestant country, and that without fault on any side, except that the country is Protestant. Neither party will understand the other, and then the old grievances in history which this country has against Rome will be revived and operate to our disadvantage. It is true that this age is far more gentle, kind and generous than former ages, and Englishmen, in their ordinary state, are not cruel, but they may easily be led to believe that their generosity may be abused on our part, that they were unwise in liberating those who are in fact their mortal enemies. And this general feeling of fear of us may be such as, even with a show of reason, to turn against us even generous minds, so that from no fault of ours, but from the natural antagonism of a religion which cannot change with the new political states into which the whole world is gradually moulding itself, may place us in temporal difficulties, of which at present we have no anticipation.

And it cannot be denied that there is just now threatening the political world such a calamity. There are many influential men who think that things are not indeed ripe as yet for such a measure, but who look forward to the times, when whether the one or the other great political party in the State may make it their cry at the elections of a new Parliament, that they propose to lessen the influence of Catholics and circumscribe their privileges. And however this may be, two things, I think, are plain, that we shall become more and more objects of distrust to the nation at large, and that our Bishops and Priests will be associated in the minds of men with the political acts of foreign Catholics, and be regarded as members of one extended party in all countries, the enemies, as will be thought, of civil liberty and of national progress. In this way we may suffer disadvantages which have not weighed upon the Catholic Church since the age of Constantine.

3. I repeat, when Catholics are a small body in a country, they cannot easily become a mark for their enemies, but our prospect in this time before us is that we shall be so large that our concerns cannot be hid, and at the same time so unprotected that we cannot but suffer. No large body can be free from scandals from the misconduct of its members. In medieval times the Church had its courts in which it investigated and set right what was wrong, and that without the world knowing much about it. Now the state of things is the very reverse. With a whole population able to read, with cheap newspapers day by day conveying the news of every court, great and small to every home or even cottage, it is plain that we are at the mercy of even one unworthy member or false brother. It is true that the laws of libel are a great protection to us as to others. But the last few years have shown us what harm can be done us by the mere infirmities, not so much as the sins, of one or two weak minds. There is an immense store of curiosity directed upon us in this country, and in great measure an unkind, a malicious curiosity. If there ever was a time when one priest will be a spectacle to men and angels it is in the age now opening upon us.

4. Nor is this all. This general intelligence of every class of society, general but shallow, is the means of circulating all through the population all the misrepresentations which the enemies of the Church make of her faith and her teaching. Most falsehoods have some truth in them; at least those falsehoods which are perversions of the truth are the most successful. Again, when there is no falsehood, yet you know how strange truth may appear to minds unfamiliar with it. You know that the true religion must be full of mysteries – and therefore to Catholicism, if to any profession, any body of men at all, applies the proverb that a fool may ask a hundred questions which a wise man cannot answer. It is scarcely possible so to answer inquiries or objections on a great number of points of our faith or practice, as to be intelligible or

persuasive to them. And hence the popular antipathy to Catholicism seems, and will seem more and more, to be based upon reason, or common sense, so that first the charge will seem to all classes of men true that the Church stifles the reason of man, and next that, since it is impossible for educated men, such as her priests, to believe what is so opposite to reason, they must be hypocrites, professing what in their hearts they reject.

5. I have more to say on this subject. There are, after all, real difficulties in Revealed Religion. There are questions, in answer to which we can only say, "I do not know." There are arguments which cannot be met satisfactorily, from the nature of the case – because our minds, which can easily enough understand the objections, are not in their present state able to receive the true answer. Nay, human language perhaps has not words to express it in. Or again, perhaps the right answer is possible, and is set down in your books of theology, and you know it. But things look very different in the abstract and the concrete. You come into the world, and fall in with the living objector and inquirer, and your answer you find scattered to the winds. The objection comes to you now with the force of a living expositor of it, recommended by the earnestness and sincerity with which he holds it, with his simple conviction of its strength and accompanied by all the collateral or antecedent probabilities, which he heaps around it. You are not prepared for his objection being part of a system of thought, each part of which bears one way and supports the other parts. And he will appeal to any number of men, friends or others, who agree with him, and they each will appeal to him and all the rest to the effect that the Catholic view and arguments simply cannot be supported. Perhaps the little effect you produce by the arguments which you have been taught is such that you are quite disheartened and despond.

6. I am speaking of evils, which in their intensity and breadth are peculiar to these times. But I have not yet spoken of the root of all these falsehoods – the root as it ever has been, but hidden; but in this age exposed to view and unblushingly

avowed – I mean, that spirit of infidelity itself which I began by referring to as the great evil of our times, though of course when I spoke of the practical force of the objections which we constantly hear and shall hear made to Christianity, I showed it is from this spirit that they gain their plausibility. The elementary proposition of this new philosophy which is now so threatening is this – that in all things we must go by reason, in nothing by faith, that things are known and are to be received so far as they can be proved. Its advocates say, all other knowledge has proof – why should religion be an exception? And the mode of proof is to advance from what we know to what we do not know, from sensible and tangible facts to sound conclusions. The world pursued the way of faith as regards physical nature, and what came of it? Why, that till three hundred years ago they believed, because it was the tradition, that the heavenly bodies were fixed in solid crystalline spheres and moved round the earth in the course of twenty-four hours. Why should not that method which has done so much in physics, avail also as regards that higher knowledge which the world has believed it had gained through revelation? There is no revelation from above. There is no exercise of faith. Seeing and proving is the only ground for believing. They go on to say, that since proof admits of degrees, a demonstration can hardly be had except in mathematics; we never can have simple knowledge; truths are only probably such. So that faith is a mistake in two ways. First, because it usurps the place of reason, and secondly because it implies an absolute assent to doctrines, and is dogmatic, which absolute assent is irrational. Accordingly you will find, certainly in the future, nay more, even now, even now, that the writers and thinkers of the day do not even believe there is a God. They do not believe either the object – a God personal, a Providence and a moral Governor; and secondly, what they do believe, viz. that there is some first cause or other, they do not believe with faith, absolutely, but as a probability.

You will say that their theories have been in the world and are no new thing. No. Individuals have put them forth, but they have not been current and popular ideas. Christianity has never yet had experience of a world simply irreligious. Perhaps China may be an exception. We do not know enough about it to speak, but consider what the Roman and Greek world was when Christianity appeared. It was full of superstition, not of infidelity. There was much unbelief in all as regards their mythology, and in every educated man, as to eternal punishment. But there was no casting off the idea of religion, and of unseen powers who governed the world. When they spoke of Fate, even here they considered that there was a great moral governance of the world carried on by fated laws. Their first principles were the same as ours. Even among the sceptics of Athens, St. Paul could appeal to the Unknown God. Even to the ignorant populace of Lystra he could speak of the living God who did them good from heaven. And so when the northern barbarians came down at a later age, they, amid all their superstitions, were believers in an unseen Providence and in the moral law. But we are now coming to a time when the world does not acknowledge our first principles. Of course I do not deny that, as in the revolted kingdom of Israel, there will be a remnant. The history of Elias is here a great consolation for us, for he was told from heaven that even in that time of idolatrous apostasy, there were seven thousand men who had not bowed their knees to Baal. Much more it may be expected now, when our Lord has come and the Gospel been preached to the whole world, that there will be a remnant who belong to the soul of the Church, though their eyes are not opened to acknowledge her who is their true Mother. But I speak first of the educated world, scientific, literary, political, professional, artistic – and next of the mass of town population, the two great classes on which the fortunes of England are turning: the thinking, speaking and acting England. My Brethren, you are coming into a world, if present appearances do not deceive, such as priests never came into before, that is, so far forth as you do go into it, so far as you go beyond your flocks, and so far as those flocks may be in great danger as under the influence of the prevailing epidemic.

That the discipline of a seminary is just that which is suited to meet the present state of things, it does not become me to attempt to suggest to you now—you, who have so much better, and so much more authoritative advisers—but I may be allowed perhaps to follow up what I have said to such conclusions as it seems to point to.

1. A seminary is the only true guarantee for the creation of the ecclesiastical spirit. And this is the primary and true weapon for meeting the age, not controversy. Of course every Catholic should have an intelligent appreciation of his religion, as St. Peter says, but still controversy is not the instrument by which the world is to be resisted and overcome. And this we shall see if we study that epistle, which comes with an authority of its own, as being put by the Holy Spirit into the mouth of him who was the chief of the Apostles. What he addresses to all Christians, is especially suitable for priests. Indeed he wrote it at a time when the duties of one and the other, as against the heathen world, were the same. In the first place he reminds them of what they really were as Christians, and surely we should take these words as belonging especially to us ecclesiastics. "You are a chosen generation, a kingly priesthood, a holy nation, a purchased people ..." (1 Pet. ii. 9).

In this ecclesiastical spirit, I will but mention a spirit of seriousness or recollection. We must gain the habit of feeling that we are in God's presence, that He sees what we are doing; and a liking that He does so, a love of knowing it, a delight in the reflection, "Thou, God, seest me." A priest who feels this deeply will never misbehave himself in mixed society. It will keep him from over-familiarity with any of his people; it will keep him from too many words, from imprudent or unwise speaking; it will teach him to rule his thoughts. It will be a principle of detachment between him and even his own people; for he who is accustomed to lean on the Unseen God, will never be able really to attach himself to any of His creatures. And thus an elevation of mind will be created, which is the true weapon which he must use against the infidelity of the world. (Hence, what St. Peter says: 1, ii, 12, 15; iii, 16.) Now this I consider to be the true weapon by which the infidelity of the world is to be met.

2. And next, most important in the same warfare, and here too you will see how it is connected with a Seminary, is a sound, accurate, complete knowledge of Catholic theology. This, though it is not controversial, is the best weapon (after a good life) in controversy. Any child, well instructed in the catechism, is, without intending it, a real missioner. And why? Because the world is full of doubtings and uncertainty, and of inconsistent doctrine – a clear consistent idea of revealed truth, on the contrary, cannot be found outside of the Catholic Church. Consistency, completeness, is a persuasive argument for a system being true. Certainly if it be inconsistent, it is not truth. [Note 2]

Notes

(adapted from those provided for the first published edition of this sermon by Fr C. Stephen Dessain)

1. In the manuscript there is a note "about Infidelity first."
2. [Summary on the last page of the manuscript]
   1 Infidelity – induction.
      Why not by science? – if not science, so much the worse for religious probability –
   2 A persecuting infidelity, because it is pure
   3 Fear
      1. Here our very growth is against us.
         It begins to fear us. Englishmen are cruel when they are frightened.
      2. Toleration is only when we go half way.
   4 Hitherto Anglicans, etc., have acted as a shelter, but this is going.
   5 Cheap publications – popular arguments
   6 And stories against Catholicism and scandals.

VII

The Tree Besides the Waters*

*"He shall be like a tree which is planted near the running
waters, which shall bring forth its fruit in due season. And his
leaf shall not fall off; and all whatever he shall do shall
prosper." Psalm i. 3*

Among the many images under which the good man is
described in Holy Scripture, perhaps there is none more vivid,
more beautiful, and more touching than that which represents
him as some favoured and thriving tree in the garden of God's
planting. Our original birth-place and home was a garden; and
the trees which Adam had to dress and keep, both in
themselves and by the sort of attention they demanded,
reminded him of the peaceful happy duties and the innocent
enjoyments which were the business of his life. A garden, in
its perennial freshness and its soothing calm, is the best type of
heaven, and its separate plants and flowers are the exactest
types of the inhabitants of heaven. Accordingly it is introduced
into the last page of Scripture as well as into the first; it makes
its appearance at the conclusion of man's eventful history as in
the record of its opening. As in the beginning we read of the
Paradise of pleasure, with the great river and its four separate
streams, with all manner of trees, fair to behold and pleasant
to eat of, and, above all, the Tree of Life, – so, in the last
chapter of the Apocalypse, we are told of the river of water of
life, clear as crystal, proceeding from the throne of God and of
the Lamb, which he that thirsteth may drink freely; and of the
Tree of Life, bearing twelve fruits, the leaves of which were
for the healing of the nations.

---

* Preached Nov. 11, 1859, in St. Mary's, Oscott, at the Funeral of the
Right Rev. H. Weedall, D.D.

And, in like manner, when we turn to that portion of the sacred volume which more than any other both reveals and supports the hidden life of the servants of God in every age, – I mean the Psalter, – we find, prefixed to the collection, the Psalm from which my Text is taken, in which the obedient and just man is set before us under the self-same image; under the image of some choice specimen of the vegetable world, that innocent portion of the divine handiwork which is deformed by no fierce passions, which has no will and pursues no end of its own, and which seems created only to please the eye of man, and to be his food, medicine, and refreshment:

Blessed is the man who hath not walked in the counsel of the ungodly, nor stood in the way of sinners, nor sat in the chair of pestilence: but his will is in the law of the Lord, and in His law he shall meditate day and night.
And he shall be like a tree which is planted near the running waters, which shall bring forth its fruit in due season. And his leaf shall not fall off; and all whatsoever he shall do shall prosper.

This spiritual plant of God is placed by the running waters; it is nourished and recruited by the never-failing, the perpetual, the daily and hourly supply of their wholesome influences. It grows up gradually, silently, without observation; and in proportion as it rises aloft, so do its roots, with still less observation, strike deep into the earth. Thus it determinately takes up its habitation in one place, from which death alone shall part it. Year after year it grows more and more into the hope and the posture of a glorious immobility and unchangeableness. What it has been, that it shall be; if it changes, it is as growing into fruitfulness, and maturing in its fruit's abundance and perfection. Nor is that fruit lost; it neither withers upon the branches nor decays upon the ground. Angels unseen gather crop after crop from the unwearied never-failing parent, and carefully store them up in heavenly treasure-houses. Its very leaf remains green to the end; not only its fruit, which is profitable for eternal life, but its very foliage, the ordinary dress in which it meets our senses, its beautiful colouring, its rich yet delicate fulness of proportion, the graceful waving of its boughs, the musical whispers and rustlings of its leaves, the fragrance which it exhales, the refreshment which it spreads around it, – all testify to that majestic, serene beneficence which is its very nature, and to a mysterious depth of life which enables it ever to give out virtue, yet never to have less of it within.

Such is the holy servant of God, considered in that condition which is both his special reward and his ordinary lot. There are those, indeed, who, for the good of their brethren, and according to the will of God, are exercised by extraordinary trials, and pass their lives amid turbulence and change. There are others, again, who are wonderfully called out of error or of sin, and have experience of much conflict within or without them before they reach the heavenly river, and the groves which line its banks. Certainly history speaks much more of martyrdom and confessorship on the one hand, and of inquiry and conversion, of sin and repentance, on the other, than of the tranquil Christian course; but history does but give the surface of what actually takes place in the heavenly kingdom. If we would really bring before us what is both the highest blessedness in God's service, and also in fact the ordinary portion of good men, we shall find it to consist in what from its very nature cannot make much show in history; – in a life barren of great events, and rich in small ones; in a life of routine duties, of happy obscurity and inward peace, of an orderly dispensing of good to others who come within their influence, morning and evening, of a growth and blossoming and bearing fruit in the house of God, and of a blessed death in the presence of their brethren. Such has been the round of days of many a pastor up and down Christendom, as even history has recorded, of many a missioner, of many a monk, of many a religious woman, of many a father or mother of a family, of many a student in sacred or profane literature, – each the centre of his own circle, and the teacher of his own people, though more or less unknown to the world. This had been the blessedness of holy Job, as he sets it before us himself: "I said, I shall die in my nest, and as a palm-tree shall multiply my days. My root is opened beside the waters, and dew shall continue in my harvest. They that heard me ... to my words durst add nothing, and my speech dropped upon them. They waited for me as for rain, and they opened their mouth as for a latter shower." [Job xxix. 18–23] It is expressed also in the words of the Canticle, which, though belonging in their fulness to our Lord Himself, yet in their measure apply to the benefits which any holy man extends to those who are within the range of his attraction: "As the apple-tree among the trees of the woods, so is my beloved among the sons. I sat down under his shadow whom I desired, and his fruit was sweet to my mouth."

I have said that the servant of God resembles a tree, not only in his graciousness, his fruitfulness, and his repose, but also in his immobility. This is a point which may be suitably enlarged upon. Like a tree, he is confined to one place, and his duties lie at home; at home he is prized; he is the blessing and the pride of his own neighbourhood or circle; but his name will be little known beyond it, much less has he a world-wide reputation. Christendom is divided into a great number of districts, each with its own character and interests; each has its own indigenous saints; each has its own patrons, its holy men, its benefactors, its patterns. Each region or province has those within it to whom it has given birth, and who in time become its teachers; who form its traditions, mould its character, and thereby separate and discriminate it from other regions. And thus it is that each part of the Catholic Church has excellences of its own which other parts have not, and is as distinct from the rest in genius and in temper as it is in place.

It is true, indeed, that in a certain sense local differences are unknown in that Religion which comes from God. What it is in one place, such it is in another, and ever must be so. The very name of Catholic is contrasted with local, and precludes any variation in revealed truth wherever it is found. This is undeniable; and St. Paul insists upon it. Christianity, he says, has destroyed all distinction of a national, or family, or party nature. He reminds us that we are citizens of one city, and partakers of one and the same new nature; and that, when old things passed away, local interests and ideas went away among them. "As many of you," he says, "as have been baptized in Christ, have put on *Christ*." There is neither Jew nor Gentile, barbarian nor Scythian, bond nor free, male nor female; "for you are all one in Christ Jesus." [Gal. iii. 27, 28. Col. iii. 11] This certainly is never to be forgotten; but it is in nowise inconsistent with the peculiarity on which I wish to insist. If St. Peter, who is the very witness and foundation of unity, has placed himself at Rome for ever, instead of wandering from kingdom to kingdom and from city to city, if he has thus given local, nay almost national attributes to the Holy See, we may be sure that there is nothing judaical, or otherwise secular or carnal, if we throw ourselves heartily and with a special warmth of attachment upon the country or the place in which we personally find ourselves, drink in its particular spirit, and glory in the characteristic tokens of a Divine Presence which have been bestowed upon it. There is nothing surely contrary to the strictest evangelical purity, and the firmest maintenance of the principles of Catholicity, and the most loyal devotion to the See of St. Peter, though we gather about us our own traditions, and sit under their shadow, and delight in their fruit; nothing unbecoming, if in this country, in England, and in this part of England, which in some sense has been the heart and centre of the ancient faith, where there have been so many old Catholic families, where there are so many religious institutions, where the sacred fire has been tended and nourished in evil times so assiduously, and whence in an especial manner it has in late years burst forth again and spread far and wide, – I say, there is nothing unseemly, – least of all within these walls, and amid these most solemn and affecting duties, and on this rare occasion, – there is nothing surely strange, nothing that demands excuse, if we remind ourselves, each in his own heart, and with an appeal to each other, of what has been the aspect which the Church has worn in these parts, what are the peculiar graces which have here been given to her children, what he was, of whom we have been just now bereaved, and whose last rites have brought us together, and how he contributed to make the mind of this diocese what we find it to be.

There is but one consideration, my Reverend Brethren, which makes such a line of thought unsuitable on this occasion; and that is, the consideration of the person who is bringing it before you. There is no need to say that I feel deeply, what every one here must understand quite well, that I am not the person who has any right, or any power, to refer back to the history of Catholicism in these parts, or to attempt to trace the connexion of the dear and venerated priest, of whom we are now taking leave, with that history. I can scarcely do more than remind you that there *is* such a characteristic history, and that there *is* such an intimate connexion; and I leave it to you individually, by your vivid recollection and actual experience of the past and present state of the diocese, to give a meaning to my words fuller than my own. Nay, putting aside his relation to things and persons about him, not even in his own personal character can I worthily describe the man whom I so much loved and so much admired; for it is plain that, however kind he was to me and mine, and whatever confidence he gave us, still I have never lived nor worked with him, I have never been partner in his anxieties, I have never witnessed his daily life, and am unable, except in that external aspect which is presented to a stranger, to record his virtues and his good works. And further still, who can understand, who can undertake to describe, the excellences of a holy man, except one who in good measure partakes of them, and can by sympathy enter into the spirit by which his words and his deeds have been governed? It is said in the lesson of the Office for St. Bonaventure's day, that when St. Thomas found him writing the life of St. Francis, he observed, "Suffer a saint to minister to a saint"; and what is true of sanctity in those highest measures, by which upon death it merits at once the heavenly crown, is true of it in all its manifestations. As well might a man who could not read attempt to estimate some literary labour, or a man without an ear attempt to judge of music, as they presume to speak of a holy servant of God, who had not themselves that key to his thoughts and his motives which sanctity like his alone can give.

But further, even putting aside this serious consideration, after all, who among us has the power to speak of any man in the presence of his friends, without paining them by the insufficient estimate which they are sure to feel that we are taking of him? Those who have known another long, who are familiar with definite aspects of his character, with special passages of his life, with the trials which have brought him out, or the unostentatious graces which have at all times adorned him, – such persons are naturally disappointed with any account which does not do justice to their own true, though it may be their private and particular, view of him; just as intimate friends are never satisfied, or at least, are never one and all satisfied, with any portrait of him, however faithful it may be in the judgment of strangers. All that I can say for my own encouragement, in speaking to you, my Reverend Brethren, in such disadvantageous circumstances, is this: – first, that his Lordship would not have asked me in his own and your name to undertake duties, which I was not likely on the whole to discharge in a manner honourable and reverential to the memory of our common friend; and next, that an external judgment, such as mine must be, is sometimes useful, whether by confirming the view which would be taken by friends, or by contributing something additional to their testimony. These considerations are my support in the duty which has been laid upon me.

The Right Reverend Dr. Weedall, the friend whom we have lost, was born September 6th, 1788 [Note 1]. He was left an orphan a few years after his birth; and at the early age of six he was sent to the school of Sedgley Park, at that time consisting of about one hundred and thirty boys, under the presidency of Dr. Kirk, a little more than thirty years after its first establishment. The history of that important place of education has been lately given to the public by a writer especially qualified for the work [Note 2]; and there is no one, I may say, who has followed his graphic narratives and his minute investigations with deeper interest and respect than myself. There is something, to my mind, exceedingly touching in watching the work of God in its silent and humble beginnings. He who is the highest, is never more awful than when He condescends to be lowest; and when I read the unpretending account, to which I am referring, of the ordinary lowly toil, the homely life, and the simple amusements of the good and faithful men who began and carried out that work amid the contempt or neglect of the world, I am drawn by an irresistible sympathy to venerate the spot on which they laboured, as if the patriarch's ladder rested upon it, and Angels were thither descending and thence ascending between earth and heaven.

To this place came Henry Weedall, on the 11th of December, 1794; and if a person could be named, whom, from knowing in age, we could fancy we had seen in the simplicity and bloom of early boyhood, it would be he. I seem to be able to picture to myself an innocent child of six years old, attracting the hundred inquisitive eyes of his new companions by the refinement and delicacy of his appearance [Note 3]. He was asked a number of questions, as is usual with fresh-comers to a school; and among other accomplishments of the child, it was found that he could sing. I wish I could relate, without a familiarity unsuitable to this place and occasion, what occurred, as it has been handed down to us in the words of a priest who, much older than our friend, was then preparing for holy orders in the house. It seems to me a type of himself, and beautifully prophetic of his whole life: it was as if his Guardian Angel on that occasion took his place, and sang the destiny of sixty-five coming years, his calm duties, and the cheerful, gentle, guileless spirit with which he met them. In a sweet voice he began a song known to us all, the substance of which is a resolve and an engagement to put aside care for ever, and be happy and joyful under all circumstances, and to make all persons about us happy and cheerful as ourselves. It is no wonder that his appearance, his manners, and his ways drew all our hearts to him: we are told that he soon became a universal favourite in the school [Note 4].

From Sedgley Park he was removed [Note 5], in June, 1804, to old Oscott College, where he received his education for the priesthood [Note 6]. This occupied close upon ten years. At the age of twenty-four, on the 26th of May, 1812, he was ordained sub-deacon; on the 15th of April following, deacon; and priest on the 6th of April, 1814. During the first years of his priesthood, he was accustomed on Sundays to come into Birmingham, and to catechise at St. Chad's small chapel as an assistant to the well-known clergyman who held the mission. He soon gained reputation as a preacher, the personal gifts, which we all recollect so well, fitting him especially for the office; and he was often selected to fill the pulpit on special occasions [Note 7].

In course of time he became Vice-president of the College [Note 8]; and in 1825, on the consecration [Note 9] of Dr. Walsh as coadjutor to Dr. Milner, he succeeded him as its President. At this time he was thirty-seven years of age.

He remained in this office till the year 1840, during which time he planned and raised the magnificent pile of buildings in which we are now assembled: which was soon to be illustrated by so much genius, and has since been associated with such memorable ecclesiastical events. It was the great work of his life, and will be his memorial to posterity.

In 1840, on the new arrangement of the Apostolic Vicariates, he was nominated to one of those in the north; but his heart was in his old work and on his old scene of action, and his excellent judgment told him, that to begin life over again in a new sphere at the age of fifty-two, was neither desirable in itself nor suited to him. He had no wish to lose the vantage-ground on which he stood, and from which he could command the co-operation in such services as might remain to him, of the many Catholics who had successively been trained up under his eye. He was quietly exerting an influence throughout Catholic England, and Oscott was a centre far more favourable to its extension than that which was offered to him elsewhere. He understood also, as all his friends would understand, that his calling was for a college life, – for the quietness and peace, for the opportunities of devotion, for the gradual formation of young minds, for the literary leisure, which a place of education afforded him. Like the Venerable Bede, it seems to be his vocation to live and die in the cloister. What should *he* do, with his graceful attainments, his delicate sensitiveness, his modest and unassuming simplicity, in the rude world, amid duties which, though they involved far higher ecclesiastical dignity and spiritual privilege, were intended for men of commanding minds, and of force as well as firmness of character? Like the trees in the parable, – with the fig-tree, and the olive, and the vine, – he was loth to leave "his sweetness and delicious fruit, his richness, and the wine which cheereth God and men," to be promoted over the other trees. If there was a man to be found who fulfilled the image with which I opened this discourse, – if there was any one who ought not to be transplanted, and was too useful in his present place to need it, – it was the heavenly-minded priest of whom I am speaking. Not only then from that sincere humility which was pre-eminently his, and was his motive principle on this occasion, but with calm prudence, he betook himself to the Apostolic Throne, and succeeded in gaining from Pope Gregory permission to decline the high honour which had been intended for him. The Pope, however, struck with his saintliness of character, told him that "he should not let him off so easily another time." [Note 10]

At this date he had been President of Oscott College for fourteen or fifteen years: he was now to be absent from the dear home of his youthful studies and his sacerdotal labours for not much short of the same time. During these years he was upon the mission at Hampton, Leamington, and Handsworth. In 1853 he returned to the College, where he has continued till his death.

As regards this latter portion of his history, which we all know so well, I am enabled to avail myself of your Lordship's circular letter.

There can be very little doubt [that letter says] but that the illness in which our venerated friend and brother in Christ so long suffered and lingered was brought on through that constant application of mind, that untiring solicitude of heart, and that unceasing energy of will, with which he devoted his declining years to the interests of the College over which he presided. In his vigour of life he raised that College up in its splendour, and, at the voice of obedience, left it prospering; at the same voice of obedience he returned again to it, in its hour of difficulty, and expended on its service all the energies of life that yet remained to him. God blessed his work, and now He has been pleased to take the workman.

One would have thought that a life so innocent, so active, so holy, I might say so faultless from first to last, might have been spared the visitation of any long and severe penance to bring it to an end; but, in order doubtless to show us how vile and miserable the best of us are in ourselves, and, even when we are in the fulness of grace and in the fervour of charity, how many imperfections we have in thought, word, and deed; and, moreover, to give us a pattern how to bear suffering ourselves, and to increase the merits and to hasten and brighten the crown of this faithful servant of his Lord, it pleased Almighty God to send upon him a disorder which, during the last six years, fought with him, mastered him, and at length has destroyed him, so far, that is, as death has still power to destroy, since the Cross of Christ has given it its death-blow. It is for those who came near him year after year to store up the many words and deeds of resignation, love, and humility which that long penance elicited. These meritorious acts are written in the Book of Life, and they have followed him whither he is gone. They multiplied and grew in strength and perfection as his trial proceeded; and they were never so striking as at its close. When a friend visited him in the last week, he found he had scrupled at allowing his temples to be moistened with some refreshing waters, and had with difficulty been brought to give his consent; he said he feared it was too great a luxury. When the same friend offered him some liquid to allay his distressing thirst, his answer was the same. As he read to him various texts of Scripture, he came, among others, to St. Paul's reflexion on his own approaching dissolution: "Bonum certamen certavi, cursum consummavi, fidem servavi. In reliquo reposita est mihi corona justitiæ." "I have fought the good fight, I have finished the course, I have kept the faith. Now there is laid up for me the crown of justice." When the last words were read, the holy old man burst into tears and remained awhile quite overcome. On the next time that his friend came, the day before his death, the sufferer recurred to the text, and repeated it. It had been his consolation ever since it had been read to him. At this time, though he was quivering with unintermitting convulsions, he repeated the alternate verses of the *Miserere* with that extreme composure, deliberateness, and measured exactness, which was so familiar with him. Within a few hours of this he died. Some time before, he had put into the hands of a friend a habit of the third order of Mount Carmel, of which he was a member, with the expression of his wish that he should be clothed in it on his death. This wish of course was carefully observed. He died at four o'clock on the morning of the 7th, last Monday, on a day of black vestments; so that his friends were able to say a Mass *pro defunctis* for the repose of his soul within a few hours after his departure. May God give him rest! Indeed, who can doubt that He has already granted it to him, and has taken him from the place of purification to His Eternal Presence?

He had lately entered upon his seventy-second year. For nearly ten years of his life he was at Sedgley Park. When close upon sixteen he went to Oscott College, where above forty years of his life, from first to last, have been spent. About the year 1830, at the instance of Dr. Walsh, his Bishop, he received the degree of Doctor in Divinity. On the erection of the Cathedral Chapter of Birmingham, in the year 1856, he was nominated its Provost; and, shortly afterwards, he received the appointment of Domestic Prelate to his Holiness. Shortly before this he had celebrated his jubilee, on the completion of the fiftieth year of his connexion with the College.

And now, my Lord, and my Reverend Brethren, I have performed, in such way as I have been able, the duty which you have imposed upon me. We are taking our last farewell of the remains of one of the old school, – of that old school of Catholics which has characteristics so great and so special. We are committing to the grave all that is mortal of a priest of solid piety, of deep and calm devotion, of mortified life, of ever wakeful, firm conscientiousness, of a spirit truly ecclesiastical, of singular consistency, equability, perfection in conduct, of virtue which ripened thoroughly upon the tree before it has been gathered. There was nothing crude, nothing extravagant, nothing fitful, nothing pretentious, in the character of our dear and venerated friend. He was ever one and the same; ever simple, single-minded, blameless, modest, and true. You ever knew where to find him. He was an unselfish spirit, which laboured, and then let others enter into his labours. His was a discriminating judgment, which found the right place for every duty that had a claim on his attention; which enabled him freely to cultivate human learning without its encroaching on the time and interest due to sacred studies; and to consecrate himself to the inward life of religion without thereby neglecting "whatever is lovely, whatever is of good fame," in his intercourse with others. A pleasing speaker, an elegant writer, with a natural playfulness of thought and manner which made him dear to friends and agreeable to all, through the whole man shone the spirit of evangelical charity, and made his gentleness and refinement seem what they really were, a growth from, or a graft upon, that pure harmony of soul which is a supernatural gift. He and his patron the venerable Dr. Walsh, the late Vicar-Apostolic of this district, fellow-disciples of Dr. Milner, entered into the intimate heart of that remarkable man, and made themselves heirs of its truest characteristic in perpetuating his devotional spirit. It was Dr. Milner, the sharp controversialist, as the world has often considered him, who set himself to soften and melt the frost which stiffened the Catholicism of his day, and to rear up, safe from our northern blasts, the tender and fervent aspirations of Continental piety. The small chapel at Maryvale, which is so well known to us all, contains the first altar dedicated in England to the Sacred Heart of our Lord.

Well did those two servants of God, his pupils, continue the work of Milner; – and now the last of the three has been taken away from us, and we are left to follow out the lessons and the patterns which they have given us. We do not lament their departure; we thank God that He gave them to us, and continued each of them to labour through a sufficient length of life for His glory and our edification. We do not lament their loss; for they are gone to their reward, and can do more for us by their intercessions before the Eternal Throne than by their prolonged presence on earth. We do not lament their absence; for they have done their work. Every one is made for his day; he does his work *in* his day; what he does is not the work of any other day, but of his own day; his work is necessary in order to the work of that next day which is *not* his, as a stepping-stone on which we, who come next, are to raise our own work. God grant that we too may do our own work, whatever it may be, as perfectly as he did his, whom we are now consigning to the grave! God in His great mercy grant, by the sacrifice of the Immaculate Lamb, once made on the Cross, daily renewed at the Altar, through the intercession of His dear Virgin Mother, for the merits of all Saints, especially those connected with this Diocese and College, – God, the Holy Trinity, Father, Son, and Holy Ghost, grant us, with unselfish hearts and pure love of Him, ever to aim at His glory, and to seek His will, and to ask for His grace, and to obey His word, labouring according to our strength, labouring to the end, – as he did, the dear friend whom we have lost, – labouring to the very end, in humility, diligence, and love!

Notes

1. "In London," says the Very Rev. Canon Macdonnell, in some notes with which he has favoured me, "his father had been contemporary with Bishop Milner, at Douay, and followed the profession of medicine."
2. "The Very Rev. Dr. Husenbeth, V. G. Provost of Northampton.
3. "The late Rev. Mr. Jones of Warwick Street," says the very same reverend correspondent, "who was a sort of parlour-boarder at Sedgley Park, took great notice of the child, and showed him much kindness. He became a sort of patron to him, and continued so for many years, even after his ordination."
4. "He became a general favourite"; I still quote from Canon Macdonnell, who came to the school two years before Weedall left it: "with superiors, for docility, piety, and general good conduct; with fellow-students, for his pacific and obliging disposition. He was pointed out to me as the head boy of the school, when I went there in 1802."
5. "He told me," says Mr. Macdonnell, "that Mr. Simkiss, the spiritual director," to whom we are indebted for the incident recorded in the foregoing page, "on Weedall leaving school, asked him how long he had been there; and when he answered nine years, Mr. S. said, that the next nine years would pass away more quickly than those."
6. "He pursued his studies with great credit, and became a good classical scholar according to the curriculum of the college, and distinguished himself by his compositions in prose and verse. He was always regular and unostentatious, and his whole demeanour inspired respect. Both at Sedgley Park and at Oscott he distinguished himself among the students in games."
7. "His prepared discourses were singularly beautiful. His first occasional sermon was at St. Peter's, for the schools. It was printed."
8. Long before this he had had the teaching of the junior classes. "He was popular with his pupils," says Canon Macdonnell. "Mild and gentle, without weakness. The ecclesiastics held conferences: his displays were remarkable for eloquent language, able argument, and happy repartee. In 1818 he succeeded to the chair of theology."

9. "Mr. Weedall preached the consecration sermon. It was a most elaborate composition, and his health gave way. He was obliged to retire from the Presidency of the College, and travel. He went to Rome and probably to other parts of Italy." Since these pages have been in type, I have received remarkable evidence of the life-long trial to which the weakness of his health subjected him.

10. "He was certainly in Italy," says Canon Macdonnell, "between 1825 and 1840, but I cannot recollect the occasion. On this visit he went to Naples."

Appendices

Appendix 1

Advice to R.F. Wilson, who had just commenced
on his first assignment in a parish

Oriel College June 15, 1834

You must not be at all surprised or put out at feeling the difficulties you describe. It is the lot of all men who are by themselves on first engaging in parochial duty, especially of those who are of an anxious turn of mind. I felt so much of it on starting that I should compassionate you very much, unless I recollected that after a while the prospect before me cleared, as doubtless it will with you thro' God's mercy. It certainly is very distressing to have to trust one's own judgement in such important matters, and the despondency resulting is made still more painful by the number of little unimportant matters which must be decided one way or the other tho' without any good reason to guide the decision, and which in consequence are very fidgeting. You will not get over this all at once, yet in time all will be easy, in spite of whatever you may have to urge about your own disposition.

So much then generally, though you tell me not to speak in that way. Then as to your coldness which you complain of, I am sorry I can give no *recipe* here either. I can only say that I have much to lament in that way myself; that I am continually very cold and unimpressed, and very painful it is; but what can be done?[1] Would we could so command our minds as to make

---

[1] Cf. *LD* vi. 57. To Henry Wilberforce, 12 April 1837: 'Let me conclude by earnestly begging any one who thinks good gained to her from what I have written . . . to do what I cannot doubt such a person would do, pray

them feel as they ought – but it is their very disease that they are not suitably affected according to the intrinsic value of the objects presented to them – that they are excited by objects of this world, not with the realities of death and judgement, and the mercies of the Gospel. Meanwhile it is our plain *duty* to speak – to explain and to pray even while we find ourselves cold – and, please God, while we thus do what *is* a plain duty, perchance He may visit us and impress us with the realities of what we are speaking of. Certain it is, looking at things merely humanly, the oftener you go to a sick person the more you are likely at last to get interested in him. How can you expect to feel anything the *first or second time*? when you know nothing of his state. Interest will grow upon you as you ascertain his frame of mind. It is an irrational despondency and an impatience, to complain because nothing comes of your *first* visit. Be sure also that what he is to get from you, is not communicated all at once – nay not in words. What he will first gain will be *the sight of your earnestness* (though you do not see it yourself) – he will witness your earnestness, and thence be impressed with the *reality* of what makes *you* earnest. Your coming day by day to him, sacrificing your own ease, your mildness, bearing with interruptions, answering objections, etc, etc will bring before him the next world, *as a fact* before he gains perhaps any definite knowledge of the way of salvation. It will enlarge his heart with the knowledge of a world which hitherto was a name to him. Doubtless you will be all the while teaching him more or less of the matter of revelation – but I lay stress upon this to show that you need not fear you are doing no good, on the mere ground you know not what to say. Job's friends sat by him a week in silence; yet who will say there was no sympathy or comfort in their doing so? Further you have the Prayers of the Visitation Service to

---

I should hold *that* as a sort of interest, which I have a fair right to expect my writings to bear. Indeed I need it much. I do not think I gain any comfort from such things as you have kindly told me, except this hope. Such things do not seem to comfort or cheer me; I feel so conscious I am like the pane of glass (to use the common simile) which transmits heat yet is cold. I dare say I *am* doing good – but I have no consciousness that I retain any portion of it myself.'

read to the sick man – you have the psalms, and Gospels – nay the whole Bible. What instruments are these, if you find you have none beside? Begin in this way, and trust to opportunity to open the ground for you to make personal and individual application of the great subjects which you are laying before him.

I did not know you were to be by yourself for any time till this letter – and now you do not say how long this solitude is to last. If it is a permanent arrangement, make a plan for calling round on all your parishioners in order, with the object of getting their names, number of family, children in schools, place they go to worship at, etc, etc (the *Speculum Gregis* is a good book for this purpose, though I believe there are others like it). This will take you five or six weeks and business will grow out of these visits without your making it. Be careful not to be *too* condescending to them. That was my fault when I was first in orders – and I believe it is the fault of the day. I am sure in many cases the clergyman is thought a servant who is bound to relieve them whenever they are in want, and to whom no thanks are due for his attentions.[2] . . .

2 *LD* iv. 281–2.

Appendix 2

*An English translation of the notes Newman made
during his pre-ordination retreat at St Eusebio, Rome*[1]

I have in my mind a wound or cancer, the presence of which
prevents me from being a good Oratorian. It cannot be
described in a few words, for it is many-sided.

I am in the state of being able to fulfil my duty
conscientiously along a prescribed course, but I cannot rise
above it to a higher level. I creep along the ground, or even
run – well enough for one who creeps or runs, but I cannot fly.
I have not in me the elements for rising or advancing.

So far as I know I do not desire anything of this world; I do
not desire riches, power or fame; but on the other hand I do
not like poverty, troubles, restrictions, inconveniences. Bad
health I fear as one does who has experienced it, and avoid
bodily pain more than I used to. I love the mean that lies
between riches and poverty, and that is a temptation for me;
yet I hope that without great difficulty I should be able to give
up all that I have, if God ordered it.

I do not like a rule of life, although for eighteen years I have
wished to live a more or less regular life. I like tranquillity,
security, a life among friends, and among books, untroubled
by business cares – the life of an Epicurean in fact. This state
of mind, never strange to me, has grown with the years.

Although I have the fixed habit of referring all things to the
will of God, and desire to do His will, and although in practice
I really observe this principle in greater matters, yet I do not
in practice seek His will in lesser things. And even in those

[1] *AW* 245–8.

greater matters, although I have often prayed earnestly to do His will, yet my actions have proceeded rather from a kind of conscientiousness which forbade me to act otherwise, from a sense of correctness, from perceiving what became me, and doing which I should be consistent, than from faith and charity.

Increasing years have deprived me of that vigour and vitality of mind which I once had and now have no more. Just as the limbs become stiff so now my mind and its powers have lost their youthful agility and versatility. I am slow and unready in performing good actions, and this causes me no little trouble and labour, now that I am a Catholic. For the holiest customs of the Church, sacred functions, works necessary for gaining indulgences, assistance at Exposition, and Benediction of the Blessed Sacrament itself, embarrass me like a person acting in a new and unfamiliar role. The Mass, visits to the Blessed Sacrament, the Rosary, litanies, the Breviary – all these give me pleasure; but whenever I have to do a number of things, and especially when they are minute (e.g. the prayers necessary for gaining certain indulgences, or other prayers which have been promised, or those for a Novena), they overwhelm my memory, are a weight on my mind, distract and almost terrify me; all the more because I am perhaps liable to be scrupulous. There is an example of this at the present moment: – I have a particular dread of making "resolutions".

In almost everything I like my own way of acting; I do not want to change the place or business in which I find myself, to undertake the affairs of others, to walk, to go on a journey, to visit others, since I prefer to remain at home. I am querulous, timid, lazy, suspicious; I crawl along the ground; feeble, downcast and despondent.

Further, I have not that practical, lively, and present faith, against the persistent working and wiles of the evil spirit in my heart, which I ought to have.

When I was growing up, and as a young man, I had confidence and hope in God, i.e. I committed myself without anxiety to His Providence, I had the greatest faith in the efficacy of prayer, in all adversities I used to say calmly that He would deliver me and mine in His own good time. I

encouraged others, and was active and joyful; and I believed
(rightly, I hope), that I received from the Merciful God many
answers to my prayers. But when I began to apply my intellect
to sacred subjects, and to read and write, twenty years ago and
more, then, although what I wrote was for the most part true
and useful, nevertheless, first, I lost my natural and inborn
faith, so that now I am much afraid of the priesthood, lest I
should behave without due reverence in something so sacred;
then too I have lost my simple confidence in the word of God.
My joyousness and agreeableness I have not lost; among
friends and others I was affable and kind, but gradually my
original confidence in God's boundless love for me, and in the
efficacy of my prayers has faded away. I have not lost either
my intimate sense of the Divine Presence in every place, not
the good conscience and the peace of mind that flows
therefrom, but I no longer thought, or at any rate, much less
than formerly, that the habit of prayer was not only a
prescribed duty but also a great talent and privilege, by which
we can do all things. That subtle and delicate vigour of faith
has become dulled in me, and remains so to this day.

What is more serious, I have for some years fallen into a
kind of despair and a gloomy state of mind. Not that I cannot
say interiorly and with my whole heart: "My God and my
All", for these words have been constantly on my lips, but I
have had many things to oppress me. In a variety of ways I
have fallen away from hope. In the Church of England I had
many detractors; a mass of calumny was hurled at me; my
services towards that Church were misrepresented by almost
everyone in authority in it. I became an exile in a solitude,
where I spent some years with certain of my friends, but not
even in that retreat was I safe from those who pursued me with
their curiosity. I believe and hope that I did not on that account
give way to anger, indignation, or the like, for in that respect
I am not especially sensitive, but I was oppressed and lost
hope. And now the cheefulness I used to have has almost
vanished. And I feel acutely that I am no longer young, but
that my best years are spent, and I am sad at the thought of the
years that have gone by; and I see myself as to be fit for
nothing, a useless log.

Then on becoming a Catholic I lost not a few of my friends, and that at a time when by death I had lost others most dear to me.

Further; – when I lived in my retreat with certain others, seeking a way of life, we were accustomed to observe many things which are proper to Catholics, – fasts, meditations, retreats, the use of the Breviary, and other practices belonging to the ecclesiastical, or rather to the religious life. And now I undergo a reaction, as they say, and have not the courage to continue those things which I did willingly in the Anglican Church.

But further still; – it is difficult to explain and strange even to myself, but I have this peculiarity, that in the movement of my affections, whether sacred or human, my physical strength cannot go beyond certain limits. I am always languid in the contemplation of divine things, like a man walking with his feet bound together. I am held as it were by a fetter, by a sort of physical law, so that I cannot be forcible in preaching and speaking, nor fervent in praying and meditating.

This besides, I can never keep my mind fixed and intent on the subject proposed for meditation, nor on the words of the daily office. My mind wanders unceasingly; and my head aches if I endeavour to concentrate upon a single subject . . .

Appendix 3

*Extracts from the prayer intentions written
in the notebooks of John Henry Newman
as presented in Ward's biography.*[1]

1853

General Objects

Friday
Increase of Priests.
Sanctification of Priests and People.
Spread of Religion.
Conversion of the Nations.
All who befriend or help us.
All who ask my prayers.
All who attend our Church.
All who are in our schools.
Catholic Education.
All in our Mission.
All in Birmingham.
All in England – the Queen.
All I have forgotten.
All who helped me in the Achilli matter.
The Faithful departed.[2]
Opponents and enemies.

[1] *Ward* ii. 361–4.
[2] With names.

Memento Defunctorum

Adam de Brome. Edward II.[3]
Sir Thomas Pope.[4]
Count Mellerio.[5] John Baptist Palma.[6]
Fr. Dominic.
Mgr. Allemani.[7]
Fathers Perrone, Buonvicino, Ripetti.[8]
All whom I have attended on their sick bed.
All whom I ought to have attended and did not.
Any who have died Protestants through me
Make up to them and forgive me
The defects of my ministrations.

General Memento

The Holy Father, for wisdom and fortitude.
The Holy Roman Church.
The Cardinals,
our Bishop and Chapter, seculars, regulars,
the whole Hierarchy, in England, throughout the world
all religious orders,
all ecclesiastical establishments and institutions,
for children and the young, rich and poor, for the sick,
prisons, reformatories, penitentiaries,
all religious associations;
for the extension and prosperity of Holy Church,
for the sanctification, intelligence, influence of her children,
for her success with heathen, infidels, misbelievers,
heretics, schismatics.
For her victory over kings, governments and people.

---

[3] Joint Founders of Oriel.
[4] Founder of Trinity College, Oxford.
[5] Count Mellerio was very kind to J. H. N. at Milan, when the latter was on his way to Rome in 1846.
[6] Author of a Life of Christ, used in Lent by J. H. N.
[7] Bishop of all California, he died Archbishop of San Francisco. He interested himself much for Newman in the Achilli trial.
[8] Jesuits in Rome. The last was at Propaganda while J. H. N. and St John were there, and was much esteemed by them. There is a further long list of names which I do not transcribe.

For her confessors, missionaries, apologists,
for her theologians, controversialists, literary men.
For our Colonies,
for Ireland, France, Germany, Italy,
Spain, Russia, Egypt, United States.
For our Oratory.
For each of its Fathers, for good novices,
Oratorium Parvum,
For its Mission, orphanage, poor schools, middle schools,
penitents and people,
for the Oratory School with its
matrons, masters, servants, old scholars.
Pro re pecuniaria nostra,
and as regards Rednal and Ravenhurst.
For the London Oratory.
For all Oratories, here and abroad.
For all who befriend me, who have a claim on my prayers.
Who attend our Church, all teachers and taught.
All my benefactors and well-wishers.
All who subscribed and prayed for me
in the Achilli matter,
in the Oxford matter,
and on my being appointed Cardinal,
for all my friends and acquaintance,
for all my work, by word, deed, or writing,
for all whom I have influenced,
for my future.

Memento Vivorum

For all the Fathers and the Brothers,
And our Novices and Scholars,
And the Little Oratory;
and our Friends and Benefactors,
And our Schools for poor and gentle,

And our Parish, past and present,
Harborne, Edgbaston, and Smethwick.

For our preaching and our singing,
For our reading and our writing,
For sufficient worldly goods.

And for all the Sacred College,
And the Papal Curia,
And our Bishops and their Clergy,
And St. Philip's London Fathers,
And the University of Ireland,
And for Trinity and Oriel,
And the state of Christendom.
For my private Benefactors,
And my penitents and pupils,
And my kindred connections,
And my friends and my acquaintance,
And my slanderers and thwarters,
Catholic and Protestant.

Appendix 4

On the Priesthood of Christ

Sermon Notes of 6 April 1851 (Passion Sunday)[1]

1. INTROD. – Go through the gospel of the day, showing the strangeness of our Lord's doctrine, and the surprise and contempt of the Jews, in detail – modes of expression, ideas, objects, different.

2. So it was: it was a different system. If the world was true, He was not; if He, the world not.

3. They felt it obscurely and in detail, though He did not speak openly. How would they have felt if our Lord had said openly, 'I am the priest of the world'? What a great expression! But this is the truth, as forced on us by today's epistle. What the gospel says obscurely the epistle speaks out.

4. What is a priest? See how much it implies: first the need of reconciliation – it has at once to do with sin; it presupposes sin. When then our Lord is known to come as a priest, see how the whole face of the world is changed. Describe the world, how it goes on, buying and selling, etc.; then the light thrown on it that it is responsible to God, and has ill acquitted itself of that responsibility.

5. Again, it implies one the highest in rank. The head of the

1 *SN* 69–70.

family was a priest – primogeniture. Hence Christ the Son of God.

6. Christ then, the Son of God, offers for the whole world, and that offering is Himself. He who is high as eternity, whose arms stretch through infinity, is lifted up on the cross for the sins of the world.

7. And He is a priest for ever. 'Thou art a priest *for ever* according to the order of Melchisedec.' The offering of the Mass. Say not it is an *historical* religion, done and over; it lasts.

8. And as, for ever, so *all things* with blood. Why? Grace of Christ, and Adam's grace before the fall. Men 'washed their robes in the blood of the Lamb'; 'the blood of Christ cleanseth,' 1 John i. 7.[2]

9. Now turn back and see how different from what we see — need of *faith*, so says our Lord in the gospel of the day.

10. And this awful addition, 'He that heareth the word of God is of God,' etc., John viii. 47.[3]

11. This a reason for these yearly commemorations, to bring on us the thought of the unseen world.

---

[2] 'We have fellowship one with another, and the blood of Jesus Christ his Son cleanseth us from all sin.'

[3] 'He that is of God heareth the words of God: therefore you hear him not, because you are not of God.'

Appendix 5

A Brief History of the Cause for the Canonization of John Henry Cardinal Newman

17 June 1958   Archbishop Grimshaw of Birmingham formally introduced the Cause for the Canonization of John Henry Cardinal Newman.

22 January 1991   Newman declared 'Venerable' by Pope John Paul II.

15 August 2001   Miraculous healing of Deacon Jack Sullivan from Boston, USA, through the intercession of the Venerable John Henry Newman.

24 April 2008   The *Consulta Medica*, a group of doctors appointed by the Congregation for the Causes of Saints, met and unanimously agreed that the cure of Deacon Jack Sullivan had no medical explanation.

2 June 2009   Ordinary Session of the Congregation for the Causes of Saints meets and votes unanimously in favour of accepting the miraculous cure of Deacon Jack Sullivan.

3 July 2009   Papal Decree of Pope Benedict XVI announcing that the Venerable John Henry Cardinal Newman was to be beatified.

Bibliography

Arnold, M., *Discourses in America,* London, 1885.

Bellasis, E., *Coram Cardinali,* London, 1916.

Bouyer, L., *Newman – His Life and Spirituality,* London, 1958.

Brook, M. G., & Curthoys, M. C. (eds), *The History of the University of Oxford,* vol. vi. *Nineteenth-century Oxford, Part I,* Oxford, 1997.

Butler, C., *The Life and Times of Bishop Ullathorne 1806–1889,* London, 1926.

Caraman, P., *Occasional Sermons of Ronald A. Knox,* London, 1960.

Church, R. W., *The Oxford Movement: Twelve Years 1833 – 1845,* London, 1900.

Coleridge, H., 'A Father of Souls', the *Month,* lxx (October 1890).

Dessain, C. S., *Cardinal Newman's Teaching About The Virgin Mary,* Birmingham.

Dulles, A., *Newman,* London & New York, 2002.

Ffoulkes, E. S., *A History of the Church of S. Mary the Virgin Oxford,* London, 1892.

Froude, J. A., *Short Studies on Great Subjects,* vol. v, London, 1907.

Fuller Russell, J., ed., *The Judgement of the Anglican Church (posterior to the Reformation) on the Sufficiency of Holy Scripture, and the Authority of the Holy Catholic Church in matters of Faith,* London, 1838.

Goulburn, E. M., *John William Burgon, Late Dean of Chichester,* London, 1892.

Gregoris, N., *"The Daughter of Eve Unfallen – Mary in the Theology and Spirituality of John Henry Newman,* Mount Pocono, 2003.

Honoré, J., *The Spiritual Journey of Newman,* New York, 1992.

Ker, I., *The Achievement of John Henry Newman,* London, 1990.

Ker, I., *John Henry Newman: A Biography,* Oxford, 1988.

Ker, I., & Merrigan, T. (eds), *The Cambridge Companion to John Henry Newman,* Cambridge, 2009.

Lake, K. (ed.), *Memorials of William Charles Lake 1869–1894,* London, 1901.

Lefebvre, P., & Mason, C. (eds), *John Henry Newman – Doctor of the Church,* Oxford, 2007.

Lefebvre, P., & Mason, C. (eds), *John Henry Newman In His Time,* Oxford, 2007.

Lockhart, W., *Cardinal Newman: Reminiscences of Fifty Years Since,* London, 1891.

Macleod, D. (ed.), *Good Words for 1881,* London, 1881.

Murray, P. (ed.), *Newman the Oratorian – His Unpublished Oratory Papers,* Leominster, 2004.

Neville, W. P. (ed.), *Addresses to Cardinal Newman, with his replies, 1879–81,* London, 1905.

Oakley, F., *Historical Notes on the Tractarian Movement 1833–1845,* London, 1865

Schofield, N., & Skinner, G., *The English Cardinals,* Oxford, 2007.

Selby, R., *The Principle of Reserve in the Writings of John Henry Cardinal Newman,* Oxford, 1975.

Seynaeve, J., *Cardinal Newman's Doctrine on Holy Scripture,* Louvain, 1953.

Shairp, J. C., *Studies in Poetry and Philosophy,* 3rd edition, Edinburgh, 1876.

Stephens, W. B., *The Victoria County History of the County of Warwick,* London, 1964.

Strange, R., *Newman and the Gospel of Christ,* Oxford, 1981.

Strange, R., *John Henry Newman: A Mind Alive,* 2008.

Trevor, M., *Newman Pillar of the Cloud,* London, 1962.

Trevor, M., *Newman Light in Winter,* London, 1962

Ullathorne, W. B., *Christian Patience,* London, 1886.

Velocci, G., *Prayer in Newman,* Leominster, 2006.

Ward, W., *The Life of John Henry Cardinal Newman,* London, 1927.

Withey, D., *John Henry Newman: the Liturgy and the Breviary – Their influence on his life as an Anglican,* London, 1992.

Fr Zeno, *John Henry Newman – His Inner Life,* San Francisco, 1987.

Lightning Source UK Ltd.
Milton Keynes UK
22 April 2010

153196UK00002B/2/P

9 780852 447369